RURAL SOCIOLOGY

RURAL SOCIOLOGY

Dr. Binoy Kumar

RANDOM

RANDOM PUBLICATIONS

NEW DELHI - 110 002 (INDIA)

Rural Sociology

ISBN 978-93-51117-32-2

Published in 2015 in India by

RANDOM PUBLICATIONS

4376-A/4B, Gali Murari Lal, Ansari Road
New Delhi-110 002
Phone: +9111-43580356, 23289044
E-mail: randomexports@gmail.com; sales@randompublications.com; info@randompublications.com

Reprinted 2026

Type Setting by: Friends Media, Delhi-110089

Preface

Rural sociology is a field of sociology traditionally associated with the study of social structure and conflict rural areas although topical areas such as food and agriculture or natural resource access transcend traditional rural spatial boundaries. Human settlements are classified as rural or urban depending on the density of human-created structures and resident people in a particular area. Urban areas can include town and cities while rural areas include villages and hamlets. While rural areas may develop randomly on the basis of natural vegetation and fauna available in a region, urban settlements are proper, planned settlements built up according to a process called urbanization. Many times, rural areas are focused upon by governments and development agencies and turned into urban areas. Of late, Rural Sociology has taken the shape of an independent social science with its own characteristic standpoint and methods. The subject matter of Rural Sociology, according to Nelson, is the description and analysis of the progress of various groups as they exist in the rural environment.

Similarly, Bertrand has treated Rural Sociology as the study of human relationships in rural environment. This, again, emphasizes the study of all types of social relationships existing in village setting. There are two schools of thought on the scope of Rural Sociology. According to the first school of thought, Rural Sociology provides only scientific knowledge about rural society. It offers a composite picture of rural life in its multifaceted dimensions. Rural Sociology is also concerned with the study of several socio-economic problems such as rural poverty, rural unemployment, illiteracy, rural indebtedness, and incidence of crimes in rural areas etc.-their causes, effects and remedial measures. Rural life is the principal pivot around which whole Indian social life revolves. India is a land of agriculture. Its history, customs and traditions, complex social organization and unity in diversity etc can be understood by the study of rural life. India is an agricultural country and village is a basic and important unit of the society. After independence the process of rural reconstruction was started and importance of the rural sociology was recognized. The need of development of the villages and speed of education in the villages were understood and to achieve this community development programme was started. It can be achieved when the planners and administrator correct knowledge of the rural life. As a scientist, rural sociologist is keenly interested in understanding rural people. He is also equally interested in the betterment of rural life. He collects facts concerning rural life and tries to interpret them in a meaningful way keeping rural development in view. Social, economic, political, educational and religious institutions in the context of rural society constitute the subject matter of rural sociology. Rural Sociology also analyses the sociological significance of these institutions.

The information presented in this book will be highly useful to the students research scholars teachers planners administrators extension workers and all those who are engaged in teaching rural development and doing research on rural sociology and educational psychology.

I thank all members of my team who have helped in the preparation of the book. My special thanks go to "Random Publications" who have published the book.

— Dr. Binoy Kumar

Contents

Chapter 1

Introduction

Literally and from the social, economic and political perspectives the statement is valid even today. Around 65% of the State's population is living in rural areas. People in rural areas should have the same quality of life as is enjoyed by people living in sub urban and urban areas. Further there are cascading effects of poverty, unemployment, poor and inadequate infrastructure in rural areas on urban centres causing slums and consequential social and economic tensions manifesting in economic deprivation and urban poverty. Hence Rural Development which is concerned with economic growth and social justice, improvement in the living standard of the rural people by providing adequate and quality social services and minimum basic needs becomes essential. The present strategy of rural development mainly focuses on poverty alleviation, better livelihood opportunities, provision of basic amenities and infrastructure facilities through innovative programmes of wage and self-employment.

The goals will be achieved by various programme support being implemented creating partnership with communities, non-governmental organizations, community based organizations, institutions, PRIs and industrial establishments, while the Department of Rural Development will provide logistic support both on technical and administrative side for programme implementation. Other aspects that will ultimately lead to transformation of rural life are also being emphasized simultaneously.

Though the percentage of persons below poverty level in Tamil Nadu has come down significantly between 1993-94 (35.03%) and 1999-2000 (21.12%) as a result of the implementation of various Central and State sponsored schemes, the level of poverty both in absolute numbers (130.40 lakh persons) and percentage of population below poverty line (21.12%) in Tamil Nadu is highest among the four southern States. In spite of huge investments on wage and self -employment programmes, the level of unemployment as per the NSSO 55th round (1999-2000) for Tamil Nadu compared to All India is the second highest among major States in 1987-88 and 1993-94 and third highest in 1999-2000. The Government's policy and programmes have laid emphasis on poverty alleviation, generation of employment and income opportunities and provision of infrastructure and basic facilities to meet the needs of rural poor. For realising these objectives, self-employment and wage employment programmes continued to pervade in one form or other. As a measure to strengthen the grass root level democracy, the Government is constantly endeavouring to empower Panchayat Raj Institutions in terms of functions, powers and finance. Grama sabha, NGOs, Self-Help Groups and PRIs have been accorded adequate role to make participatory democracy meaningful and effective.

Review of Ninth Plan Performance

An outlay of ₹2000 crores was provided for Rural Development sector during Ninth Plan period. The budgetary support and allocation from 1997-98 to 2001-02 for various schemes/programmes was ₹2498.30 crores. The year-wise outlay and expenditure are indicated below:

Financial Performance		***(₹in crores)***
Year	*Budget Provision*	*Expenditure*
1997-98	*330.68*	*440.76*
1998-99	*490.51*	*526.45*
1999-2000	*498.27*	*484.27*
2000-01	*423.31*	*543.50*
2001-02	*755.53*	*725.14*
Total	***2498.30***	***2720.12***

Table: *Physical Performance*

Year	*I. R. D. P No. of families benefited*	*TRYSEM No. of persons trained*	*DWCRA No. of groups formed*	*No. of SHGs formed*	*SGSY economic assistance provided*	*Families benefited*	*Individual assisted*
1997-98	*180696*	*16479*	*2041*	—	—	—	—
1998-99	*142813*	*12381*	*2917*	—	—	—	—
1999-2000	*New scheme-SGSY introduced*			*18661*	*3198*	*47264*	*18163*
2000-01				*25324*	*4712*	*71503*	*11890*
2001-02				*12132*	*2158*	*34098*	*1259*
Total	***323509***	***28860***	***4958***	***56117***	***10068***	***152865***	***31312***

During the Ninth Five Year Plan, under IRDP, income generating assets were provided to 3.235 lakh families through subsidy and credit. Under TRYSEM 28,860 rural youths in the age group of 18 to 35 from the families of below poverty line were provided with training enabling them to take up income generating activities.

Under DWCRA 4,958 women groups covering 12.40 lakh beneficiaries were formed and they were provided with revolving fund, credit and subsidy so as to enable them to participate in social developmental activities towards achieving economic self-reliance. During 1999-2000 the IRDP, TRYSEM, DWCRA were merged to form a new self-employment programme called *Swarna Jayanthi Gram Swarojgar Yojana* (SGSY) with effect from 1-4-99. Under SGSY 56,117 Women Self Help Groups (SHGs) were formed from the families of below poverty line.

Out of this, 10,068 SHGs have been provided with economic assistance under various trades enabling them to take up income generating activities. Under SGSY 31,312 individual beneficiaries have also been provided with economic assistance.

Table: *Mandays generated and Community assets created under Centrally Sponsored Schemes during Ninth Five Year Plan*

Sl. No.	*Name of the scheme*	*Unit*	*Mandays generated /Assets created*
1	*JRY/JGSY*	*Lakh mandays*	*1048.95*
2	*EAS*		*1344.38*
	IAY		
3	*New houses*	*Nos.*	*2,08,441*
4	*IAY Kutcha houses*	*Nos.*	*41,239*
5	*PMGY Rural shelter*	*Nos.*	*6880*
6	*Credit cum subsidy*	*Nos.*	*5577*
7	*Million Wells Scheme*	*Nos.*	*9588*

The total man-days generated under Employment Oriented Schemes like JRY/JGSY and EAS works out to 2393.33 lakhs. These schemes in addition to the creation of infrastructural facilities such as roads, school buildings, improvement of tanks etc. provided employment and income opportunities to the rural poor.

Regarding provision of housing facilities, 2.08 lakh new houses were constructed and 41,239 kutcha houses upgraded under IAY, 6880 new houses were constructed under PMGY-Rural Shelter for benefit of rural poor living below poverty line. Under Credit cum subsidy scheme, 5,577 houses were constructed for the benefit the people above poverty line.

Access to pucca dwelling provides basic housing as well as better environment for the beneficiaries and raises the social status of the members of the household. Under Jeevandhara Irrigation Wells Scheme (Million Wells Scheme), totally 9588 beneficiaries were assisted to dig irrigation wells during 1997-98 and 1998-99.

During the Ninth Five Year Plan, the State Government introduced new schemes such as Member of Legislative Assembly Constituency Development Schemes (MLACDS), Annamarumalrchi Thittam (AMT) and Namakku Naame Thittam.

Under MLACDS, 42,954 works were taken up at a total cost of ₹580.46 crores, 1,05,605 works were taken up a total cost of ₹301.86 under AMT and 28,421 works were taken up at a total cost of ₹157.11 crores under Namakku Naame Thittam.

Goals, Objectives and Strategy

The prime goal of rural development is to improve the quality of life of the rural people by alleviating poverty through the instrument of self-employment and wage employment programmes, by providing community infrastructure facilities such as drinking water, electricity, road connectivity, health facilities, rural housing and education and promoting decentralization of powers to strengthen the Panchayat raj institutions.

The Chief Minister's 15 Point Programme is a visionary programme which seeks to make Tamil Nadu the best State in the country by way of creating growth opportunities in rural areas and eradicating rural poverty. To achieve the objectives, the following priorities and thrust areas have been identified during the Tenth Five Year Plan period:

- The goal is reduction of poverty from 21.12% in 1999-2000 to 10% by 2006-07 and near elimination by 2012. Poverty reduction will be attempted
  - By organizing the rural masses into self-help groups and the establishment of micro-enterprises, training, credit linkages, market support, etc.
  - By substantial flow of investment in physical infrastructure like roads, water supply and social infrastructure like health, education and nutrition.
- Special efforts for generation of adequate employment and creation of durable community assets to improve the rural

people especially the small farmers, marginal farmers, rural artisans etc., through programmes like Sampoorna Grameen Rozgar Yojana (SGRY).

- Decentralization of the process of planning by entrusting major role to the Panchayat raj bodies in the preparation of local level planning.
- Improving the efficiency and capacity of the officials and elected local body representatives.
- Providing all weather roads to all rural habitations having a population above 500 by 2004.
- Strengthening of Grama Sabha the governing body of village assembly as an agency of social audit and to review the implementation of programmes.
- Special efforts will be made to converge various schemes and programmes for accelerating the development process through special schemes like Village Self-sufficiency scheme etc.
- Emphasis will be given for the maintenance of the assets created under various schemes.

Tenth Five Year Plan proposals

The schemes / programmes proposed to be implemented during the Tenth plan period to achieve the above cherished objectives are:

Centrally Sponsored Schemes

Poverty Alleviation Programmes: *Swarnajayanthi Gram Swarozgar Yojana (SGSY):* The magnitude of poverty and disparities that existed between the various social groups necessitated planned state intervention to provide succor and relief particularly to the disadvantaged and marginalised groups such as SC/ST, women etc. Keeping this in view and having regard to the positive aspects as well as deficiencies, the earlier self employment programmes like TRYSEM, SITRA, GKY, DWCRA, IRDP and MWS were merged and a new self employment programme *viz.*, SGSY was launched w. e. f.1-4-1999.

The SGSY is conceived as a holistic programme of micro enterprises covering all aspects of self-employment and establishing effective linkages between the various components *viz.*, organization of the rural poor into Self Help Groups (SHGs), their capacity building, planning of activity clusters, infrastructure build up, technology, credit and marketing etc. The main objective of the programme is to bring the existing poor families above the poverty line. Among the rural poor, special emphasis will be given for the welfare of SCs/STs, women and disabled. The programme lays emphasis on organization of poor into Self Help Groups (SHGs) and their capacity building.

The SHGs may consist of 10 to 20 persons 4 to 5 key activities will be identified in each block based on the resource endowments, occupational skills of the people and availability of markets and these activities will be implemented in clusters. 10% of the SGSY fund will be set apart for training, wherein emphasis will be given for skill development through well designed courses. SGSY is a Credit cum Subsidy programme with the involvement of banking and financial institutions. The expenditure under SGSY is shared by the Centre and the States in the ratio of 75:25. Subsidy will be provided at 30% of the project cost subject to a maximum of `7,500 and 50% for SC/ST subject to a maximum of `10,000. For groups, the subsidy is 50% subject to a ceiling of `1.25 lakhs.

During the Tenth Five Year Plan under SGSY it has been proposed:

1. To form 1.25 lakhs Self Help Groups benefiting 25 lakh women beneficiaries in rural areas.
2. To impart EDP and Vocational training for about 5 lakh rural women to start micro enterprise for economic independency.
3. To train 3 lakh unemployed youth to take up self-employment.
4. To construct one Self Help Group Centre per Panchayat to conduct meeting, store and display their products and to hold training programmes for the members of SHGs.
5. To establish District Information Service Centre in each district to provide backward and forward linkages in marketing.

The State's share of the SGSY scheme during the Tenth Plan will be `131.45 crores.

Sampoorna Grameen Rozgar Yojana (SGRY): Creation of sustained employment opportunities for securing a minimum level of employment and income for the rural poor necessitated continuous need for special employment programmes.

Keeping the above aim and to strengthen the need based infrastructure at the village level to boost the rural economy the erstwhile wage employment programmes JGSY and EAS were merged and a new scheme namely SGRY was launched from 15th August 2001. The main objective of the new programme is to provide additional wage employment in the rural areas as food security by creation of durable community social and economic assets and infrastructure development in rural areas.

Towards this end the SGRY envisages distribution of food grains @ 5 kg per manday to the workers as part wages. While the cash component will be shared by the Centre and States in the ratio of 75:25, the Central Government will supply the food grains free of cost to the States. The scheme will be implemented in two streams.

The first stream will be implemented at the District and Panchayat Union levels 50% of the funds and food grains available under the programme will be distributed between the District Panchayat and the Panchayat Union in the ratio of 40:60.

The second stream will be implemented at the Village Panchayat level. The entire allocation under this stream will be distributed among the Village Panchayats through the DRDAs/District Panchayats. To augument the storage capacity of the tanks maintained by the local bodies towards increasing the availability of water for drinking, irrigation and other purposes it has been proposed to renovate one tank per panchayat under this scheme. During Tenth Plan, the State's share will be ₹303.80 crores.

Rural Housing

The aim of the State Government is to provide a dwelling for each family giving special emphasis to rural poor and deprived. The on going rural housing programmes will be given a new thrust.

Indira Awaas Yojana: With a view to meeting the housing needs of the rural poor, Indira Awaas Yojana (IAY) was launched in May 1985 as a subscheme of Jawahar Rozgar Yojana. It is being implemented as an independent scheme since 1 January 1996. It aims at helping below poverty line rural households belonging to SCs/STs, free bonded labourers, widows of next of kin of defence personnel, ex-servicemen and retired members of the paramilitary forces and also non SC/ST rural poor by providing them with grant-in-aid for construction of new dwelling units and upgradation of existing unserviceable kutcha houses. 3% of funds are reserved for the benefit of disabled poor below the poverty line in rural areas.

The assistance ceiling for each house in plain area is fixed at ₹20,000/-and for hill/difficult areas ₹22,000. In order to enable fire proof RCC roofed houses to be provided, the State Government provides additionally ₹12,000 per house as additional cost apart from its usual matching share to the Central grant. The expenditure towards provision of RCC roofing is met under Adi-dravida Welfare head.

Therefore, the unit cost including sanitary latrine under this scheme is ₹32,000/-in normal terrain and ₹34,000 in difficult terrain.80%

of the IAY funds is earmarked for construction new houses and 20% is towards upgradation of unserviceable kutcha houses at the rate of ₹10,000/-per unit. The funds under IAY are shared between Centre and States in the ratio of 75:25. During the Tenth Plan it has been proposed to construct 1,54,090 new houses and to upgrade 78,970 unserviceable kutcha houses into pucca houses. The proposed outlay during the Tenth plan under IAY under SCP is ₹292.89 crores.

Credit/cum/Subsidy Scheme: The Credit-cum-Subsidy Scheme has been conceived for rural households having an annual income upto ₹32,000/-. Subsidy upto ₹10,000/-and loan up to ₹40,000/-from commercial or co-op banks is provided to eligible households for construction of houses. Out of the total outlay of ₹9.15 crores, 25% share of the State Government will be ₹2.29 crores. The physical target under the scheme will be 914.

Innovative Stream for Rural House and Habitat Development Scheme: This scheme intends to popularize low cost technology and usage of locally available materials in construction of buildings in rural areas.

Innovative technology adopted for the rural house type design in the scheme are:

- Rat-trap bond brick work, hollow blocks and soil stabilized cement mortar for construction of walls.
- Filler slab roofing using Mangalore tiles as filler material for roofing.
- Ferro cement/pre cast RCC doors, window, frame and shelter and
- Brick with plastering for flooring.

Under this scheme free houses are constructed for the rural poor. Infrastructure facilities such as drinking water, drainage, street formation etc., are provided by dovetailing funds under other ongoing schemes in the habitations developed under this scheme. This scheme is fully funded by the Government of India. The scheme will be taken up in the districts of Tiruvannamalai, Salem, Dharmapuri, Nilgiris, Nagapattinam, Tiruvarur, Theni, Ramanathapuram, Sivagangai and Villupuram during the Tenth Plan at a total cost of ₹5 crores.

Pradhan Mantri Gramodaya Yojana (PMGY) (Rural Shelter Component): This scheme has been introduced by the Government of India under additional Central assistance for providing shelter in the rural areas to supplement the efforts in the sphere of rural housing considering the magnitude of the task.

The guidelines of Indira Awaas Yojana are applied for this scheme also. 60% of the total allocation is earmarked for SC/ST beneficiaries. During Tenth Plan it has been proposed to construct 34,475 rural shelters with an allocation of ₹111.14 crores.

Member of Parliament Local Area Development Programme

The Government of India introduced this scheme in 1993. Each MP (Lok Sabha and Rajya Sabha) was allotted ₹2 crore per annum to take up developmental works in his constituency. The District Collectors and in respect of Chennai, the Commissioner of Chennai Corporation implement the scheme.

In Tamil Nadu, there are 39 Lok Sabha MPs and 18 Rajya Sabha MPs and hence ₹114 crores is received annually from Government of India under this scheme.

A Member of Rajya Sabha may select any district of the State for exercising the choice of works under the scheme. The executive authorities concerned after studying the feasibility of the proposals of members will exccute the works by following open tender system.

The list of works that can be taken up under this scheme includes school buildings, village roads/approach roads, and irrigation canals, bus shelters, desilting of village ponds etc. An outlay of ₹570 crores has been proposed under this scheme during Tenth Plan period, which will be directly released to the District Collectors by GOI for executing the works.

Pradhan Manthri Gram Sadak Yojana (PMGSY)

The Pradhan Mantri Gram Sadak Yojana (PMGSY) is a Government of India Scheme introduced in the year 2000-2001 with the objective of providing road connectivity through good all weather roads to all unconnected rural habitations having population above 1000 by 2003 and all unconnected habitations having population of 500 and above by end of Tenth Plan period (2007).

Under this programme the approved works are grouped into packages costing more than ₹1 crore but less than ₹5 crores and executed through tender system. The guidelines stipulate that district master plans would be prepared.

A District Rural Road Plan is prepared for each district indicating the habitations in each block with the existing status of road connectivity. The scheme will be fully funded by the Government of India and an allocation of ₹750 crores has been proposed for the Tenth Plan.

National Project on Biogas Development

Biogas Development programme aims to promote an eco-friendly Non-conventional Energy Source with multiple benefits. The role of biogas as a major source of renewable energy has been recognized by the Government of India by including this scheme as an item in the 20 Point Programme. Prevention of deforestation, production of enriched manure and to improve sanitation and hygiene by linking sanitary toilets with biogas plants are the objectives of this rural energy programme.

This is a Centrally sponsored programme with a subsidy component of ₹1800/-for general category and ₹2300/-for scheduled category and ₹3500/-for hilly areas. An amount of ₹500/-is provided in addition for installation and maintenance of the plant to the Turnkey agent. 10,000 bio-gas plants will be constructed during the Tenth Plan. The scheme is fully funded by the Government of India and ₹8.05 crores is provided for the Tenth Plan which will be directly released to the District Collectors.

Eleventh Finance Commission Grant

This grant is provided to Village Panchayats and Panchayat Unions for maintenance of civic services. Under Eleventh Finance Commission grant, a sum of ₹186.45 crores for 2000-01 and 2001-02 was allocated. Out of this, ₹171.92 crores is provided to Village Panchayats and Panchayat Unions for maintenance of civic services and ₹14.53 crores for maintenance of accounts and audit and for development of database. An outlay of ₹659.47 crores has been proposed during the Tenth Plan period under this scheme.

Rashtriya Sam Vikas Yojana (RSVY)

During Tenth Plan a new scheme viz, Rashtriya Sam Vikas Yojana (RSVY) Development and Reform Facility will be launched by Government of India. The prime objective of RSVY is to address the problems of pockets of high poverty, low growth, low agricultural productivity, unemployment and poor governance by putting in place programmes and policies, which would remove barriers to growth and accelerate the development process.

An amount of ₹15 crores per year will be provided for implementation of various developmental programmes such as drought proofing (soil conservation, afforesation, social forestry, wasteland development and minor irrigation), agriculture, horticulture etc. infrastructure (road and power), social sector (health and education) and livelihood support (income generating activities such as handloom, information technology, agricultural processing etc.). Under the scheme 15% of the funds will be earmarked for maintenance of assets in health, education and veterinary sectors.

The main focus and strategy of the scheme will be on infrastructure development and income generation for under-privileged. The scheme will be implemented through people's participation, involvement of PRIs, NGOs and Self Help Groups at every stage including plan formulation, implementation and monitoring. Tiruvannamalai district has been selected on pilot basis for implementation of RSVY scheme. During Tenth Plan period the total amount of `225 crores is proposed under the scheme.

State schemes

Construction of office Buildings for Village Administrative Officers

Administration at the door steps of the people is the slogan of the Government. In order to achieve this objective the scheme for construction of buildings for the office of the Village Administrative Officers has been proposed during Tenth plan period. There are about 16000 revenue villages in the state, each having a Village Administrative Officer.

The VAO's office buildings would be constructed adjacent to every panchayat office building so that public can have easy access to both. It has been proposed to construct the VAO's office building through state budgetary support and by dovetailing funds under MLA Constituency Development Scheme. The outlay proposed for the scheme during the Tenth Plan is `19.80 crores.

Village Fair Development Scheme

The Agro-based industries play a vital role in the development of rural economy. It is essential that the farmers should have remunerative returns and the agricultural labourers should have high wages.

To enhance the livelihood security of the farmers and agricultural labourers, the Village Fair Development Scheme has been launched. Presently the agriculture produces are marketed in shandies maintained by village panchayats and panchayat unions.

These shandies are being maintained without adequate infrastructure facilities. It is proposed to provide facilities such as stalls, drinking water to cattle/people, public convenience, lighting facilities, improvement to inner roads between the stalls etc., These will also facilitate the rural masses to have an access to agriculture produce besides improved income to the local bodies. The scheme will be implemented in 25 districts with (NABARD) assistance costing ₹5.00 crores during the Tenth Plan period.

Village Self-sufficiency Scheme

The main objective of the Scheme is to promote self-reliant and self help attitude among the rural people. This scheme attempts to reverse growing dependency syndrome in the rural areas on Govt. and bring back to the mainstream of development process by inculcating community involvement and participatory approach in development.

Community needs are articulated by the public through Grama Sabha and after thorough deliberations, their needs are prioritized and converted as implementable projects where the public themselves actively contribute in cash, kind or through labour to supplement the government funds and execute the works. The Government provides necessary technical support to execute the works.

This scheme maximizes the utility value of the funds allocated by the Government. Apart from expediting the execution and improving the quality of work, it also promotes the concept of community maintenance of public assets. The outlay proposed for this scheme during Tenth Plan period is ₹120 crores.

Member of Legislative Assembly Constituency Development Scheme (MLACD)

The Member of Legislative Assembly Constituency Development Scheme is fully funded by the State Government. The main objective of the scheme is to bridge the critical infrastructural gap in the Assembly Constituencies.

Under this scheme each member of Legislative Assembly shall identify the works that should be executed in his constituency. The allocation for each Assembly Constituency is ₹82 lakhs.

Important works like Integrated Sanitary Complexes for Women, construction of hostels for SC/STs, BC/MBCs students, construction of office buildings for VAOs and provision of drinking water in drought-affected areas are taken up on priority basis. The remaining works will be proposed by MLA should be in accordance with the guidelines issued in this regard. An outlay of ₹1059.85 crores has been proposed under the scheme during Tenth Plan period.

State Finance Commission Grant

A devolution formula has been adopted for devolving resources to urban and rural local bodies based on the recommendations of the

Second State Finance Commission for the award period 2002-07 coinciding with the Tenth Plan period. The rural and urban local bodies will receive 8 per cent of the States' Own Tax Revenue after excluding Entertainment Tax receipts.

The vertical sharing of resources between rural and urban local bodies will be in the ratio of 58:42. Of the total devolutions to the urban local bodies, the resources will be shared between the Corporations, Municipalities and Town Panchayats in the ratio 31:34:35. The devolution to rural local bodies will be shared among the Village Panchayats, Panchayat Unions and the District Panchayats in the ratio of 47:45:8. Further the State Finance Commission grants will be released to the local bodies on a monthly basis. An outlay of ₹659.47 crores is provided for this purpose

Integrated Sanitary Complex for Women

Tamil Nadu's coverage in rural sanitation is presently at 11% which is lower than national average of 15%. To protect dignity and privacy of the women the Government have launched a new scheme called the Integrated Sanitary Complex for women to provide toilets and facilities for bathing and washing for women under one roof. Each sanitary complex will be spread over approximately 750 sq. ft. with 10 toilets and 3 cubicles for bathing. Each complex has an independent water connection to ensure that the users have a steady and continued supply of water.

A pump room and water tank will also form part of the sanitary complex. The operation and maintenance of these sanitary complexes will be the responsibility of the village panchayats and self-help groups.

Monitoring committees will also be formed for proper maintenance of these sanitary complexes. An outlay of ₹284 crores has been proposed under this scheme during the Tenth Plan period.

Other Programmes/Schemes

The outlay proposed in respect of other Rural Development programmes during Tenth Plan is as follows:

Sl. No.	*Name of scheme/programme*	*Proposed outlay (₹ in crores)*
1	*Capital programme of Infrastructure Development by rural local bodies*	*100.00*
2	*DRDA Administration cost*	*20.08*
3	*Other Rural Development Programmes*	*113.14*
	Total	***233.22***

Area Development Programme

Western Ghats Development Programme

Provision of infrastructure facilities like drinking water, street lights, formation of link roads, construction of school buildings and health subcentres have been proposed to be taken up in the Western Ghats taluks under WGDP.

These works will be planned and executed by the concerned local bodies. The outlay proposed under the above head during the Tenth Plan period is `1.90 crores.

Drought Prone Area Programme

The Drought Prone Area Programme (DPAP) is an integrated watershed development programme with the prime objective of promoting the over all economic development of watershed community by optimally utilizing natural resources so as to mitigate the adverse effects of drought, prevent further ecological degradation and create employment through non-farm activities.

This programme is being implemented in 16 districts viz:

- Dharmapuri (14),
- Thoothukudi (18)
- Sivagangai (7),
- Ramanathapuram (7),
- Virudhunagar (7),
- Pudukottai (4),
- Tirunelveli (1),
- Salem (5),
- Namakkal (3),
- Coimbatore (5),
- Thiruvannamalai (1),
- Dindigul (3),
- Vellore (6),
- Tiruchirappali (1).
- Perambalur (6), and
- Karur (2).

This programme is sponsored by the Government of India and the expenditure is shared in the ratio of 75:25 between and Central and State Governments.

The DPAP is implemented on watershed approach. Each watershed covers an area of approximately 500 ha. The allocation per hectare is ₹6,000.

This programme consists of 5 major components, namely,

1. Entry point activity
2. Community organization,
3. Training,
4. Developmental activities and
5. Project administration.

The Developmental works carried out under DPAP are as follows:

- Land Development including land levelling, summer ploughing, institutional and moisture conservation measures like contour and graded bunds fortified by vegetation, bench terracing in hilly terrain.
- Drainage line treatment with a combination of vegetative and engineering structures.
- Development of small water harvesting structures such as low cost farm ponds, nulla bunds, check dam and percolation ponds.
- Nursery raising for fodder, timber, fuelwood and horticultural species.
- Afforestation activities including block plantations, avenue plantation, shelter belts, sand dune stabilization etc.,
- Agro-forestry and horticultural development.
- Pasture development either by itself or in conjunction with plantations.
- Repair, restoration and upgradation of existing common property assets and structures in watershed to obtain optimum and substained benefits from previous public investments.
- Crop demonstration for popularizing new crops/varieties or innovative management practices.

Proposals

Development works in 297 watersheds sanctioned in the first batch during 1995-96 to 1999-2000 have already been successfully completed with a total outlay of ₹53.57 crores covering 42,090 hec. Watersheds sanctioned during 1999-2000 and 2001-02 will be continued during Tenth Plan period. In addition it is expected that 700 more watershed projects will be taken up during Tenth plan period. The outlay proposed under DPAP would be ₹210 crores during Tenth plan out of which the State's share will be ₹52.50 crores. The total outlay towards Special Programme for Rural Development is ₹3500 crores.

Table: *Proposed outlay for Special Programmes for Rural Development (Rs. ₹in crores)*

Sl. No.	*Name of the scheme/Programme*	*Outlay for Tenth Plan (State share)*
1	*Member of Legislative Assembly Constituency Development scheme (MLACD)*	*1059.85*
2	*Village Self-sufficiency scheme*	*120.00*
3	*Capital Programme of Infrastructure Development by Rural Local bodies*	*100.00*
4	*Rural Sanitary Complex for Women*	*284.00*
5	*Construction of building for VAO's Office*	*19.80*
6	*Villlage Fair Development scheme*	*5.00*
7	*SGSY*	*131.45*
8	*SGRY*	*303.79*
9	*IAY under Special Component Programme*	*292.89*
10	*Special Component Plan for rural shelter*	*111.14*
11	*District Reform facility*	*225.00*
12	*Finance Commission Grants to Local bodies*	*659.47*
13	*DRDA Administration cost*	*20.07*
14	*Other Rural Development Programme*	*113.14*
	Area Development Programme	
15	*Western Ghats Development Programme*	*1.90*
16	*Drought Prone Area Programme*	*52.50*
	Total	***3500.00***

Community Development

Formation of rural roads, construction of small bridges and culverts, provision of water supply and sanitation facilities, improvement and maintenance of minor irrigation tanks constitute Community Development activities.

Rural Sanitation

To provide more and more sanitation facilities to rural population, generate awareness about health education and eradicate manual scavenging, the Total Sanitation Campaign scheme under RCRSP will be continued during the Tenth Five Year Plan period.

The Total Sanitation Campaign envisages a demand driven approach with greater public participation and more emphasis given for IEC activities to create awareness among the rural masses.

The project would be implemented in 24 months spread over 3 years in select districts with the ultimate objective of covering 80% rural population under sanitation. The expenditure on this scheme is shared by the Central and State Government on 80:20 basis. An outlay of `19.15 crores has been provided under the Tenth plan.

Integrated Rural Sanitation and Water Supply Project with DANIDA Assistance

This scheme aims to improve the health and sanitary condition in the project area villages through integrated approach to provide safe drinking water and sanitation through participatory and demand driven approach. This programme is being implemented with DANIDA assistance. Water supply works, individual household latrines and institutional latrines are taken up in the project area. The outlay provided is `16.27 crores.

Improvement of Rural roads, bridges and drainage structures

At present panchayats and panchayat unions are maintaining 52% of the total length of the roads in the state. The road transport has emerged as the most eminent mode of transport in the light of its inherent advantages of lower cost of travel and flexibility in operation. The rural roads also provide outlet to market centres, taluk headquarters and other main roads.

Hence, it is essential to improve village roads to all weather roads *i.e.,* by black topping. The improvement of road works has been taken up under Rural Infrastructure Development Fund (RIDF) under NABARD. An outlay of `93.75 crores has been proposed under this head during Tenth plan. It has also been proposed to avail a loan amount of `93.76 crores under RIDF-V.

Provision of Infrastructural facilities in Tribal blocks

The objectives of the schemes are:

- To assist the ST families to cross the poverty line with special emphasis on improving agriculture, irrigation and education in tribal areas and
- To provide basic infrastructure facilities for better living conditions. An outlay of `2.39 crores has been proposed during the Tenth Plan.

Provision of Infrastructure facilities for Rural local bodies

With a view to provide basic infrastructure facilities such as drinking water, street lights, link roads, construction of school buildings, health subcentres etc., an outlay of 294.68 crores has been proposed during the Tenth Plan.

Local Bodies Incentive Scheme

An outlay of `80 crores has been proposed during the Tenth Plan. Thus the total outlay for Community Development for the Tenth Plan is `600 crores.

Table: *Proposed outlay for Community Development (`in crores)*

Sl.	*Name of the scheme/Programme*	*Outlay (State No. share)*
1	*Improvement of rural roads, bridges and drainage structures under RIDF*	*93.75*
2	*Loans for improvement of rural roads, bridges and drainage structures under RIDF-V*	*93.76*
3	*Integrated Rural sanitation and water supply project with DANIDA assistance*	*16.27*
4	*Central Rural Sanitation Programme*	*19.15*
5	*Local Bodies incentive scheme*	*80.00*
6	*Formation of Tribal blocks in Hill areas*	*2.39*
7	*Provision of infrastructure facilities for rural local bodies*	*294.68*
	Total	***600.00***

Chapter 2

Overview of Rural Sociology

Origin and Development of Rural Sociology

Rural sociology is a new branch of sociology with studies being carried out from 19th century. The prominent scholars engaged in rural sociology during this period were-Sir Henry Maine, Etton, Stemann, Baden Powell, Slater and Pallock etc. The period of 1890-1920 in America saw the rural societies facing many socio-economic problems which attracted the attention of the intelligentsia thus establishing study of rural society as an academic discipline. The appointment of Country life Commission by Theodore Roosevelt was an important landmark in the history of rural sociology. In 1916 the first text book on sociology was published by J.N Gillettee.

It was first originated in the United States of America. It has taken more than half a century to become established as a distinct academic field or professional study. The main contributors to the development of rural sociology are-Charles Sanderson, Burtherfield, Ernast Burnholme, John Morris Gillin, Franklin H. Giddings and Thomas Nixon Carver. It was President Roosevelt who, through the appointment of 'Country Life Commission' gave a good encouragement to the development to the rural sociology in 1908. The report of this Commission encouraged the studies of rural society.

In 1917 the Department of Rural Sociology was set up by the American Sociological Society. In 1919, a 'Rural Sociology Department' was established under the chairmanship of Dr. C. J. Galpin. The Great Depression of 1930 provided another stimulus to the growth of rural sociology.

In 1937, 'Rural Sociological Society' was formed. It started publishing a professional journal 'Rural Sociology' containing results of rural sociological research. C. J. Galpin of University of Wisconsin developed techniques for defining and delimiting the rural community. His approach is still popular today.

The Great Second World War gave yet another fillip to the growth of rural sociology. The destruction caused by the war demanded reconstruction. The reconstruction work brought further encouragement to the science. By 1958 there were about 1000 professional rural sociologists in America. Rural sociology crossed the boundaries of America and became popular in Europe. A European Society for Rural Sociology was formed in 1957, and a similar organisation was started in Japan also. In developing countries, the role of the rural sociologists is primarily in the applied field of more effective planning and operation of rural community development programmes.

The Second World War caused heavy destruction and damage to human society which needed reconstruction. As a result rural sociology got an impetus in USA. The main concern of rural sociology came to be the understanding and diagnosing of the social and economic problems of farmers. More emphasis was placed on issues such as the internal structures of community life and the changing composition of rural populations than on their relationships with land or the social aspects of agricultural production.

Theoretically rural sociology remained caught up in bipolar notions of social change whereas rural often got defined as the opposite of urban. Rurality was conceptualized as an autonomous sociological reality. The identification of rural sociology with rural society has also raised questions about its relevance in the western context where no rural areas were left anymore and almost the entire population had become urbanized.

In response to these critiques of rural sociology a new sub-discipline of sociology emerged that operated largely within the functionalist paradigm and was preoccupied with the study of the community life of rural people. This sub-discipline known as sociology of agriculture focused its attention on understanding and analysing the social framework of agricultural production and the structures of relations centered on land. It raised questions about how and on what terms the agrarian sector was being integrated into the system of commodity production and about the unequal distribution of agricultural incomes and food among the different social categories of people.

The sociology of agriculture also distinguished itself from peasant studies on the grounds that its focus was on capitalist farming where the production was primarily for the market, not on peasants producing for their own consumption by using family labour. Thus it claimed more kinship with the tradition of the political economy of agriculture or agrarian studies.

At the methodological level, historical inquiries became as relevant as ethnographic/empirical studies. This conceptual shift during the early 1970s also helped in bringing sociologists working on agrarian issues in the western countries closer to those concerned with agrarian transformations in the third world.

Scope of Rural Sociology

The scope or subject-matter of rural sociology is basically the study of rural society with all its complexities. According to Lawry and Nelson, 'The subject-matter of rural sociology is the description and analysis of the progress of various groups as they exist in the rural environment.' The main tasks of rural sociology can be mentioned here.

They are as follows:

1. *Rural Community and Rural Problems:* This includes the characteristics and nature of rural community and its problems.
2. *Rural Social Life:* This includes various aspects of the rural people.
3. *Rural Social Organization:* This includes the study of various rural social organizations and institutions including family and marriage.
4. *Rural Social Institutions and Structure:* This includes the study of dogmas, customs, traditions, morals, conventions, practices and various political, economic, religious and cultural institutions
5. *Rural Planning and Reconstruction:* Rural sociology has great practical applications. Hence rural planning and reconstruction are also the main tasks of rural sociology to be dealt with.
6. *Social Change and Social Control in Rural Social Setup:* It is here we study the impact of city on rural life. The mechanisms of social control of the rural society are also examined here.
7. *Religion and Culture in Rural Society:* Religion plays an important role in the rural set up. Culture of rural society exhibits striking peculiarities. These come within the domain of rural sociology.

8. *Rural Social Processes:* Different social processes such as cooperation, competition, integration, differentiation, isolation etc., that take place in rural society are also studied in rural sociology.
9. *Differences between Urban and Rural Society:* The study of rural society includes the differences between urban and rural society also.

Importance of Rural Sociology

The practical value of the study of rural sociology is widely recognised today. As long as the villages and the rural society assume importance, the rural sociology shall continue to acquire importance. The value of rural sociology can be understood by the following points:

1. Rural Population is in Majority: The world's is more rural than urban. More than two-third of people of the world live in villages. It is the village that forms the basis of society. Rural sociology is inevitable for the study of the majority of the population.
2. Intimate Relationship between the Land and Man: Man is born out of land and his entire culture depends on it. Land has been the part of and parcel of human life. Progress starts from the village. The type of land partially conditions the type of society and the opportunities for human development. This close relationship between man and land has also been recognised by economists and political scientists.
3. Villages and Rural Life from the Source of Population: Cities normally grow out of towns and villages. No city can come into existence all of a sudden without having a rural background. A village, when improved and thickly populated, becomes a town or city. Thus it is the village population that forms the source of urban life.
4. Psychological Approach to the Rural Life: Rural progress, rural reconstruction or improvement of rural societies is possible only when the people have correct idea about the rural way of life and problems. Rural sociology touches upon the rural psychology and provides a good understanding of the rural people and their society.

"All of us know," for example, that people prefer to live in cities because there are more opportunities, services, and great personal fulfillment. "Everyone knows" that successful business and economic development must stay focused on metropolitan locations to maximize transportation and labor costs. "Everyone knows" that many of our small towns and villages are in distress and that even though the *unsettling* of the countryside may be a national tragedy, it amounts to no more than a natural process that will continue to occur over the next century.

Defining Rural

There are many ways to define areas that are "rural." Although the general idea of specifically conceptualizing "rural" areas came into use in the 1920s with its basis in sociology, many, if not most, of the current explanatory frameworks evolved to provide guidance for the distribution of government monies or to perform a census of places and people. As a corollary to these classification systems, there persists the traditional assumptions that tend to go along with the word "rural," assumptions that are often ungrounded and at best belie the diversity inherent in areas typically grouped together as "rural" or "nonmetropolitan."

For instance, it is a commonly held belief that farming is a mainstay of most rural economies. In fact, fewer than one-fifth of rural counties in North America now have a significant economic dependence on farming, and the 20% of nonmetro counties that have farming as their principal economic base contain less than 10% of the nonmetro population (Deavers, 1992). Moreover, the geopolitical boundaries that usually serve as the basis for these classifications often are not optimal.

The Urban-Rural Imbalance

Since 1950 it should be clear that metropolitan settlement structure leading to urban conglomerations is the dominant growth form of the world. Metropolitan areas will account for 70 percent of the net growth in world population during the 1990s-an additional 67 million people every year. Other than natural increase, the prime engine of metropolitan growth is rural-to-urban migration. It is, however, important to note that rural-to-metropolitan trends have changed directions several times in the latter part of the 20 Century. It would appear that change, rather than stability, is the typical demographic and economic situation for most of the world's rural and nonmetropolitan areas at the end of the 20th Century.

The United Nations reports that 43 percent of the world's population lived in urban areas in 1990; a 34 percent increase since 1960. In the next several years (2005), the world will pass a historic milestone: more than half of its population — or more than three billion people — will live in cities. At the turn of the century, only 14 percent of the Earth's population called cities home — and just 11 centres on the planet had more than one million inhabitants.

Now there are 400 cities with populations of at least one million, and 20 megacities with populations exceeding 10 million, with a half dozen of them approaching or exceeding the 20 million level. While the developing world still flocks to core cities, much of Europe, North America, the Russian Federation, and Australia are reversing the process: emptiness at the center and growth on the edges-or the new "Edge City" metropolitan areas.

At the halfway mark of the 21st Century, more than 70 percent of the world's population will live within the metropolitan framework (an area now loosely defined up to 40-100 kilometres from the older urban cores). In most more developed nations, especially in North America and Europe, the urban-rural distribution now stands at 75-80 percent metropolitan to 20-25 percent rural.

The most common factor contributing to rural-to-urban migration is rural unemployment resulting in part from rural areas having higher fertility levels than urban areas, according to Lori S. Ashford, a senior policy analyst with the Population Reference Bureau (PRB). A shortage of basic technology in rural areas also promotes out-migration and environmental degradation; it has led to a serious shortage of arable land in many communities throughout the developing world. While the growth of cities can contribute to economic progress, the study notes that problems arise when urbanization "occurs so rapidly that it strains the ability of urban governments to provide housing, sanitation, public safety, and other necessary services— and when there are not enough jobs."

The New Paradigm

The relationship between government and economic development began to change marked during the late 1970's and early 1980's. The beginning of the 1980's saw many less developed countries heavily borrowed and unable to service their debt. The physical plant and infrastructure fashioned in the 1950s and 1960s-often of exceptionally poor quality-created high levels of service costs that even the most developed nations could not bear. Hardest hit were the rural economies and regional settlement patterns resulting in a virtually unabated flow of resources to the metropolitan areas. The final result was the beginning of the demise of the centrally-planned economy and the ushering of the "Age of Austerity." The concept of integrated population and development planning had to be adjusted in light of the changes brought about by this austerity.

Many planners and development analysts regarded the goals of development under austerity as self-evident and non-problematic, seeing the only problems as concerning how to attain them. The new paradigm recognized that both the environment and human settlement where *open* systems and regulated by things happening beyond local and national boundaries-*the Global Economy*-and greatly affected by natural and human imbalances. In short, the *urbancentric* view of the world was called into question, especially the prevalent notion that the purpose of rural areas was to provide food, fuel, and cheap workers. The new paradigm not only recognizes the connectivity of the urban-rural spheres, but also addresses the issue of rural vitality. For, unless rural areas are revitalized, the metropolitan centres must ultimately provide the rescue funds and resources to support the countryside. The solution is what we typically call *economic development*. In principle, the new paradigm called for self-sustaining economic growth and social policy designed to provide the requisites of existence and citizenship. While the former can help provide the fuel for the latter, we must be under no illusion that growth itself will fulfil basic needs.

The New Century Approach to Rural Planning

The most important question to be asked is "are rural areas and country towns sustainable as working and living communities?" Many rural areas have proven to be *persistent*-they have sustained while both inner city and suburban area have declined in the face of metropolitan spread. The only reasonable conclusion that can be reached concerning this persistence is their *diversity*. Less than a century ago the rural economy depended almost entirely on resource extraction, agriculture (and support service to agriculture), and fishing.

Economic Diversity

The rural areas that show the most favorable growth and economic strength have their economies based on recreation and tourism. Throughout most of North and South America, Western Europe, Australia, and New Zealand the lure of the natural environment and tourism (place and historicity) are significant parts of their economies. Firms and industries built around the exploitation of amenities show exceptionally strong growth and are a world leader in providing new jobs.

Are rural economies built around tourism and amenities sustainable? Thought on this question is decidedly mixed and generally negative. Tourism, in one form or another is the world's second largest industry. As a whole, this activity *mines* and *extracts* wealth in the form of money and exports the final resources to metropolitan areas where the corporations and trusts reside. Tourism is dependent on wealth and increasing affluence-it is not an activity within reach of the world's poor. Thus, there is a closed cycle of events whereby tourism and amenity based economies demand ever increasing affluence and affluence itself is associated with migration to metropolitan areas. Tourism and amenity jobs are among the lowest paying service industries in the world-or what is termed minimum or subsistence wage in most countries. The firms that service the local industries are labor intensive and built around employment in food service, lodging and accommodation, information assistance, maintenance, and service sales to the travelling public.

Since most tourism is seasonal, the industry depends on high migration rates based on *boom and bust* seasons that in turn demand the cheapest labor available. Factors such as poor seasonal weather, higher transportation costs due to both profit taking and increasing costs for fuels can send a local economy into shambles within a short period of time-causing some of the highest unemployment rates in any industry. Finally, there is the long term (and often conflicting) goal of greater economic sustainability in local areas based on tourism and amenities. The goal is to extend visiting seasons by creating greater opportunity to capture market share of tourism monies. Since 1980 the most popular methods in the western world are gaming or gambling, conventions/meetings, and multiple use recreation (golfing, theme parks, and similar facilities). The controversy over gaming/gambling as a supplement to economic diversity continues in a worldwide debate. Regardless, it has achieved phenomenal rates of return and now appears to be reaching saturation as larger scale enterprises are developed. Wage and salary incomes paid to industry employees are among the highest in rural areas.

Remoteness

Remoteness is the one characteristic that all true rural areas share in common. It is viewed as both an asset and a major liability. Many development specialists and rural sociologists take the stance that remoteness and isolation is an asset. They argue that small structure, vertical leadership, and cooperation are important strengths that contribute to ethic and social identity.

Although they acknowledge that interlocal cooperation with regional towns is important, they also counter that individual community ties are the most important process in local development. They imply that to dismiss the importance of local pride, concern, and problem solving capabilities would ignore much of the community's true resource base.

On the other hand, current economic development practice now strongly encouraged in rural areas promotes inter-community cooperation, assimilation with other communities, and common work towards development. This is based on the theory that small size and remoteness is *the* major inhibitor of development efforts. Thus, the other side of the problem is how to overcome distance factors in rural areas. In general, remoteness factors are related to four major policy choices in central planning: transportation, critical service deliver, communications, and jobs skills/training.

Communications, more specifically telecommunications amounting to both advanced systems of current technologies, and emerging forms of real time delivery, are predicted by many to be the total planning solution for rural areas. Unlike transportation outcomes, which must overcome *place to place* remoteness, telecommunications offers the hope of *in-place* service and need delivery. It is attractive, if for no other reason, because it offers quick and incremental *upgrade paths*-often at a decreasing marginal costs-rather than enormous sunk costs experienced in transportation and regional development.

The final factor to be discussed, because it serves to impact the cost of remoteness, is job skills/training. No society or societal sector in the global world can afford to concentrate its educational and development resources solely in metropolitan areas.

Yet, decentralization of educational resources and development ranks exceptionally high on the list of major expenditures of any nation aspiring to greater sustainability and vitality. Both public and private systems have responded throughout this century to deliver education, jobs skills, and general training to remote areas-both in-place and through regional centres coordinating with outlying communities. But, it would appear that, even with local self-help and capacity building programs, the delivery of these vital services is reaching maximum effort under present funding and technology.

Lack of Resources

A lack of basic resources to meet rural residences' needs is repeatedly shown as a major factor in a community's inability to sustain and maintain community identity and commitment. Resources are understood to mean both fiscal (material) and human and therefore most planning solutions employ a two-pronged set of policies designed to increase resource capacity.

Efforts to redirect material resources to rural areas have been ongoing throughout the 20th Century and far out number programs targeted towards urban areas. Worldwide, major efforts include wide-ranging programs such as education (extension), farm and price supports, direct grants-in-aid, revenue sharing, new towns, and health care-to mentioned but a few. No comprehensive assessment of the effectiveness of these programs exists, but few will venture to say that trillions of dollars poured into rural development has not made a difference in the shape of the nonmetropolitan sectors of our countries. Many rural sociologists argue that it is the scarceness of resources, the need for austerity, and the concomitant appreciation for the assets that do exist that creates the unique blend of community and sustainability thought to be prevalent in the world's nonmetropolitan areas. On the other hand, it is also widely argued that it is the dependence of small communities on others for aid that creates a limited perspective or community vision and a clearly articulated path into the future. Whatever blend of perspective, it is abundantly clear that the request for resources is an all-consuming factor in the life of small communities.

Work Diversity and New Rural Industries

Much of the local economic development (L.E.D.) literature promotes the development of new rural industries (RIs) as one path to a sustainable countryside. There is little argument that one of the keys to attaining a vital, living countryside is increased job opportunity and quality employment. Although RIs lag behind new service enterprises as the fastest growing component of the rural economy, nevertheless, they play a critically important role in rural economic diversification. However, a minority of rural researchers point to the rise of RIs, specifically in developing regions, as a sign of distress rather than positive rural development.

Tambunan [1995] and others argue that there are two quite different conditions under which rural labor might shift from traditional agriculture, fishing, forestry and extractive pursuits: (a) when labor is pulled or "attracted" out of agriculture into better non-agricultural opportunities; or, (2) when labor is "pushed" or forced out of agriculture by declining employment opportunities into relatively worse RIs (marginal occupations) whose capacity to absorb large quantities is achieved at the cost of extremely low, and possibly declining incomes.

The first type of RIs (attracted) are typically run on a more or less stable basis with a business goal of surplus generation and growth using hired labor and a certain degree of technical sophistication. This is in contrast to the second type of RIs which are often seasonal, run with the help of unpaid family labor, using rather primitive technology catering mainly to local markets.

The argument against sustainability and a total planning solution is that a heavy presence of the second type of RIs denotes increasing poverty in the region. Some researchers note, therefore, that the presence of the second type of RIs can only be justified on the basis of their labor intensity and not productivity or income gains.

Building Local Capacity as a Route to Sustainability

Throughout North America, much of Western Europe, Australia, and New Zealand, community generated rural revitalization (generally termed Local Economic Development-or LED) is currently a matter of considerable profile.

A prominent feature of this activity is what is termed the *process related dimensions* of rural LED-meaning that the capacity of individual communities to bring about a better future for themselves depends in no small measure on how well they are equipped in terms of leadership and team related skills. The root challenge of all rural communities must be the shaping of new strategies responsive to the enduring realities of rural economies and cultural life-high unemployment; persistent poverty; deteriorated social well-being; lower earnings; and diminished health care-as well as changing national and global circumstances.

Revitalizing “rural” must include the participation of small communities in search of positive change, whereby local people are encouraged to think more about their futures and to put into practice their ideas for securing those futures. Capacity building, therefore, deals mostly with the ability of local people to solve problems. These *process dimension programs* seek to bring about change by forging new skills within rural communities related to leadership, mediation and conflict resolution, group processes, understanding the business of government, and the articulation of a shared vision. In the simplest terms, capacity building can be defined as increasing the ability of people and institutions to do what is required of them [Newlands, 1981].

Counterurbanizing the Countryside-Evidence of Change?

Throughout this century migration flows worldwide follow a recognizable pattern: from rural to urban, from mountains to plains, from undeveloped countries to developed countries. These population flows are marked by diversity, complexity, and change leaving many of the small, remote rural areas in a final stage of disintegration. Thus, population reversal (*counterurbanization*) has become one of the hallmarks of a sustainable, living rural countryside.

On a worldwide scale, recent literature assesses counterurbanism as occurring throughout much of the world-albeit at very diverse rates. In truth, the evidence for urban population dispersal is strong while the proof for rural rejuvenation is weak. As noted, the reasons for this phenomena are diverse and complex, and should not be confused with temporary labor migration, but from an overall standpoint there are three controlling factors.

First, it is important to understand that the predominant growth form in the world today-metropolitanism-is undergoing considerable change. Traditional rural communities lying within 65 to 120 kilometres of the metropolitan fringe show a strong propensity to expand in population size and economic diversity. This large sphere of distance influencing surrounding fringe areas, sometimes called *penturbia* or the *component economic area*, is quite possible the final wave of spatial development of large urban centres before urban agglomeration occurs. Forces associated with this change are many, but predictable. In the U.S., it is often associated with the quest for more affordable housing, less computing to work, educational opportunities for children, lifestyle and amenities. Since most-if not nearly all-of the communities within the 65-120 k growth ring are classified as rural or small town (ranging from 15,000 to 5,000 and under), it is not surprising that demographers report new rural growth and counterurbanism.

Second, not all of the more remote rural areas have experienced depopulation. Fully 25-30 percent of communities in the more developed countries report that small towns have gained in population during the past 30 years. Again, the factors associated with this growth are complex, but can be said to center around several major causes. The presence of tertiary (university) education systems is important, as is the location near major transportation links. The main factor, however, at least in North America and Western Europe, are amenity rich areas attracting lifestyles, tourism, recreation, elderly retirement, and land investment opportunities.

Third, although the most remote rural communities show considerable aggregate population loss, some (but not many) seem to have beat the odds and sustained or even exhibit growth while their neighboring communities have perished. The evidence for this counterurbanism is sketchy at best and relies mainly on individual case studies rather than aggregate data, and for every success story there appears to be dozens of declining towns.

There is solid evidence that renewed local leadership from in migrant entrepreneurs (especially retirements) plays a role in some counter-urbanization. Governmental and private economic development programs must surely account for a portion of this reversal-although the evidence is not clear. The economic phenomena of *clustering of related economic activities* may, in fact, play a greater role. Governmental direction of capital expenditures, often using triage concepts, seems to have an impact in larger remote rural communities when prisons, hospitals, and related facilities are constructed.

Regional Country Towns and Rural Stabilization

Certainly one of the bright spots among rural researchers is the role played by the Country Towns in remote, rural areas. Called *"growth poles"* or *"regional centres"* in the 1960s, these large towns-or small cities, as some prefer-appear to provide a major stabilizing force in all nonmetropolitan areas.

Regional country towns display a wide population variance, depending on the degree of remoteness and economic function. In North America, regional towns rarely display a population base less than 10,000 persons, but the median size is 25,000 and will range upwards to 50,000 persons.

Diverse dependency will typically begin to appear around the 10,000 person level and becomes statistically significant at 25,000 persons. Diverse dependency is a term coined by the United States Bureau of Economic Research and rests on the concept of local economic function.

Economic Dependency Types include:

1. Farming-dependent—Farming contributes a weighted annual average of 35 percent or more of total labor and proprietor income.
2. Mining-dependent—Mining contributes a weighted annual average of 25 percent or more of total labor and proprietor income.
3. Manufacturing-dependent—Manufacturing contributes a weighted annual average of 35percent or more of total labor and proprietor income.
4. Government-dependent—Government contributes a weighted annual average of 25 percent or more of total labor and proprietor income.
5. Services-dependent—Service activities (private and personal services, agricultural services, wholesale and retail trade, finance and insurance, transportation and public utilities) contribute a weighted annual average of 50 percent or more of total labor and proprietor income.
6. Non-specialized— Not classified as a specialized economic type.

There is worldwide evidence that the larger regional country towns are rapidly approaching non-specialized economies, although employment tends to be heavily weighted in favor of services and manufacturing, as they assume the leading provider roles in their spheres of influence. It also appears that they have or will soon gain the necessary concentration of capital, population mass, and economies of scale to provide the essential development functions, health care services, manufacturing and employment opportunities, and cultural assets to sustain large and remote rural hinterlands.

The concept of rural *triage* is especially important for centralized decision makers considering policies on regional towns.

Triage is, of course, an emergency medical technique for concentrating on those patients that show the best promise of recovery rather than those in critical condition or those that will probably stabilize. Given the assumption that small, remote rural centres have little hope of a sustainable future unless they are linked to unique resources, and that rural communities tied to metropolitan influence will be sustainable in the future, the best policy may be to concentrate on all but the most critical resources on those communities which, given immediate attention, demonstrate great promise.

Regional country towns fit this classification nicely. First, they are survivors in their spheres of influence-they have managed to gain supremacy over their economic hinterlands. Second, they are sustainable from the standpoint that they have the capacity to provide both employment, food, and shelter at some of the most reasonable costs in the world today, Third, they can provide a partial solution to the *exit roads syndrome* from smaller rural areas by providing retirement opportunities for the elderly and educational chances for youth who would otherwise naturally migrate to metropolitan areas. Finally, they provide an excellent occasion for government to decentralize their social and service functions in the more remote areas of a nation. If the concept of local economic redevelopment holds promise, then it must decentralized empowerment to the local place.

The Impact of Telecommunications

"While we weren't looking, the future arrived"! Since the middle 1980s, futurists such as Alvin Toffler [Toffler, 1985] have said that "it is certainly no secret that our society is moving away from a manufacturing focus and becoming an information driven machine... The nascent markets of the next century are based on value-added service which are typically the result of adept information management.". The heart of this new information *Third Wave* technology is the digital network and digital communications via the computer modem, faxes, and wireless telephones.

The true, large scale impact of telecommunications on rural areas lies some distance in the future; some would say between the year 2030 and 2050 before global wireless is a truly dependable and integrated source of doing business. Even now in 1997, digital communications through the *Internet* are reforming some selected market relationships between rural and metro locations. Without a doubt, telecommunications will have a marked impact on the two overriding factors that affect non-metropolitan performance: remoteness and labor pools.

Reliable, real time telecommunications cannot solve, but will certainly diminish the impact of distance between more remote rural locations and their major markets and suppliers in metro areas. The bourgeoning service sector worldwide that is essentially responsible for the assimilation, interpretation, and management of information will no longer be place bound-location will be irrelevant assuming that global communications will be the same everywhere.

Telecommunications will be a major factor in transforming, rather than reforming, the way rural communities do business and live their lives. No amount of digital information can reform the basic distinction between the urbanized and the small place given the massive imbalance of resources. It cannot be *a total planning solution*, but it can help to create a greater competitiveness in the way rural people receive their education, medical and social care, market their goods, acquire their supplies, and conduct their affairs.

It is assumed that rural areas already showing signs of great vitality will be best positioned to benefit from the new technologies and more remote centres already in decline the least. There is, however, a counter hypothesis to this argument. Telecommuting may contribute to further suburbanization and urban sprawl by releasing households from location constraints related to maximum acceptable commute time and distance. Because the practical use of modern digital telecommunications is such a relatively new activity, no studies have been able to confirm or deny this hypothesis (Handy, 1994). If this indeed occurs, the environmental costs of further sprawl could far outweigh benefits received by reduced automobile and office use. It is difficult to estimate the likelihood of this scenario because there are so many factors contributing to housing location decisions.

The second overriding factor related to rural-metro imbalance likely to be impacted by telecommunications is the labor pool itself.

Remote, rural areas may (at least according to some studies and many common perceptions in local economic development) be good places to start both services and new start-up firms, but they cannot sustain the need for increased capital and labor due to lack of available resources and worker pools.

The concept of *telecommuting*-large groups of workers who are place bound throughout a nation, but who work for a remote and centralized firm via digital communications-will diminish the need for regional labor. The argument that telecommunications can never supplant the need for specific site, skilled labor in manufacturing and fabrication will always remain valid, however it is necessary to realize that most now agree that the distinction between value-added activities and services is becoming less important.

Conclusions-Century's End and a New Millennium

Change is the price of the rejuvenation of the countryside and the survival of small towns. In most cases, adequate levels of employment and income cannot be expected from traditional sectors-especially if rural areas are expected to decouple from metros. The real choice, as Galston suggests, will be between decline and forms of innovation that will leave neither individual lives nor the structure of social relations unchanged. Some, perhaps many, rural residents will both resent and regret these changes, but they cannot be avoided.

Every way of life requires some economic basis, but a commitment to preserving a *total way of life* in the face of profound economic and social change cannot hope to succeed. Individuals who are devoted to continuity of place, who want a sustainable base for the generations who follow, must therefore accept some degree of discontinuities of economic and social life.

"To be successful, efforts to rejuvenate the rural countryside must rest on genuine local preferences. Underlying these preferences is some understanding of what rural individuals, considered simply as citizens of a country, are thought to deserve. Since the 1940s many countries have made the political determination that all citizens, regardless of place, were entitled to electricity, decent roads, schools, and adequate water/wastewater facilities.

The question in the next century is whether access to information management through digitalization and fiber optics will be similarly defined as elements of social citizenship. The question is on the table, and the viability of most of our rural areas hangs in the balance."

Rural Sociology in Europe

Rural sociology as it is understood in the United States came into being in Europe only after World War II. On the surface, this seems somewhat surprising. An important part of the population of Europe is still rural. During the last few decades in most European countries the percentage of the active population engaged in agriculture was higher than in the United States, in several countries much higher. Sociology as a science originated from Europe. So why no rural sociology at an earlier date?

There are several reasons which help to explain this phenomenon. First of all, one has to bear in mind that rural sociology as we know it now is not just *the* sociology of rural life. One could imagine a rural sociology in many respects quite different from the present. Rural sociology as we know it in America and elsewhere has strong roots in practice. Even if it would not be right to call rural sociology just an applied science, it would be equally wrong to deny its strong interest in the problems of daily life and its striving for applicability. Rural sociology never would have developed in the way it did if it had not shown its importance for the betterment of rural life. But before World War II, sociology in Europe was hardly seen by nonprofessionals as a science which had a practical value. This conclusion was right. Sociology as it was taught and studied in Europe before the war was, for the greater part, highly theoretical and often even philosophical in character. Thus, there was no place for a rural sociology with a strong orientation to applicability.

Many sociologists even sought generalizations at such a high level that differences between rural and nonrural society hardly came into consideration, so that on a more abstract level there were not many chances for a special study of rural life either. At any rate, one can state that the kind of rural sociology which has been developed in America did not fit into the dominating concept of sociology in Europe before 1940.

You may reply that more or less the same was true for America. Rural sociology was not conceived as a welcome child of general sociology m your country either. As you know, rural sociology originated here in fact from the Land Grant Colleges, that means from institutes for applied higher education, and not from the general universities. I know that it took some time before it was accepted as a legitimate daughter of general sociology. Even in 1951, when I visited your country, I had the feeling that at some of your institutes of higher learning there was still some tension between rural sociology and general sociology. Not all general sociologists seemed to be convinced that rural sociology was a respectable kind of sociology. But I have the impression, nevertheless, that already during the thirties the chances for the acceptance of rural sociology as a branch of sociology in general were much better in America than in Europe.

The climate for the acceptance of rural sociology in Europe would have been better, perhaps, if the communication between scholars in the field of sociology in Europe and America before the war had been as good as it was after the war. In fact, the contacts between scientists in Europe and America in general, and between the sociologists in particular, before the war were rather few. It would not be right to say that American sociology was unknown in Europe, but the European sociologists, in general, were not quite aware of what was going on in America.

Of the fathers of sociology in the United States, one could find some publications on their bookshelves, but one could not say that they had an influence of importance on sociological thinking in Europe. Only a few in Europe were conscious of the fact that already at the end of the twenties American sociologists were beginning to write a new page in the history of sociology.

With few exceptions, the European sociologists did not know that by careful gathering of data by means of fieldwork and by an equally careful processing of these data by statistical methods, the Americans were introducing a new type of research which would change the face of sociology drastically. Only at the end of the thirties did they become gradually aware that in this respect something of great importance was developing, but this had hardly any effect before the end of the war.

The fact that in Europe there was no rural sociology in the modern sense did not mean, of course, that more or less systematic knowledge about rural life was totally lacking. In several countries other disciplines showed an interest in rural life. In France, for example, human geographers of the group of *Vidal de la Blache* were strongly interested in the study of the socio-economic way of life—*genre de vie—oi* rural regions. In Germany elements of the study of social life of the countryside were incorporated in the so-called *Agrarpolitik* (agricultural policy), which was taught to the students in agriculture at the German universities and colleges.

The many problems which tried to be solved during the years of reconstruction after the war and the growing consciousness of rapid social change led to the increasing awareness that, for the foundation of a well-balanced policy, systematic scientific knowledge of the conditions and processes in social life is indispensable. That Was true also with regard to agriculture and rural life. Both experienced extremely rapid changes in Europe after the war, which created problems for the ministries of agriculture and other agencies. In almost all European countries sociologists were called to help these countries solve their difficulties.

People in charge o£ the extension services gradually began to see that the economie problems of the farmer could not be solved by purely technical and economie approaches. They began to see that advisory work is not just a thing to be learned by trial and error only, but that the extension worker can find a sound basis for his work in scientific knowledge provided by sociology and psychology. Today it has become clear that the countryside needs a drastic physical reconstruction to adjust it to modern social, economie, and technical conditions; and physical planners £eel that they cannot do the job without the help o£ sociology. Churches, village communities, farmers unions, and other voluntary associations in the countryside, including cooperatives, all feel a need for change or at least for a reconsideration of their own position. Often they ask the advice of sociologists. Rural family life, including problems of retirement, demands much more attention than it got formerly; and it is again the sociologist who has to find out the real character of the problems and of their causes.

Thus, in almost all countries in Western Europe sociological research in rural areas started. Even in some countries behind the Iron Curtam there is an interest in rural sociology. Poland and Yugoslavia have to be mentioned especially, but in Czechoslovakia there seems to be some interest also. Does this mean that rural sociology in Europe is in a satisfactory state at the moment and that we can expect that it will show a continuous growth in the near future? Let me try to give you a picture of its present state so you can form your own judgment.

It seems that in Europe not much is to be expected for rural sociology from the general universities, at least as far as they do not have agricultural faculties. In the survey of rural sociology in Europe which was published by Mendras in the first issue of *Sociologia Ruralis,* he mentions only one university (the University of Stockholm) where rural sociology was taught as a separate part of a course in general sociology. I can only add that in my own country students in general sociology from other universities are permitted to come to my university, the Agricultural University of Wageningen, to take rural sociology as a part of the study for their final degree, and a number of them do so. The universities of the European continent have, in general, a strong urban background and show—much more than in America—a great resistance to the introduction of anything which could be considered as appüed science. Thus, almost the only hope in academie life for rural sociology Hes with agricultural universities and colleges and faculties of agriculture in general universities. That hope certainly is not vain. In almost all Western European countries, at one or more institutes for higher education in agriculture, rural sociology is taught. But it would be a mistake to suppose that means an education of rural sociologists.

Methods of Study

Sociological research methods may be divided into two broad categories:

Quantitative Designs

In the social sciences, quantitative research refers to the systematic empirical investigation of quantitative properties and phenomena and their relationships. The objective of quantitative research is to develop and employ mathematical models, theories and/or hypotheses pertaining to phenomena. The process of measurement is central to quantitative research because it provides the fundamental connection between empirical observation and mathematical expression of quantitative relationships.

Quantitative research is used widely in social sciences such as psychology, sociology, anthropology, and political science. Research in mathematical sciences such as physics is also 'quantitative' by definition, though this use of the term differs in context. In the social sciences, the term relates to empirical methods, originating in both philosophical positivism and the history of statistics, which contrast qualitative research methods.

Qualitative methods produce information only on the particular cases studied, and any more general conclusions are only hypotheses. Quantitative methods can be used to verify, which of such hypotheses are true. A comprehensive analysis of 1274 articles published in the top two American sociology journals between 1935 and 2005 found that roughly two thirds of these articles used quantitative methods.

Overview

Quantitative research is generally made using scientific methods, which can include:

- The generation of models, theories and hypotheses
- The development of instruments and methods for measurement
- Experimental control and manipulation of variables
- Collection of empirical data
- Modeling and analysis of data
- Evaluation of results.

In the social sciences particularly, quantitative research is often contrasted with qualitative research which is the examination, analysis and interpretation of observations for the purpose of discovering underlying meanings and patterns of relationships, including classifications of types of phenomena and entities, in a manner that does not involve mathematical models. Approaches to quantitative psychology were first modelled on quantitative approaches in the physical sciences by Gustav Fechner in his work on psychophysics, which built on the work of Ernst Heinrich Weber. Although a distinction is commonly drawn between qualitative and quantitative aspects of scientific investigation, it has been argued that the two go hand in hand.

For example, based on analysis of the history of science, Kuhn (1961) concludes that "large amounts of qualitative work have usually been prerequisite to fruitful quantification in the physical sciences". Qualitative research is often used to gain a general sense of phenomena and to form theories that can be tested using further quantitative research. For instance, in the social sciences qualitative research methods are often used to gain better understanding of such things as intentionality (from the speech response of the researchee) and meaning (why did this person/group say something and what did it mean to them?)(Kieron Yeoman). Although quantitative investigation of the world has existed since people first began to record events or objects that had been counted, the modern idea of quantitative processes have their roots in Auguste Comte's positivist framework.

Use of Statistics

Statistics is the most widely used branch of mathematics in quantitative research outside of the physical sciences, and also finds applications within the physical sciences, such as in statistical mechanics. Statistical methods are used extensively within fields such as economics, social sciences and biology. Quantitative research using statistical methods starts with the collection of data, based on the hypothesis or theory. Usually a big sample of data is collected-this would require verification, validation and recording before the analysis can take place. Software packages such as SPSS and R are typically used for this purpose. Causal relationships are studied by manipulating factors thought to influence the phenomena of interest while controlling other variables relevant to the experimental outcomes.

In the field of health, for example, researchers might measure and study the relationship between dietary intake and measurable physiological effects such as weight loss, controlling for other key variables such as exercise. Quantitatively based opinion surveys are widely used in the media, with statistics such as the proportion of respondents in favor of a position commonly reported. In opinion surveys, respondents are asked a set of structured questions and their responses are tabulated. In the field of climate science, researchers compile and compare statistics such as temperature or atmospheric concentrations of carbon dioxide.

Empirical relationships and associations are also frequently studied by using some form of General linear model, non-linear model, or by using factor analysis. A fundamental principle in quantitative research is that correlation does not imply causation. This principle follows from the fact that it is always possible a spurious relationship exists for variables between which covariance is found in some degree. Associations may be examined between any combination of continuous and categorical variables using methods of statistics.

Measurement

Views regarding the role of measurement in quantitative research are somewhat divergent. Measurement is often regarded as being only a means by which observations are expressed numerically in order to investigate causal relations or associations. However, it has been argued that measurement often plays a more important role in quantitative research. For example, Kuhn argued that within quantitative research, the results that are shown can prove to be strange. This is because accepting a theory based on results of quantitative data could prove to be a natural phenomenon.

When measurement the parts from theory, it is likely to yield mere numbers, and their very neutrality makes them particularly sterile as a source of remedial suggestions. But numbers register the departure from theory with an authority and finesse that no qualitative technique can duplicate, and that departure is often enough to start a search (Kuhn, 1961).

In classical physics, the theory and definitions which underpin measurement are generally deterministic in nature. In contrast, probabilistic measurement models known as the Rasch model and Item response theory models are generally employed in the social sciences. Psychometrics is the field of study concerned with the theory and technique for measuring social and psychological attributes and phenomena. This field is central to much quantitative research that is undertaken within the social sciences.

Quantitative research may involve the use of *proxies* as stand-ins for other quantities that cannot be directly measured. Tree-ring width, for example, is considered a reliable proxy of ambient environmental conditions such as the warmth of growing seasons or amount of rainfall. Although scientists cannot directly measure the temperature of past years, tree-ring width and other climate proxies have been used to provide a semi-quantitative record of average temperature in the Northern Hemisphere back to 1000 A.D. When used in this way, the proxy record (tree ring width, say) only reconstructs a certain amount of the variance of the original record. The proxy may be calibrated (for example, during the period of the instrumental record) to determine how much variation is captured, including whether both short and long term variation is revealed. In the case of tree-ring width, different species in different places may show more or less sensitivity to, say, rainfall or temperature: when reconstructing a temperature record there is considerable skill in selecting proxies that are well correlated with the desired variable.

Quantitative Methods

Quantitative methods are research techniques that are used to gather quantitative data-information dealing with numbers and anything that is measurable. Statistics, tables and graphs, are often used to present the results of these methods. They are therefore to be distinguished from qualitative methods.

In most physical and biological sciences, the use of either quantitative or qualitative methods is uncontroversial, and each is used when appropriate. In the social sciences, particularly in sociology, social anthropology and psychology, the use of one or other type of method has become a matter of controversy and even ideology, with particular schools of thought within each discipline favouring one type of method and pouring scorn on to the other. Advocates of quantitative methods argue that only by using such methods can the social sciences become truly scientific; advocates of qualitative methods argue that quantitative methods tend to obscure the reality of the social phenomena under study because they underestimate or neglect the non-measurable factors, which may be the most important. The modern tendency (and in reality the majority tendency throughout the history of social science) is to use eclectic approaches. Quantitative methods might be used with a global qualitative frame. Qualitative methods might be used to understand the meaning of the numbers produced by quantitative methods. Using quantitative methods, it is possible to give precise and testable expression to qualitative ideas. This combination of quantitative and qualitative data gathering is often referred to as mixed-methods research.

Examples

- Research that consists of the percentage amounts of all the elements that make up Earth's atmosphere.
- Survey that concludes that the average patient has to wait two hours in the waiting room of a certain doctor before being selected.
- An experiment in which group x was given two tablets of Aspirin a day and Group y was given two tablets of a placebo a day where each participant is randomly assigned to one or other of the groups. The numerical factors such as two tablets, percent of elements and the time of waiting make the situations and results quantitative.

Qualitative Designs

Qualitative research is a method of inquiry appropriated in many different academic disciplines, traditionally in the social sciences, but also in market research and further contexts. Qualitative researchers aim to gather an in-depth understanding of human behaviour and the reasons that govern such behaviour. The qualitative method investigates the *why* and *how* of decision making, not just *what*, *where*, *when*. Hence, smaller but focused samples are more often needed, rather than large samples. Qualitative methods produce information only on the particular cases studied, and any more general conclusions are only hypotheses (informative guesses). Quantitative methods can be used to verify which of such hypotheses are true.

History

Until the 1970s, the phrase 'qualitative research' was used only to refer to a discipline of anthropology or sociology. During the 1970s and 1980s qualitative research began to be used in other disciplines, and became a significant type of research in the fields of education studies, social work studies, women's studies, disability studies, information studies, management studies, nursing service studies, political science, psychology, communication studies, and many other fields. Qualitative research occurred in the consumer products industry during this period, with researchers investigating new consumer products and product positioning/advertising opportunities.

The earliest consumer research pioneers including Gene Reilly of The Gene Reilly Group in Darien, CT, Jerry Schoenfeld of Gerald Schoenfeld & Partners in Tarrytown, NY and Martin Calle of Calle & Company, Greenwich, CT, also Peter Cooper in London, England, and Hugh Mackay in Mission, Australia. There continued to be disagreement about the proper place of qualitative versus quantitative research. In the late 1980s and 1990s after a spate of criticisms from the quantitative side, new methods of qualitative research evolved, to address the perceived problems with reliability and imprecise modes of data analysis. During this same decade, there was a slowdown in traditional media advertising spending, so there was heightened interest in making research related to advertising more effective.

In the last thirty years the acceptance of qualitative research by journal publishers and editors has been growing. Prior to that time many mainstream journals were prone to publish research articles based upon the natural sciences and which featured quantitative analysis.

Distinctions from quantitative research (In simplified terms-Qualitative means a non-numerical data collection or explanation based on the attributes of the graph or source of data. For example, if you are asked to explain in qualitative terms a thermal image displayed in multiple colours, then you would explain the colour differences rather than the heat's numerical value.)

First, in qualitative research, cases can be selected purposefully, according to whether or not they typify certain characteristics or contextual locations. Second, the researcher's role receives greater critical attention. This is because in qualitative research the possibility of the researcher taking a 'neutral' or transcendental position is seen as more problematic in practical and/or philosophical terms. Hence qualitative researchers are often exhorted to reflect on their role in the research process and make this clear in the analysis.

Third, while qualitative data analysis can take a wide variety of forms, it differs from quantitative research in its focus on language, signs and meaning. In addition, qualitative research approaches analysis holistically and contextually, rather than being reductionistic and isolationist. Nevertheless, systematic and transparent approaches to analysis are almost always regarded as essential for rigor. For example, many qualitative methods require researchers to carefully code data and discern and document themes consistently and reliably.

Perhaps the most traditional division between the uses of qualitative and quantitative research in the social sciences is that qualitative methods are used for exploration (i.e., hypothesis-generating) or for explaining puzzling quantitative results. Quantitative methods, by contrast, are used to test hypotheses. This is because establishing content validity-do measures measure what a researcher thinks they measure?-is seen as one of the strengths of qualitative research.

Some consider quantitative methods to provide more representative, reliable and precise measures through focused hypotheses, measurement tools and applied mathematics. By contrast, qualitative data is usually difficult to graph or display in mathematical terms.

Qualitative research is often used for policy and program evaluation research since it can answer certain important questions more efficiently and effectively than quantitative approaches. This is particularly the case for understanding how and why certain outcomes were achieved (not just what was achieved) but also for answering important questions about relevance, unintended effects and impact of programs such as: Were expectations reasonable? Did processes operate as expected?

Were key players able to carry out their duties? Did the program cause any unintended effects? Qualitative approaches have the advantage of allowing for more diversity in responses as well as the capacity to adapt to new developments or issues during the research process itself. While qualitative research can be expensive and time-consuming to conduct, many fields of research employ qualitative techniques that have been specifically developed to provide more succinct, cost-efficient and timely results. Rapid Rural Appraisal is one formalised example of these adaptations but there are many others.

Data Collection

Qualitative researchers may use different approaches in collecting data, such as the grounded theory practice, narratology, storytelling, classical ethnography, or shadowing. Qualitative methods are also loosely present in other methodological approaches, such as action research or actor-network theory. Forms of the data collected can include interviews and group discussions, observation and reflection field notes, various texts, pictures, and other materials.

Qualitative research often categorizes data into patterns as the primary basis for organizing and reporting results. Qualitative researchers typically rely on the following methods for gathering information: *Participant Observation, Non-participant Observation, Field Notes, Reflexive Journals, Structured Interview, Semi-structured Interview, Unstructured Interview, and Analysis of documents and materials.*

The ways of participating and observing can vary widely from setting to setting. Participant observation is a strategy of reflexive learning, not a single method of observing In participant observation researchers typically become members of a culture, group, or setting, and adopt roles to conform to that setting. In doing so, the aim is for the researcher to gain a closer insight into the culture's practices, motivations and emotions. It is argued that the researchers' ability to understand the experiences of the culture may be inhibited if they observe without participating.

Some distinctive qualitative methods are the use of focus groups and key informant interviews. The focus group technique involves a moderator facilitating a small group discussion between selected individuals on a particular topic. This is a particularly popular method in market research and testing new initiatives with users/workers.

One traditional and specialized form of qualitative research is called cognitive testing or pilot testing which is used in the development of quantitative survey items. Survey items are piloted on study participants to test the reliability and validity of the items.

In the academic social sciences the most frequently used qualitative research approaches include the following:

1. Ethnographic Research, used for investigating cultures by collecting and describing data that is intended to help in the development of a theory. This method is also called "ethnomethodology" or "methodology of the people". An example of applied ethnographic research, is the study of a particular culture and their understanding of the role of a particular disease in their cultural framework.
2. Critical Social Research, used by a researcher to understand how people communicate and develop symbolic meanings.
3. Ethical Inquiry, an intellectual analysis of ethical problems. It includes the study of ethics as related to obligation, rights, duty, right and wrong, choice etc.
4. Foundational Research, examines the foundations for a science, analyses the beliefs and develops ways to specify how a knowledge base should change in light of new information.

5. Historical Research, allows one to discuss past and present events in the context of the present condition, and allows one to reflect and provide possible answers to current issues and problems. Historical research helps us in answering questions such as: Where have we come from, where are we, who are we now and where are we going?
6. Grounded Theory, is an inductive type of research, based or "grounded" in the observations or data from which it was developed; it uses a variety of data sources, including quantitative data, review of records, interviews, observation and surveys.
7. Phenomenology, describes the "subjective reality" of an event, as perceived by the study population; it is the study of a phenomenon.
8. Philosophical Research, is conducted by field experts within the boundaries of a specific field of study or profession, the best qualified individual in any field of study to use an intellectual analyses, in order to clarify definitions, identify ethics, or make a value judgment concerning an issue in their field of study.

Data Analysis

Interpretive Techniques

The most common analysis of qualitative data is observer impression. That is, expert or bystander observers examine the data, interpret it via forming an impression and report their impression in a structured and sometimes quantitative form.

Coding

Coding is an interpretive technique that both organizes the data and provides a means to introduce the interpretations of it into certain quantitative methods. Most coding requires the analyst to read the data and demarcate segments within it. Each segment is labeled with a "code" – usually a word or short phrase that suggests how the associated data segments inform the research objectives. When coding is complete, the analyst prepares reports via a mix of: summarizing the prevalence of codes, discussing similarities and differences in related codes across distinct original sources/contexts, or comparing the relationship between one or more codes.

Some qualitative data that is highly structured (e.g., open-end responses from surveys or tightly defined interview questions) is typically coded without additional segmenting of the content. In these cases, codes are often applied as a layer on top of the data. Quantitative analysis of these codes is typically the capstone analytical step for this type of qualitative data.

Contemporary qualitative data analyses are sometimes supported by computer programs. These programs do not supplant the interpretive nature of coding but rather are aimed at enhancing the analyst's efficiency at data storage/retrieval and at applying the codes to the data. Many programs offer efficiencies in editing and revising coding, which allow for work sharing, peer review, and recursive examination of data.

A frequent criticism of coding method is that it seeks to transform qualitative data into quantitative data, thereby draining the data of its variety, richness, and individual character. Analysts respond to this criticism by thoroughly expositing their definitions of codes and linking those codes soundly to the underlying data, therein bringing back some of the richness that might be absent from a mere list of codes.

Recursive Abstraction

Some qualitative datasets are analysed without coding. A common method here is recursive abstraction, where datasets are summarized, those summaries are then further summarized, and so on. The end result is a more compact summary that would have been difficult to accurately discern without the preceding steps of distillation.

A frequent criticism of recursive abstraction is that the final conclusions are several times removed from the underlying data. While it is true that poor initial summaries will certainly yield an inaccurate final report, qualitative analysts can respond to this criticism. They do so, like those using coding method, by documenting the reasoning behind each summary step, citing examples from the data where statements were included and where statements were excluded from the intermediate summary.

Mechanical Techniques

Some techniques rely on leveraging computers to scan and sort large sets of qualitative data. At their most basic level, mechanical techniques rely on counting words, phrases, or coincidences of tokens within the data. Often referred to as content analysis, the output from these techniques is amenable to many advanced statistical analyses.

Mechanical techniques are particularly well-suited for a few scenarios. One such scenario is for datasets that are simply too large for a human to effectively analyze, or where analysis of them would be cost prohibitive relative to the value of information they contain.

Another scenario is when the chief value of a dataset is the extent to which it contains "red flags" (e.g., searching for reports of certain adverse events within a lengthy journal dataset from patients in a clinical trial) or "green flags" (e.g., searching for mentions of your brand in positive reviews of marketplace products).

A frequent criticism of mechanical techniques is the absence of a human interpreter. And while masters of these methods are able to write sophisticated software to mimic some human decisions, the bulk of the "analysis" is nonhuman. Analysts respond by proving the value of their methods relative to either a) hiring and training a human team to analyze the data or b) letting the data go untouched, leaving any actionable nuggets undiscovered.

Paradigmatic Differences

Contemporary qualitative research has been conducted from a large number of various paradigms that influence conceptual and metatheoretical concerns of legitimacy, control, data analysis, ontology, and epistemology, among others. Research conducted in the last 10 years has been characterized by a distinct turn toward more interpretive, postmodern, and critical practices. Guba and Lincoln (2005) identify five main paradigms of contemporary qualitative research: positivism, postpositivism, critical theories, constructivism, and participatory/cooperative paradigms. Each of the paradigms listed by Guba and Lincoln are characterized by axiomatic differences in axiology, intended action of research, control of research process/ outcomes, relationship to foundations of truth and knowledge, validity, textual representation and voice of the researcher/participants, and commensurability with other paradigms. In particular, commensurability involves the extent to which paradigmatic concerns "can be retrofitted to each other in ways that make the simultaneous practice of both possible". Positivist and postpositivist paradigms share commensurable assumptions but are largely incommensurable with critical, constructivist, and participatory paradigms. Likewise, critical, constructivist, and participatory paradigms are commensurable on certain issues (e.g., intended action and textual representation).

Validation

A central issue in qualitative research is validity (also known as credibility and/or dependability). There are many different ways of establishing validity, including: member check, interviewer corroboration, peer debriefing, prolonged engagement, negative case analysis, auditability, confirmability, bracketing, and balance. Most of these methods were coined, or at least extensively described by Lincoln and Guba (1985)

Academic Research

By the end of the 1970s many leading journals began to publish qualitative research articles and several new journals emerged which published only qualitative research studies and articles about qualitative research methods.

In the 1980s and 1990s, the new qualitative research journals became more multidisciplinary in focus moving beyond qualitative research's traditional disciplinary roots of anthropology, sociology, and philosophy. The new millennium saw a dramatic increase in the number of journals specializing in qualitative research with at least one new qualitative research journal being launched each year.

Sociologists are divided into camps of support for particular research techniques. These disputes relate to the epistemological debates at the historical core of social theory. While very different in many aspects, both qualitative and quantitative approaches involve a systematic interaction between theory and data. Quantitative methodologies hold the dominant position in sociology, especially in the United States. In the discipline's two most cited journals, quantitative articles have historically outnumbered qualitative ones by a factor of two. (Most articles published in the largest British journal, on the other hand, are qualitative.) Most textbooks on the methodology of social research are written from the quantitative perspective, and the very term "methodology" is often used synonymously with "statistics." Practically all sociology PhD program in the United States require training in statistical methods. The work produced by quantitative researchers is also deemed more 'trustworthy' and 'unbiased' by the greater public, though this judgment is continues to be challenged by antipositivists.

The choice of method often depends largely on what the researcher intends to investigate. For example, a researcher concerned with drawing a statistical generalization across an entire population may administer a survey questionnaire to a representitive sample population. By contrast, a researcher who seeks full contextual understanding of an individuals' social actions may choose ethnographic participant observation or open-ended interviews. Studies will commonly combine, or 'triangulate', quantitative *and* qualitative methods as part of a 'multi-strategy' design. For instance, a quantitative study may be performed to gain statistical patterns or a target sample, and then combined with a qualitative interview to determine the play of agency.

Sampling

Quantitative methods are often used to ask questions about a population that is very large, making a census or a complete enumeration of all the members in that population infeasible. A 'sample' then forms a manageable subset of a population. In quantitative research, statistics are used to draw inferences from this sample regarding the population as a whole. The process of selecting a sample is referred to as 'sampling'. While it is usually best to sample randomly, concern with differences between specific subpopulations sometimes calls for stratified sampling. Conversely, the impossibility of random sampling sometimes necessitates nonprobability sampling, such as convenience sampling or snowball sampling.

Methods

The following list of research methods is neither exclusive nor exhaustive:

- *Archival research or the Historical method:* draws upon the secondary data located in historical archives and records, such as biographies, memoirs, journals, and so on.
- *Content analysis:* The content of interviews and other texts is systematically analysed. Often data is 'coded' as a part of the 'grounded theory' approach using qualitative data analysis (QDA) software, such as NVivo.
- *Experimental research*: The researcher isolates a single social process and reproduces it in a laboratory (for example, by creating a situation where unconscious sexist judgments are possible), seeking to determine whether or not certain social variables can cause, or depend upon, other variables (for instance, seeing if people's feelings about traditional gender roles can be manipulated by the activation of contrasting gender stereotypes). Participants are randomly assigned to different groups which either serve as controls—acting as reference points because they are tested with regard to the dependent variable, albeit without having been exposed to any independent variables of interest—or receive one or more treatments. Randomization allows the researcher to be sure that any resulting differences between groups are the result of the treatment.
- *Survey research:* The researcher produces data using interviews, questionnaires, or similar feedback from a set of people sampled from a particular population of interest. Survey items from an

interview or questionnaire may be open-ended or closed-ended. Data from surveys is usually analysed statistically on a computer.

- *Longitudinal study:* An extensive examination of a specific person or group over a long period of time.
- *Observation:* Using data from the senses, the researcher records information about social phenomenon or behaviour. Observation techniques may or may not feature participation. In participant observation, the researcher goes into the field (such as a community or a place of work), and participates in the activities of the field for a prolonged period of time in order acquire a deep understanding of it. Data acquired through these techniques may be analysed either quantitatively or qualitatively.

Computational Sociology

Sociologists increasingly draw upon computationally intensive methods to analyze and model social phenomena. Using computer simulations, artificial intelligence, complex statistical methods, and new analytic approaches like social network analysis, computational sociology develops and tests theories of complex social processes through bottom-up modeling of social interactions.

Although the subject matter and methodologies in social science differ from those in natural science or computer science, several of the approaches used in contemporary social simulation originated from fields such as physics and artificial intelligence.

By the same token, some of the approaches that originated in computational sociology have been imported into the natural sciences, such as measures of network centrality from the fields of social network analysis and network science. In relevant literature, computational sociology is often related to the study of social complexity. Social complexity concepts such as complex systems, non-linear interconnection among macro and micro process, and emergence, have entered the vocabulary of computational sociology.

A practical and well-known example is the construction of a computational model in the form of an "artificial society", by which researchers can analyze the structure of a social system.

Practical Applications of Social Research

Social research informs politicians and policy makers, educators, planners, lawmakers, administrators, developers, business magnates, managers, social workers, non-governmental organizations, non-profit organizations, and people interested in resolving social issues in general. There is often a great deal of crossover between social research, market research, and other statistical fields.

Village through History

A village is a clustered human settlement or community, larger than a hamlet with the population ranging from a few hundred to a few thousands (sometimes tens of thousands), Though often located in rural areas, the term urban village is also applied to certain urban neighbourhoods, such as the West Village in Manhattan, New York City and the Saifi Village in Beirut, Lebanon, as well as Hampstead Village in the London conurbation. Villages are normally permanent, with fixed dwellings; however, transient villages can occur. Further, the dwellings of a village are fairly close to one another, not scattered broadly over the landscape, as a dispersed settlement.

Historically, villages were the usual form of community for societies that practise subsistence agriculture, and also for some non-agricultural societies. In Great Britain, a hamlet earned the right to be called a village when it built a church.

In many cultures, towns and cities were few, with only a small proportion of the population living in them. The Industrial Revolution attracted people in larger numbers to work in mills and factories; the concentration of people caused many villages to grow into towns and cities. This also enabled specialization of labor and crafts, and development of many trades. The trend of urbanisation continues, though not always in connection with industrialisation. Villages have been eclipsed in importance as units of human society and settlement.

Traditional Villages

Although many patterns of village life have existed, the typical village was small, consisting of perhaps 5 to 30 families. Homes were situated together for sociability and defence, and land surrounding the living quarters was farmed. Traditional fishing villages were based on artisan fishing and located adjacent to fishing grounds.

South Asia

India

"The soul of India lives in its villages", declared M. K. Gandhi at the beginning of 20th century. According to the 2001 Indian census, 74% of Indians live in 638,365 different villages. The size of these villages varies considerably. 236,004 Indian villages have a population less than 500, while 3,976 villages have a population of 10,000+. Most villages have their own temple, mosque or church depending on the local religious following.

Southeast Asia

Brunei, Indonesia and Malaysia

The term kampung (sometimes spelling *kampong*) in the English language has been defined specifically as "a Malay hamlet or village in a Malay-speaking country" In other words, a *kampung* is defined today as a village in Brunei, Indonesia or Malaysia.

In Malaysia, a *kampung* is determined as a locality with 10,000 or fewer people. Since historical times, every Malay village came under the leadership of a *penghulu* (village chief), who has the power to hear civil matters in his village. A Malay village typically contains a *"masjid"* (mosque) or *"surau"* (Muslim chapel), paddy fields and Malay houses on stilts.

Malay and Indonesian villagers practice the culture of helping one another as a community, which is better known as "joint bearing of burdens" (*gotong royong*), as well as being family-oriented (especially the concept of respecting one's family [particularly the parents and elders]), courtesy and believing in God (*"Tuhan"*) as paramount to everything else. It is common to see a cemetery near the mosque, as all Muslims in the Malay or Indonesian village want to be prayed for, and to receive Allah's blessings in the afterlife.

In Indonesia, the terms differ, villages are called *desa/kelurahan*, and village heads *kepala desa* but the same general concept applies, there is some variation among the vast numbers of Austronesian ethnic groups. In some areas such as Tanah Toraja, elders take turns watching over the village at a command post.

Philippines

In urban areas of the Philippines, the term "village" most commonly refers to private subdivisions, especially gated communities. These villages emerged in the mid-20th century and were initially the domain of elite urban dwellers. Now they are now common in Metro Manila and other major cities in the country and their residents have a wide range of income levels.

Such villages may or may not correspond to administrative units (usually barangays) and/or be privately administered. Well-known villages in Metro Manila include Forbes Park and Dasmariñas Village. Barangays more correspond to the villages of old times, and the chairman (formerly a village datu) now settles intrapersonal matters or polices the village, though with much less authority and respect than in Indonesia or Malaysia.

Central and Eastern Europe

Slavic Countries

Selo is a Slavic word meaning "village" in Bosnia and Herzegovina, Bulgaria, Croatia, Macedonia, Russia, Serbia, and Ukraine. For example there are numerous *sela* (plural of *selo*) called Novo Selo in Bulgaria, Croatia, Montenegro and others in Serbia, and Macedonia. In Slovenia, the word *selo* is used for very small villages (less than a thousand people) and in dialects; the Slovene word *vas* is used all over Slovenia.

Bulgaria

In Bulgaria the different types of *Sela* vary from a small selo of 5 to 30 families to one of several thousand people. According to a 2002 census, in that year there were 2,385,000 Bulgarian citizens living in settlements classified as *villages*. A 2004 Human Settlement Profile on Bulgaria conducted by the United Nations Department of Economic and Social Affairs stated that: The most intensive is the migration "city – city". Approximately 46% of all migrated people have changed their residence from one city to another. The share of the migration processes "village – city" is significantly less – 23% and "city – village" – 20%. The migration "village – village" in 2002 is 11%. It also stated that, the state of the environment in the small towns and villages is good apart from the low level of infrastructure.

In Bulgaria it is becoming popular to visit villages for the atmosphere, culture, crafts, hospitality of the people and the surrounding nature. This is called *selski tourism*, meaning "village tourism".

Russia

In Russia, the bulk of the rural population are concentrated in rural localities. Two most common types of rural localities are *derevnya* and *selo*. Historically, the formal indication of status was religious: a city (*gorod*) had a cathedral, a *selo* had a church, while a *derevnya* had neither.

The lowest administrative unit of the Russian Empire, *volost*, or its Soviet or modern Russian successor, *selsoviet*, was usually headquartered in a *selo* and embraced a few neighboring villages.

Between 1926 and 1989, Russia's rural population shrank from 76 million people to 39 million, due to urbanization, collectivization, dekulakization, and the World War II losses, but has nearly stabilized since. During 1930–1937, mass starvation in Russia and other parts of the Soviet Union lead to the death of at least 14.5 million peasants (including 5-7 million in the Holodomor).

Most Russian rural localities have populations of less than 200 people, and the smaller places take the brunt of depopulation: e.g., in 1959, about one half of Russia's rural population lived in villages of fewer than 500 people, while now less than one third does. In the 1960s–1970s, the depopulation of the smaller villages was driven by the central planners' drive to get the farm workers out of smaller, "prospect-less" hamlets and into the collective or state farm's main village, with more amenities.

Most Russian rural residents are involved in agricultural work, and it is very common for villagers to produce their own food. As prosperous urbanites purchase village houses for their second homes, Russian villages somctimes are transformed into dacha settlements, used mostly for seasonal residence.

The historically Cossack regions of Southern Russia and parts of Ukraine, with their fertile soil and absence of serfdom, had a rather different pattern of settlement from central and northern Russia. While peasants of central Russia lived in a village around the lord's manor, a Cossack family often lived on its own farm, called *khutor*. A number of such *khutors* plus a central village made up the administrative unit *stanitsa*. Such a *stanitsa* village, often with a few thousand residents, was usually larger than a *selo* in central Russia.

The term *aul/aal* is used to refer mostly Muslim-populated villages in Caucasus and Idel-Ural, without regard to the number of residents.

Ukraine

In Ukraine *Selo* is the lowest administrative unit. *Khutir* and *Stanytsia* are not part of the administrative division anylonger due to the collectivization. There is a higher level of the rural administrative division, *Selysche*.

Western & Southern Europe

United Kingdom

A village in the UK is a compact settlement of houses, smaller in size than a town, and generally based on agriculture or, in some areas, mining, quarrying or sea fishing.

The major factors in the type of settlement are location of water sources, organization of agriculture and landholding, and likelihood of flooding. For example, in areas such as the Lincolnshire Wolds, the villages are often found along the spring line halfway down the hillsides, and originate as spring line settlements, with the original open field systems around the village. In northern Scotland, most villages are planned to a grid pattern located on or close to major roads, whereas in areas such as the Forest of Arden, woodland clearances produced small hamlets around village greens.

Some villages have disappeared (for example, deserted medieval villages), sometimes leaving behind a church or manor house and sometimes nothing but bumps in the fields. Some show archaeological evidence of settlement at three or four different layers, each distinct from the previous one. Clearances may have been to accommodate sheep or game estates, or enclosure, or may have resulted from depopulation, such as after the Black Death or following a move of the inhabitants to more prosperous districts. Other villages have grown and merged and often form hubs within the general mass of suburbia — such as Hampstead, London and Didsbury in Manchester. Many villages are now predominantly dormitory locations and have suffered the loss of shops, churches and other facilities. For many British people, the village represents an ideal of Great Britain, as with Adlestrop. Seen as being far from the bustle of modern life, it is represented as quiet and harmonious, if a little inward-looking. This concept of an unspoilt Arcadia is present in many popular representations of the village such as the radio serial *The Archers* or the best kept village competitions.

Many villages in South Yorkshire, North Nottinghamshire, North East Derbyshire, County Durham, South Wales and Northumberland are known as pit villages. These (such as Murton, County Durham) grew from hamlets when the sinking of a colliery in the early 20th century resulted in a rapid growth in their population and the colliery owners built new housing, shops, pubs and churches. Some pit villages outgrew nearby towns by area and population; for example, Rossington in South Yorkshire came to have over four times more people than the nearby town of Bawtry. Some pit villages grew to become towns; for example, Maltby in South Yorkshire grew from 500 people in the 19th century to over 17,000 in 2007.

In the UK, the main historical distinction between a hamlet and a village was that the latter had a church, and so usually was the centre of worship for an ecclesiastical parish. However, some civil parishes may contain more than one village. The typical village had a pub or inn, shops, and a blacksmith. But many of these facilities are now gone, and many villages are dormitories for commuters. The population of such settlements ranges from a few hundred people to around five thousand. A village is distinguished from a town in that:

- A village should not have a regular agricultural market, although today such markets are uncommon even in settlements which clearly are towns.
- A village does not have a town hall nor a mayor.
- If a village is the principal settlement of a civil parish, then any administrative body that administers it at parish level should be called a parish council or parish meeting, and not a town council or city council. However, some civil parishes have no functioning parish, town, or city council nor a functioning parish meeting. In Wales, where the equivalent of an English civil parish is called a Community, the body that administers it is called a Community Council. However, larger councils may elect to call themselves town councils. Unlike Wales, Scottish community councils have no statutory powers.
- There should be a clear green belt or open fields surrounding its parish borders. However this may not be applicable to urbanised villages: although these may not considered to be villages, they are often widely referred to as being so; an example of this is Horsforth in Leeds.

France

Same general definition as in the UK.

An independent association named *Les Plus Beaux Villages de France*, was created in 1982 to promote assets of small and picturesque French villages of quality heritage. As of 2008, 152 villages in France have been labelled as "The Most Beautiful Villages of France".

Spain

Spain has plenty of little villages around its territory. Country life is more usual in Castile and Aragón. Every village has a church or hermitage.

Portugal

Same general definition as in Spain.

Netherlands

In the flood prone districts of the Netherlands, villages were traditionally built on low man-made hills called terps before the introduction of regional dyke-systems. In modern days, the term *dorp* (lit. "village") is usually applied to settlements no larger than 20,000, though there's no official law regarding status of settlements in the Netherlands.

Middle East

Lebanon

Like France, villages in Lebanon are usually located in remote mountainous areas. The majority of villages in Lebanon retain their Aramaic names or are derivative of the Aramaic names, and this is because Aramaic was still in use in Mount Lebanon up to the 18th century.

Many of the Lebanese villages are a part of districts, these districts are known as "kadaa" which includes the districts of Baabda (Baabda), Aley (Aley), Matn (Jdeideh), Keserwan (Jounieh), Chouf (Beiteddine), Jbeil (Byblos), Tripoli (Tripoli), Zgharta (Zgharta/Ehden), Bsharri (Bsharri), Batroun (Batroun), Koura (Amioun), Miniyeh-Danniyeh (Minyeh/Sir Ed-Danniyeh), Zahle (Zahle), Rashaya (Rashaya), Western Beqaa (Jebjennine/Saghbine), Sidon (Sidon), Jezzine (Jezzine), Tyre (Tyre), Nabatiyeh (Nabatiyeh), Marjeyoun (Marjeyoun), Hasbaya (Hasbaya), Bint Jbeil (Bint Jbeil), Baalbek (Baalbek), and Hermel (Hermel).

The district of Danniyeh conists of thirty six small villages, which includes Almrah, Kfirchlan, Kfirhbab, Hakel al Azimah, Siir, Bakhoun, Miryata, Assoun, Sfiiri, Kharnoub, Katteen, Kfirhabou, Zghartegrein, Ein Qibil. Danniyeh is a region located in Miniyeh-Danniyeh District in the North Governorate of Lebanon. The region lies east of Tripoli, extends north as far as Akkar District, south to Bsharri District and Zgharta District and as far east as Baalbek and Hermel. Dinniyeh has an excellent ecological environment filled with woodlands, orchards and groves. Several villages are located in this mountainous area, the largest town being Sir Al Dinniyeh.

An example of a typical mountainous Lebanese village in Dannieh would be Hakel al Azimah which is a small village that belongs to the district of Danniyeh, situated between Bakhoun and Assoun's boundaries. It is in the centre of the valleys that lie between the Arbeen Mountains and the Khanzouh.

Syria

Syria contains a large number of villages that vary in size and importance, including the ancient, historical and religious villages, such as Ma'loula, Sednaya, and Brad (Mar Maroun's time). The diversity of the Syrian environments creates significant differences between the Syrian villages in terms of the economic activity and the method of adoption. Villages in the south of Syria (Huran, Jabal Al-Arab), the north-east (the Syrian island) and the Orontes River basin depend mostly on agriculture, mainly grain, vegetables and fruits. Villages in the region of Damascus and Aleppo depend on trading. Some other villages, such as Marmarita depend heavily on tourist activity.

Mediterranean cities in Syria, such as Tartus and Latakia have similar types of villages. Mainly, villages were built in very good sites which had the fundamentals of the rural life, like water. An example of a Mediterranean Syrian village in Tartus would be Al-Annaze, which is a small village that belongs to the area of Al Sauda. The area of Al Sauda is called a nahiya, which is a subdistrict.

Sub-Saharan Africa

Australasia & Oceania

Pacific Islands Communities on pacific islands were historically called villages by English speakers who traveled and settled in the area. Some communities such as several Villages of Guam continue to be called villages despite having large populations that can exceed 40,000 residents.

New Zealand

The traditional Mâori village was the pâ, a fortified hill-top settlement. Tree-fern logs and flax were the main building materials.

Australia The term village often is used in reference to small planned communities such as retirement communities or shopping districts, and tourist areas such as ski resorts. Small rural communities are usually known as townships. Larger settlements are known as towns.

South America

Argentina Usually set in remote mountainous areas, some also cater to winter sports and/or tourism, see: Uspallata, La Cumbrecita, Villa Traful and La Cumbre

North America

United States

In the United States, the meaning of "village" varies by geographic area and legal jurisdiction. In many areas, "village" is a term, sometimes informal, for a type of administrative division at the local government level. Since the Tenth Amendment to the United States Constitution makes local government for the most part a matter for the states rather than the federal government, the states are free to have political subdivisions called "villages," or not to do so, and to define the word in many different ways.

Typically, a village is a type of municipality, although it can also be a special district or an unincorporated area. It may or may not be recognized for governmental purposes.

Informal Usage

In informal usage, a U.S. village may be simply a relatively small clustered human settlement without formal legal existence. In colonial New England, a village typically formed around the church meetinghouses that was located in the center of each town. Many of these colonial settlements still exist as town centres. With the advent of the Industrial Revolution, industrial villages also sprang up around water-powered mills, mines, and factories.

Because most New England villages were contained within the boundaries of legally established towns, many such villages were never separately incorporated as municipalities. A relatively small unincorporated community, similar to a hamlet in New York state, or even a relatively small community within an incorporated city or town, may be termed a village. This informal usage may be found even in states that have villages as an incorporated municipality and is similar to the usage of the term "unincorporated town" in states having town governments.

Formal Usage

States that formally recognize villages vary widely in the definition of the term. Most commonly, a village is either a special district or a municipality. As municipalities, a village may:

1. differ from a city or town in terms of population;
2. differ from a city in terms of dependence on a township; or
3. be virtually equivalent to a city or town.

Alaska

While municipalities in Alaska are not called villages, Alaska native villages are recognized under the Alaska Native Claims Settlement Act. Although not officially called villages, the natives and other Alaska residents refer to most small towns as villages.

Delaware

Municipalities in Delaware are called cities, towns, or villages. There are no differences among them that would affect their classification for census purposes.

Florida

Municipalities in Florida are called cities, towns, or villages. They are not differentiated for census purposes.

Idaho

All municipalites in Idaho are called cities, although the terms "town" and "village" are sometimes used in statutes.

Illinois

Municipalities in Illinois are called cities, towns, or villages. A village has up to a few hundred people.

Louisiana

A village in Louisiana is a municipality having a population of 1,000 or fewer.

Maine

In Maine, village corporations or village improvement corporations are special districts established in towns for limited purposes.

Massachusetts

All of the land area in Massachusetts is allocated to incorporated municipalities called either a city or town. Some municipalities (such as Newton, Massachusetts) have villages, and where they exist they are the equivalent of neighborhoods, which usually have no corporate existence and no official boundaries or government recognition. Sometimes villages and neighborhoods are recognized incidentally, through declarative signs, parking districts, or names used by the United States Post Office.

Maryland

In Maryland, a locality designated "Village of..." may be either an incorporated town or a special tax district. An example of the latter is the Village of Friendship Heights.

Michigan

In Michigan, villages differ from cities in that, whereas villages remain part of the townships in which they are formed, thereby reducing their home-rule powers, cities are not part of townships. Because of this, village governments are required to share some of the responsibilities to their residents with the township.

Minnesota

Villages that existed in Minnesota as of January 1, 1974, became statutory cities, as opposed to charter cities. Cities may or may not exist within township areas.

Mississippi

A village in Mississippi is a municipality of 100 to 299 inhabitants. They may no longer be created.

Missouri

The municipalities of Missouri are cities and villages. Unlike cities, villages have no minimum population requirement.

Nebraska

In Nebraska, a village is a municipality of 100 through 800 inhabitants, whereas a city must have at least 800 inhabitants. All villages, but only some cities, are within township areas. A city of the second class (800-4,999 inhabitants) may elect to revert to village status.

New Hampshire

In New Hampshire, a village district or precinct may be organized within a town. Such a village district or precinct is a special district with limited powers. The New Hampshire Association of Village Districts has a website at www.NHAVD.org

New Jersey

A village in the context of New Jersey local government, refers to one of five types and one of eleven forms of municipal government. Villages, like other municipalities, are not part of a township.

New Mexico

The municipalities in New Mexico are cities, towns, and villages. There are no differences among them that would affect their classification for census purposes.

New York

In New York State, a village is an incorporated area that differs from a city in that a village is within the jurisdiction of one or more towns, whereas a city is independent of a town. Villages thus have less autonomy than cities. A village is usually, but not always, within a single town. A village is a clearly defined municipality that provides the services closest to the residents, such as garbage collection, street and highway maintenance, street lighting and building codes.

Some villages provide their own police and other optional services. Those municipal services not provided by the village are provided by the town or towns containing the village. As of the 2000 census, there are 553 villages in New York. There is no limit to the population of a village in New York; Hempstead, the largest village in the state, has 55,000 residents, making it more populous than some of the state's cities. However, villages in the state may not exceed five square miles (13 km^2) in area. Present law requires a minimum of 500 residents to incorporate as a village.

North Carolina

The municipalities in North Carolina are cities, towns, and villages. There are no differences among them that would affect their classification for census purposes.

Ohio

In Ohio, a village is an incorporated municipality with fewer than 5,000 inhabitants. The minimum population for incorporation as a village is 1,600 inhabitants, but this was not always the case, resulting in many very small villages. If a village grows to 5,000 residents, it is automatically designated as a city. Cities or villages may be within township areas; however, if a city or village becomes coterminous with a township, the township ceases to exist as a separate government.

Oklahoma

In Oklahoma, unincorporated communities are called villages and are not counted as governments.

Oregon

In Oregon, one county — Clackamas County — permits the organization of unincorporated areas into villages and hamlets. The boards of such entities are advisory to the county.

Pennsylvania

In Pennsylvania, villages are unincorporated areas within townships. Villages are oftentimes census-designated places. The largest village in Pennsylvania is Upper Darby.

Texas

In Texas, villages may be Type B or Type C municipalities, but not Type A municipalities. The types differ in terms of population and in terms of the forms of government that they may adopt.

Vermont

In Vermont, villages are named communities located within the boundaries of a legally established town. Villages may be incorporated or unincorporated.

Washington

In Washington state, there is no legal definition of a village. Local municipalities are classified as first-class cities, second-class cities, and towns (also called fourth-class cities), with successively fewer governing powers, based on population at the time of incorporation. Colloquially, some areas are called villages, such as the Town of Beaux Arts Village.

West Virginia

In West Virginia, towns and villages are Class IV municipalities, i.e., having 2,000 or fewer inhabitants.

Wisconsin

In Wisconsin, cities and villages are both outside the area of any town. Cities and villages differ in terms of the population and population density required for incorporation.

Incorporated Villages

In twenty U.S. states, the term "village" refers to a specific form of incorporated municipal government, similar to a city but with less authority and geographic scope. However, this is a generality; in many states, there are villages that are an order of magnitude larger than the smallest cities in the state. The distinction is not necessarily based on population, but on the relative powers granted to the different types of municipalities and correspondingly, different obligations to provide specific services to residents.

In some states such as New York, Wisconsin, or Michigan, a village is an incorporated municipality, usually, but not always, within a single town or civil township. Residents pay taxes to the village and town or township and may vote in elections for both as well. In some cases, the village may be coterminous with the town or township. There are also many villages which span the boundaries of more than one town or township, and some villages may even straddle county borders.

There is no limit to the population of a village in New York; Hempstead, the largest village in the state, has 55,000 residents, making it more populous than some of the state's cities. However, villages in the state may not exceed five square miles (13 km^2) in area.

In the state of Wisconsin a village is always legally separate from the towns that it has been incorporated from. The largest village is Menomonee Falls, which has over 32,000 residents.

Michigan and Illinois also have no set population limit for villages and there are many villages that are larger than cities in those states.

Villages in Ohio are often legally part of the township from which they were incorporated, although exceptions such as Hiram exist, in which the village is separate from the township. They have no area limitations, but become cities if they grow a population of more than 5,000.

In Maryland, a locality designated "Village of..." may be either an incorporated town or a special tax district. An example of the latter is the Village of Friendship Heights.

In states that have New England towns, a "village" is a center of population or trade, including the town center, in an otherwise sparsely-developed town or city — for instance, the village of Hyannis in the city of the Barnstable, Massachusetts.

Unincorporated Villages

In many states, the term "village" is used to refer to a relatively small unincorporated community, similar to a hamlet in New York state. This informal usage may be found even in states that have villages as an incorporated municipality, although such usage might be considered incorrect and confusing.

Village Life

Medieval villages consisted of a population comprised of mostly of farmers. Houses, barns sheds, and animal pens clustered around the center of the village, which was surrounded by plowed fields and pastures. Medieval society depended on the village for protection and a majority of people during these centuries called a village home. Most were born, toiled, married, had children and later died within the village, rarely venturing beyond its boundaries.

Common enterprise was the key to a village's survival. Some villages were temporary, and the society would move on if the land proved infertile or weather made life too difficult. Other villages continued to exist for centuries. Every village had a lord, even if he didn't make it his permanent residence, and after the 1100's castles often dominated the village landscape. Medieval Europeans may have been unclear of their country's boundaries, but they knew every stone, tree, road and stream of their village. Neighboring villages would parley to set boundaries that would be set out in village charters. Medieval peasants were either classified as free men or as "villeins," those who owed heavy labor service to a lord, were bound to the land, and subject to feudal dues. Village life was busy for both classes, and for women as well as men. Much of this harsh life was lived outdoors, wearing simple dress and subsisting on a meager diet.

Village life would change from outside influences with market pressures and new landlords. As the centuries passed, more and more found themselves drawn to larger cities. Yet modern Europe owes much to these early medieval villages.

India is an agriculture country and most of its people live in villages. A village is a collection of small huts in the midst of fields on which the village farmers work. Some villages are big while others are comparatively smaller. They are generally cut off from the cities and have a different kind of life.

The villagers live in the midst of natural surroundings. The charm of nature justify the remark of the famous poet Cowper, "God made the country and man made the town", As we rise early in the morning, we can listen to the sweet songs of birds. We can enjoy the beauty of the rising sun and the sweet breeze of the greenery of fields around, are the various pleasures that abound in the countryside.

The villagers pass a healthy, peaceful life. There is no smoke and noise of the city factories. They breathe fresh air which promotes their health. They also get pure ghee and milk. There is no hustle and bustle and no worry as in the modern life. The villagers, therefore, are happy and healthy. They lead a simple life and their desires are few. They are satisfied with what they have and never dream of those luxuries and comforts that modern science has provided us with in such ample measure.

Most of the people who live in villages are farmers. They cultivate their farms situated in the neighbored of the villages. They go to their fields early in the morning where they work till evening, ploughing, sowing or reaping, according to seasons. Spinning and weaving is one of the most important cottage industries of a village. It helps to increase their meager income. Beside this, some people keep shops and provided the necessities of life of the villagers. Other works as potters, carpenters, blacksmith, etc, to fulfil their needs.

The villagers are deeply religious. They worship a number of gods and goddesses. They devote regular time to player and worship. The village priest enjoys great respect. But they are highly orthodox and any change is dislike and opposed. Many kinds of superstitions flourish among them. They live in constant fear of ghost. They believe in a number of omens.

The villagers are socially knit together. Their life is co-operate and interdependent. They depend on each other for the supply of their daily wants. They share in the joys and sorrow of each other. They help each other in time of need. Their social sense is so strong that the guest of one is considered as the guest of all. In a town or city, one does not care to know even one's neighbour. But each villages is familiar with the family history of other villagers. In the evening they assemble in the village "Chopal" with there 'hukkas' and chatting and talking goes on till late the night. This is their simple recreation.

But the village life has also some serious drawbacks. The villagers are extremely poor. They live in one roomed "*kachcha*" mud houses, which often fall to the ground in the rains. In this way, they are put to great hardship. Suitable houses must be constructed for them. At present there are only a few *Pucca* houses in villages. In spite of their hard work, they are not able to earn enough to provide themselves with even two square meals a day. They are ill-clad and ill-fed. As they are not able to save anything, in a need they have to borrow from the village money lender. They are frequently in debt which they are often never able return. Scientific methods of agriculture must be used, and government should provide facilities of this purpose. There is no doubt that much improvement has been made in this respect in recent times but it is not enough.

The villages are illiterate. Most of them do not even know how to write their names. There are no suitable arrangements for their education or for the education of their children. Even when there is a school, it is highly unsatisfactory. The teachers is ill-paid and takes no interest in his work. Their ignorance makes them superstitious and conservative. They are content with their old methods of cultivation and do not like scientific methods.

In villages, there are no suitable arrangement for treatment of the sick. Often there is no qualified doctor. The village Vaids and Hakims are mere quacks who kill more patients than they cure. The villages are highly in sanitary and many infectious disease breakout from time to time. Thousands of people die every year, uncared for an without any medical aid. However, now things are fast changing. Good hospitals have been constructed near each village. Good, qualified doctors are now there in most villages.

Such is the life in an Indian village. In spite of its various drawbacks, it is a better life than that of the city. If I were given the choice, I would prefer to live in the village. The Government has already taken in hand various measures to improve the conditions of the villages. "Jawahar Rozgar Yojana" and "Panchayati Raj" are two of the important steps taken in this direction. Let us hope, in the near feature, their poverty and illiteracy shall be eradicated. A village will then really by a paradise on earth, as God intended it to be.

Indian Village life is a mixture of tranquility, serenity, quietude and innocence. Along with numerous small and big grass fields, several rivers, chirping of birds, swinging of emerald trees, speaking in a low voice the tale of languishment and love to the big and clear blue sky give a mesmerizing, captivating and bewitching effect to the Indian villages. Ever since the country's independence from the British colonial rule in 1947, the economy of the nation has banked upon its agrarian society.

A majority of the persons living in India have involved themselves in agriculture and associated industries, and have thus made the country the quickest developing world economy. The country is hope to people of different castes and creeds which rightly demonstrates the principles of 'Unity in Diversity'. Indian village life is fully relied on agriculture and innate all over the land.

The lifestyle maintained by the people of Indian villages as well as their working styles are as fascinating as the balance offered by the metropolitan city lifestyles.

The primary occupation of the people living in the India villages is agriculture and is therefore reckoned as an unchangeable part of the Indian village culture. Traditionally, village and caste are regarded as similar to each other and the villages in India also follow the same trend. In Indian village life the presence of all the four castes with the hierarchy of the Brahmin is noticed.

The caste system which originated long back has however remained unchanged in the village life in India. Although, caste system in its original sense has collapsed yet caste identities are very much present there in the village life in India.

People belonging to different castes in a village deal with each other in kinship terms, which shows the fictive kinship relationships distinguished within each settlement.

Habitually the Indian villagers manifest a deep loyalty to their villages. A rural family which has its root seated deeply in a specific village does not move easily to another. The uniqueness of the village life in India lies in this deep loyalty which is again marked with a rich culture. The mystic charm and the cultural diversities of the village life in India, make the Indian villages that never never land where beauty never fades away, and dream never cease to exist.

The village life in India is idyllic, unchanging with its immense beauty. The villagers of India are normally habituated in sharing and using the common facilities of the village including the village shrines and temples, the village pond, schools, grazing grounds, sitting places, etc. This interdependence of the village life in India perhaps provides a matchless unity amongst the villagers which supports them in surviving amidst thousands of odds. Village unity is therefore the primary concern of the village life in India.

Characteristically, each of the Indian villages recognizes a particular deity as the protector of the concerned village and the people of that village get together to worship the deity. Religion, which is deeply instilled in the village life in India, further supports the villagers to consider this as an essential part of village prosperity. The uninterrupted village life in India entertain themselves amidst the color of the festivals like Diwali, Holi, Muharram, Dussehra, etc, in the captivating pulse of dance and songs and of course in the emotion of rural theatres.

In the Indian village life, there is a headman who is recognized often to respectfully listen to the village panchayat's decision. The village panchayat comprises of some important men from the major castes of the village. The panchayat in Indian villages are responsible to clarify the disputes within the village boundaries as much as possible, with occasional choices of the interference of police or the court system. In the recent era, the Government supports an elective Panchayat system in the Indian villages.

The Government of India helped the villages with advanced technology for farming implements and presently most of the villages in India have access to modern farming equipments. Now-a-days, the Indian village outskirts boast up with food packaging plants, textile industries, sugar industries and steel plants.

These have created for the village youth suitable employment opportunities. Continuous reform is made by the government in order to fashion the country a 'motor' for the economy of the world. Developments in the agrarian infrastructure, public sector reforms, rural development, righted labor norms, etc have changed the Indian village life. The village life in India blessed with its innocence, purity and uncomplicated saga makes the villages as the quaint, archaic, mystic yet charming places to rediscover nature.

New Trends

Up until recently, large part of the marketing that was done in this country was done, targeting the urban population of the country. Now the marketing potential of the rural part of the country is rapidly growing. Let us get an understanding of the urban and rural break up of the country. 26% of the population lives in the cities or in urban India. The remaining 74% lives in the villages or in rural India. The population of the country is spread over the villages but is very concentrated in the cities. India has six of the largest cities in the world. These are-Calcutta, Bombay, Delhi, Madras, Bangalore and Hyderabad. Besides these cities, there are six other cities that are growing at a very rapid rate and have a huge concentration of the population. These are-Ahmedabad, Kanpur, Pune, Nagpur, Lucknow and Jaipur. In addition to these cities, there are around 4000 towns that have concentrations of the population.

In the cities, there are a lot of jobs available now-a-days due to call centres and BPO's. This has given many more people purchasing power. Items that were luxury items a few years a go are seen in every house in the cities.

Besides the cities 74% of Indian population lives in the villages. As the standard of living in the villages also improves, many modern facilities are available in almost every house hold in the villages too. Now a days the TV is there in most of the houses in the villages too. This has exposed them to a lot of advertising lifestyles and products. The villages have become a huge market that will be of great consequence in the near future. In the future, companies with a strong product distribution system reaching all the villages will have a very strong advantage over the rest.

The country is growing, and is a place where business will thrive in the near future. To understand this better consider the following favorable shifts that have taken place in the consumer patters of buying.

Chapter 3

Rural Economy

The success story of Indian economy is spreading its wings towards India's districts and rural areas which accounts for over 65% of the nation's total populace. Currently, the rural sector of India is not only observing a massive increase in its per capita income but also in its expenditure and production. To enhance the rural economy of India, the Indian government has increased the monetary incentives allotted for the National Rural Employment Guarantee Act (NREGA) to USD 8.04 bn in its 2009 Union Budget. Moreover, the government has also allotted USD 34.74 bn in its Bharat Nirman Programme for enhancing rural road and rail network.

Surprisingly, the rural economy was unaffected by the recent global financial meltdown as per the research conducted by Rural Marketing Association of India (RMAI). The research also revealed that the rural economy in India is soon to witness an increase in its earnings which will be largely triggered by the incessant expansion in agriculture for the last four successive years.

Rural Consumer Market of India

The rural consumer market of India is expected to attain its target of USD 425 bn by 2010-2011, which can be translated as double of 2004-05 economy size, as per the report by CII-Technopark.

Indian Rural Retail Industry

As per the report by Associated Chambers of Commerce and Industry of India (ASSOCHAM), the Indian rural retail economy is worth USD 113 bn which can be translated as 40% of the total Indian retail market worth USD 280 bn. Some of the firms which have already established their base in rural areas are Reliance, AV Birla and Godrej, while firms like DCM, Pantaloon-Godrej JV, Tata, Hindustan Unilever, etc. are all set to expand their retail business in rural market.

Demand for FMCG in Indian Rural Areas

During the fourth quarter of the FY 2009, the demand for fast moving consumer goods (FMCG) increased steadily as compared to its urban counterparts, as per the research conducted by AC Nielsen.

Companies like Dabur, HUL, Godrej, etc have started recruiting more and more deserving candidates from rural districts in an attempt to elevate their network and market. Firms like Nestle and GlaxoSmithkline Consumer Healthcare (GSK) are all set to introduce new products for the rural areas in order to promote their brand.

This indicates that the FMCG firms no longer treat rural markets as an appendage to their metropolitan strongholds and are targeting the market for positioning their brands and for industrial set-ups.

Indian rural Healthcare Industry

The Indian rural Healthcare market is expected to expand at a pace of 44% by 2015, totaling its worth to USD 8.8 bn, according to a survey carried out by McKinsey. Conglomerates like Sanofi-Aventis, has currently introduced a promotional activity to advertise generics in rural provinces called 'Prayas'. This initiative is considered as an attempt to share medicinal information with practicing medicos in rural districts through seminars.

Indian Rural Automobiles Industry

The recent development that the Indian rural Automobiles Industry saw was the declaration of the establishment of new sales and service channels in rural India by the President of Mahindra and Mahindra Group (M&M) Rajeev Dubey. These service outlets have a premeditated target of manufacturing 1,00,000 automobiles by FY 2015.

Indian Rural Services Industry

Surprisingly, more than 60% of the services industry of the nation is based in the rural areas, as per the research conducted by National Sample Survey Organisation (NSSO). In the fiscal year 2007, there were around 85% of the own account enterprises (OAEs) in India which deployed 76% of the manpower in rural districts of India.

Indian Rural Telecommunication Industry

According to the research carried out by Confederation of Indian Industries (CII), the Indian rural Telecommunication Industry is expected to account for more than 65% of the entire telecom subscribers in India.

In an attempt to envelop rural subscribers, many telecom giants in India have willingly invested in rural telecom industry to benefit from its massive potential. Mobile equipments manufacturing firms like Intex Technologies, Karbonn, etc have allocated USD 21.03 mn for its promotional activities for 2010.

Indian Rural Agricultural System

Although agriculture contributes only 21% of India's GDP, its importance in the country's economic, social, and political fabric goes well beyond this indicator. The rural areas are still home to some 72 percent of the India's 1.1 billion people, a large number of whom are poor. Most of the rural poor depend on rain-fed agriculture and fragile forests for their livelihoods.

The sharp rise in foodgrain production during India's Green Revolution of the 1970s enabled the country to achieve self-sufficiency in foodgrains and stave off the threat of famine. Agricultural intensification in the 1970s to 1980s saw an increased demand for rural labor that raised rural wages and, together with declining food prices, reduced rural poverty.

Sustained, although much slower, agricultural growth in the 1990s reduced rural poverty to 26.3 percent by 1999/00. Since then, however, the slowdown in agricultural growth has become a major cause for concern. India's rice yields are one-third of China's and about half of those in Vietnam and Indonesia. With the exception of sugarcane, potato and tea, the same is true for most other agricultural commodities.

The Government of India places high priority on reducing poverty by raising agricultural productivity.

However, bold action from policymakers will be required to shift away from the existing subsidy-based regime that is no longer sustainable, to build a solid foundation for a highly productive, internationally competitive, and diversified agricultural sector.

Issues and Challenges

Slow Down in Agricultural and Rural Non-Farm Growth: Both the poorest as well as the more prosperous 'Green Revolution' states of Punjab, Haryana and Uttar Pradesh have recently witnessed a slow-down in agricultural growth. Some of the factors hampering the revival of growth are:

- Poor composition of public expenditures: Public spending on agricultural subsidies is crowding out productivity-enhancing investments such as agricultural research and extension, as well as investments in rural infrastructure, and the health and education of the rural people. In 1999/2000, agricultural subsidies amounted to 3 percent of GDP and were over 7 times the public investments in the sector.
- Over-regulation of domestic agricultural trade: While economic and trade reforms in the 1990s helped to improve the incentive framework, over-regulation of domestic trade has increased costs, price risks and uncertainty, undermining the sector's competitiveness.
- Government interventions in labor, land, and credit markets: More rapid growth of the rural non-farm sector is constrained by government interventions in factor markets — labor, land, and credit — and in output markets, such as the small-scale reservation of enterprises.
- Inadequate infrastructure and services in rural areas.

Weak Framework for Sustainable Water Management and Irrigation:

- Inequitable allocation of water: Many states lack the incentives, policy, regulatory, and institutional framework for the efficient, sustainable, and equitable allocation of water.
- Deteriorating irrigation infrastructure: Public spending in irrigation is spread over many uncompleted projects. In addition, existing infrastructure has rapidly deteriorated as operations and maintenance is given lower priority.

Inadequate Access to Land and Finance:

- Stringent land regulations discourage rural investments: While land distribution has become less skewed, land policy and regulations to increase security of tenure (including restrictions or bans on renting land or converting it to other uses) have had the unintended effect of reducing access by the landless and discouraging rural investments.
- Computerization of land records has brought to light institutional weaknesses: State government initiatives to computerize land records have reduced transaction costs and increased transparency, but also brought to light institutional weaknesses.

- Rural poor have little access to credit: While India has a wide network of rural finance institutions, many of the rural poor remain excluded, due to inefficiencies in the formal finance institutions, the weak regulatory framework, high transaction costs, and risks associated with lending to agriculture.

Weak Natural Resources Management: One quarter of India's population depends on forests for at least part of their livelihoods.

- A purely conservation approach to forests is ineffective: Experience in India shows that a purely conservation approach to natural resources management does not work effectively and does little to reduce poverty.
- Weak resource rights for forest communities: The forest sector is also faced with weak resource rights and economic incentives for communities, an inefficient legal framework and participatory management, and poor access to markets.

Weak delivery of basic services in rural areas:

- Low bureaucratic accountability and inefficient use of public funds: Despite large expenditures in rural development, a highly centralized bureaucracy with low accountability and inefficient use of public funds limit their impact on poverty.

  In 1992, India amended its Constitution to create three tiers of democratically elected rural local governments bringing governance down to the villages.

  However, the transfer of authority, funds, and functionaries to these local bodies is progressing slowly, in part due to political vested interests. The poor are not empowered to contribute to shaping public programs or to hold local governments accountable.

Priority Areas for the World Bank Support

Enhancing Agricultural Productivity, Competitiveness, and Rural Growth

Enhancing productivity: Creating a more productive, internationally competitive and diversified agricultural sector would require a shift in public expenditures away from subsidies towards productivity enhancing investments.

Second it will require removing the restrictions on domestic private trade to improve the investment climate and meet expanding market opportunities.

Third, the agricultural research and extension systems need to be strengthened to improve access to productivity enhancing technologies. The diverse conditions across India suggests the importance of regionally differentiated strategies, with a strong focus on the lagging states.

Improving Water Resource and Irrigation/Drainage Management: Increase in multi-sectoral competition for water highlights the need to formulate water policies and unbundle water resources management from irrigation service delivery.

Other key priorities include:

(i) modernizing Irrigation and Drainage Departments to integrate the participation of farmers and other agencies in irrigation management;

(ii) improving cost recovery;

(iii) rationalizing public expenditures, with priority to completing schemes with the highest returns; and

(iv) allocating sufficient resources for operations and maintenance for the sustainability of investments.

Strengthening rural non-farm sector growth: Rising incomes are fueling demand for higher-value fresh and processed agricultural products in domestic markets and globally, which open new opportunities for agricultural diversification to higher value products (e.g. horticulture, livestock), agro-processing and related services. The government needs to shift its role from direct intervention and overregulation to creating the enabling environment for private sector participation and competition for agribusiness and more broadly, the rural non-farm sector growth. Improving the rural investment climate includes removing trade controls, rationalizing labor regulations and the tax regime (i.e. adoption of the value added tax system), and improving access to credit and key infrastructure (e.g. roads, electricity, ports, markets).

Improving Access to Assets and Sustainable Natural Resource use

Balancing poverty reduction and conservation priorities: Finding win-win combinations for conservation and poverty reduction will be critical to sustainable natural resource management. This will involve addressing legal, policy and institutional constraints to devolving resource rights, and transferring responsibilities to local communities.

Improving access to land: States can build on the growing consensus to reform land policy, particularly land tenancy policy and land administration system.

States that do not have tenancy restrictions can provide useful lessons in this regard. Over the longer term, a more holistic approach to land administration policies, regulations and institutions is necessary to ensure tenure security, reduce costs, and ensure fairness and sustainability of the system.

Improving access to rural finance: It would require improving the performance of regional rural banks and rural credit cooperatives by enhancing regulatory oversight, removing government control and ownership, and strengthening the legal framework for loan recovery and the use of land as collateral. It would also involve creating an enabling environment for the development of micro-finance institutions in rural areas.

Strengthening Institutions for the Poor and Promoting Rural Livelihood

Promoting Community-Based Rural Development: State Government efforts in scaling up livelihood and community-driven development approaches will be critical to build social capital in the poorest areas as well as to expand savings mobilization, promote productive investments, income generating opportunities and sustainable natural resource management.

Direct support to self-help groups, village committees, user's associations, savings and loans groups and others can provide the initial 'push' to move organizations to higher level and access to new economic opportunities. Moreover, social mobilization and particularly the empowerment of women's groups, through increased capacity for collective action will provide communities with greater "voice" and bargaining power in dealing with the private sector, markets and financial services.

Strengthening Accountability for Service Delivery: As decentralization efforts are pursued and local governments are given more prominence in the basic service delivery, the establishment of accountability mechanisms becomes critical. Local governments' capacity to identify local priorities through participatory budgeting and planning needs to be strengthened. This, in turn, would improve the rural investment climate, facilitating the involvement of the private sector, creating employment opportunities and linkages between farm and non-farm sectors.

Agriculture Sector

Agriculture in India has a long history dating back to ten thousand years. Today, India ranks second worldwide in farm output. Agriculture and allied sectors like forestry and logging accounted for 16.6% of the GDP in 2007, employed 52% of the total workforce and despite a steady decline of its share in the GDP, is still the largest economic sector and plays a significant role in the overall socio-economic development of India. India is the largest producer in the world of milk, cashew nuts, coconuts, tea, ginger, turmeric and black pepper. It also has the world's largest cattle population (281 million).

It is the second largest producer of wheat, rice, sugar, groundnut and inland fish. It is the third largest producer of tobacco. India accounts for 10% of the world fruit production with first rank in the production of banana and sapota. India's population is growing faster than its ability to produce rice and wheat.

Initiatives

The required level of investment for the development of marketing, storage and cold storage infrastructure is estimated to be huge. The government has not been able to implement various schemes to raise investment in marketing infrastructure. Among these schemes are *Construction of Rural Go downs, Market Research and Information Network*, and *Development/Strengthening of Agricultural Marketing Infrastructure, Grading and Standardization.*

The Indian Agricultural Research Institute (IARI), established in 1905, was responsible for the research leading to the "Indian Green Revolution" of the 1970s. The Indian Council of Agricultural Research (ICAR) is the apex body in agriculture and related allied fields, including research and education. The Union Minister of Agriculture is the President of the ICAR.

The Indian Agricultural Statistics Research Institute develops new techniques for the design of agricultural experiments, analyses data in agriculture, and specializes in statistical techniques for animal and plant breeding. Recently Government of India has set up Farmers Commission to completely evaluate the agriculture program.. However the recommendations have had a mixed reception.

Mixed Farming

In August 2001 India's Parliament passed the Plant Variety Protection and Farmers' Rights Act, a sui generis legislation. Being a WTO member, India had to comply with TRIPS and include PVP.

However, farmers' rights are of particular importance in India and thus the Act also allows for farmers to save, sow and sell seeds as they always have, even if it is of a protected variety. This not only saves the livelihoods of many farmers, it also provides an environment for the continuing development and use of landraces, says Suman Sahai. The way it always was

Problems

Slow agricultural growth is a concern for policymakers as some two-thirds of India's people depend on rural employment for a living. Current agricultural practices are neither economically nor environmentally sustainable and India's yields for many agricultural commodities are low.

Poorly maintained irrigation systems and almost universal lack of good extension services are among the factors responsible. Farmers' access to markets is hampered by poor roads, rudimentary market infrastructure, and excessive regulation. —World Bank: "India Country Overview 2008".

The low productivity in India is a result of the following factors:

- According to World Bank, Indian Branch: Priorities for Agriculture and Rural Development", India's large agricultural subsidies are hampering productivity-enhancing investment. Overregulation of agriculture has increased costs, price risks and uncertainty. Government intervenes in labour, land, and credit markets. India has inadequate infrastructure and services. World Bank also says that the allocation of water is inefficient, unsustainable and inequitable. The irrigation infrastructure is deteriorating. The overuse of water is currently being covered by over pumping aquifers, but as these are falling by foot of groundwater each year, this is a limited resource.
- Illiteracy, general socio-economic backwardness, slow progress in implementing land reforms and inadequate or inefficient finance and marketing services for farm produce.
- Inconsistent government policy. Agricultural subsidies and taxes often changed without notice for short term political ends.
- The average size of land holdings is very small (less than 20,000 m^2) and is subject to fragmentation, due to land ceiling acts and in some cases, family disputes. Such small holdings are often over-manned, resulting in disguised unemployment and low productivity of labour.

- Adoption of modern agricultural practices and use of technology is inadequate, hampered by ignorance of such practices, high costs and impracticality in the case of small land holdings.
- Irrigation facilities are inadequate, as revealed by the fact that only 52.6% of the land was irrigated in 2003–04, which result in farmers still being dependent on rainfall, specifically the Monsoon season.

  A good monsoon results in a robust growth for the economy as a whole, while a poor monsoon leads to a sluggish growth. Farm credit is regulated by NABARD, which is the statutory apex agent for rural development in the subcontinent. At the same time overpumping made possible by subsidized electric power is leading to an alarming drop in aquifer levels.

History

Indian agriculture began by 9000 BC as a result of early cultivation of plants, and domestication of crops and animals. Settled life soon followed with implements and techniques being developed for agriculture. Double monsoons led to two harvests being reaped in one year. Indian products soon reached the world via existing trading networks and foreign crops were introduced to India. Plants and animals—considered essential to their survival by the Indians—came to be worshiped and venerated.

The middle ages saw irrigation channels reach a new level of sophistication in India and Indian crops affecting the economies of other regions of the world under Islamic patronage. Land and water management systems were developed with an aim of providing uniform growth.

Despite some stagnation during the later modern era the independent Republic of India was able to develop a comprehensive agricultural program.

Agricultural Produces

Agriculture is the production, processing, marketing, and use of foods, fibers and byproducts from plant crops and animals. Agriculture was the key development that led to the rise of human civilization, with the husbandry of domesticated animals and plants (i.e. crops) creating food surpluses that enabled the development of more densely populated and stratified societies.

The study of agriculture is known as agricultural science. Agriculture is also observed in certain species of ant and termite.

Agriculture encompasses a wide variety of specialties and techniques, including ways to expand the lands suitable for plant raising, by digging water-channels and other forms of irrigation. Cultivation of crops on arable land and the pastoral herding of livestock on rangeland remain at the foundation of agriculture. In the past century there has been increasing concern to identify and quantify various forms of agriculture. In the developed world the range usually extends between sustainable agriculture (e.g. permaculture or organic agriculture) and intensive farming (e.g. industrial agriculture).

Modern agronomy, plant breeding, pesticides and fertilizers, and technological improvements have sharply increased yields from cultivation, but at the same time have caused widespread ecological damage and negative human health effects. Selective breeding and modern practices in animal husbandry such as intensive pig farming (and similar practices applied to the chicken) have similarly increased the output of meat, but have raised concerns about animal cruelty and the health effects of the antibiotics, growth hormones, and other chemicals commonly used in industrial meat production.

The major agricultural products can be broadly grouped into foods, fibers, fuels, and raw materials. In the 21st century, plants have been used to grow biofuels, biopharmaceuticals, bioplastics, and pharmaceuticals. Specific foods include cereals, vegetables, fruits, and meat. Fibers include cotton, wool, hemp, silk and flax. Raw materials include lumber and bamboo. Other useful materials are produced by plants, such as resins. Biofuels include methane from biomass, ethanol, and biodiesel. Cut flowers, nursery plants, tropical fish and birds for the pet trade are some of the ornamental products.

In 2007, one third of the world's workers were employed in agriculture. The services sector has overtaken agriculture as the economic sector employing the most people worldwide. Despite the size of its workforce, agricultural production accounts for less than five percent of the gross world product (an aggregate of all gross domestic products).

Overview

Agriculture has played a key role in the development of human civilization. Until the Industrial Revolution, the vast majority of the human population labored in agriculture. Development of agricultural techniques has steadily increased agricultural productivity, and the widespread diffusion of these techniques during a time period is often called an agricultural revolution. A remarkable shift in agricultural practices has occurred over the past century in response to new technologies. In particular, the Haber-Bosch method for synthesizing ammonium nitrate made the traditional practice of recycling nutrients with crop rotation and animal manure less necessary.

Synthetic nitrogen, along with mined rock phosphate, pesticides and mechanization, have greatly increased crop yields in the early 20th century. Increased supply of grains has led to cheaper livestock as well. Further, global yield increases were experienced later in the 20th century when high-yield varieties of common staple grains such as rice, wheat, and corn (maize) were introduced as a part of the Green Revolution.

The Green Revolution exported the technologies (including pesticides and synthetic nitrogen) of the developed world to the developing world. Thomas Malthus famously predicted that the Earth would not be able to support its growing population, but technologies such as the Green Revolution have allowed the world to produce a surplus of food.

Many governments have subsidized agriculture to ensure an adequate food supply. These agricultural subsidies are often linked to the production of certain commodities such as wheat, corn (maize), rice, soybeans, and milk. These subsidies, especially when instituted by developed countries have been noted as protectionist, inefficient, and environmentally damaging.

In the past century agriculture has been characterized by enhanced productivity, the use of synthetic fertilizers and pesticides, selective breeding, mechanization, water contamination, and farm subsidies. Proponents of organic farming such as Sir Albert Howard argued in the early 20th century that the overuse of pesticides and synthetic fertilizers damages the long-term fertility of the soil. While this feeling lay dormant for decades, as environmental awareness has increased in the 21st century there has been a movement towards sustainable agriculture by some farmers, consumers, and policymakers.

In recent years there has been a backlash against perceived external environmental effects of mainstream agriculture, particularly regarding water pollution, resulting in the organic movement. One of the major forces behind this movement has been the European Union, which first certified organic food in 1991 and began reform of its Common Agricultural Policy (CAP) in 2005 to phase out commodity-linked farm subsidies, also known as decoupling. The growth of organic farming has renewed research in alternative technologies such as integrated pest management and selective breeding. Recent mainstream technological developments include genetically modified food.

In late 2007, several factors pushed up the price of grains consumed by humans as well as used to feed poultry and dairy cows and other cattle, causing higher prices of wheat (up 58%), soybean (up 32%), and maize (up 11%) over the year. Food riots took place in several countries across the world. Contributing factors included drought in Australia and elsewhere, increasing demand for grain-fed animal products from the growing middle classes of countries such as China and India, diversion of foodgrain to biofuel production and trade restrictions imposed by several countries.

An epidemic of stem rust on wheat caused by race Ug99 is currently spreading across Africa and into Asia and is causing major concern. Approximately 40% of the world's agricultural land is seriously degraded. In Africa, if current trends of soil degradation continue, the continent might be able to feed just 25% of its population by 2025, according to UNU's Ghana-based Institute for Natural Resources in Africa.

History

Agricultural practices such as irrigation, crop rotation, fertilizers, and pesticides were developed long ago, but have made great strides in the past century. The history of agriculture has played a major role in human history, as agricultural progress has been a crucial factor in worldwide socio-economic change. Division of labor in agricultural societies made commonplace specializations rarely seen in hunter-gatherer cultures. So, too, are arts such as epic literature and monumental architecture, as well as codified legal systems. When farmers became capable of producing food beyond the needs of their own families, others in their society were freed to devote themselves to projects other than food acquisition. Historians and anthropologists have long argued that the development of agriculture made civilization possible.

Ancient Origins

The Fertile Crescent of Western Asia, Egypt, and India were sites of the earliest planned sowing and harvesting of plants that had previously been gathered in the wild. Independent development of agriculture occurred in northern and southern China, Africa's Sahel, New Guinea and several regions of the Americas. The eight so-called

Neolithic founder crops of agriculture appear: first emmer wheat and einkorn wheat, then hulled barley, peas, lentils, bitter vetch, chick peas and flax.

By 7000 BC, small-scale agriculture reached Egypt. From at least 7000 BC the Indian subcontinent saw farming of wheat and barley, as attested by archaeological excavation at Mehrgarh in Balochistan. By 6000 BC, mid-scale farming was entrenched on the banks of the Nile. About this time, agriculture was developed independently in the Far East, with rice, rather than wheat, as the primary crop. Chinese and Indonesian farmers went on to domesticate taro and beans including mung, soy and azuki.

To complement these new sources of carbohydrates, highly organized net fishing of rivers, lakes and ocean shores in these areas brought in great volumes of essential protein. Collectively, these new methods of farming and fishing inaugurated a human population boom that dwarfed all previous expansions and continues today.

By 5000 BC, the Sumerians had developed core agricultural techniques including large-scale intensive cultivation of land, monocropping, organized irrigation, and the use of a specialized labor force, particularly along the waterway now known as the Shatt al-Arab, from its Persian Gulf delta to the confluence of the Tigris and Euphrates. Domestication of wild aurochs and mouflon into cattle and sheep, respectively, ushered in the large-scale use of animals for food/fiber and as beasts of burden. The shepherd joined the farmer as an essential provider for sedentary and seminomadic societies. Maize, manioc, and arrowroot were first domesticated in the Americas as far back as 5200 BC.

The potato, tomato, pepper, squash, several varieties of bean, tobacco, and several other plants were also developed in the New World, as was extensive terracing of steep hillsides in much of Andean South America. The Greeks and Romans built on techniques pioneered by the Sumerians, but made few fundamentally new advances. Southern Greeks struggled with very poor soils, yet managed to become a dominant society for years. The Romans were noted for an emphasis on the cultivation of crops for trade.

In the Americas, a parallel agricultural revolution occurred, resulting in some of the most important crops grown today. In Mesoamerica wild teosinte was transformed through human selection into the ancestor of modern maize, more than 6000 years ago. It gradually spread across North America and was the major crop of

Native Americans at the time of European exploration. Other Mesoamerican crops include hundreds of varieties of squash and beans. Cocoa was also a major crop in domesticated Mexico and Central America.

The turkey, one of the most important meat birds, was probably domesticated in Mexico or the U.S. Southwest.

In the Andes region of South America the major domesticated crop was potatoes, domesticated perhaps 5000 years ago. Large varieties of beans were domesticated, in South America, as well as animals, including llamas, alpacas, and guinea pigs. Coca, still a major crop, was also domesticated in the Andes.

A minor center of domestication, the indigenous people of the Eastern U.S. appear to have domesticated numerous crops. Sunflowers, tobacco, varieties of squash and Chenopodium, as well as crops no longer grown, including marshelder and little barley were domesticated. Other wild foods may have undergone some selective cultivation, including wild rice and maple sugar. The most common varieties of strawberry were domesticated from Eastern North America.

Middle Ages

During the Middle Ages, farmers in North Africa, the Near East, and Europe began making use of agricultural technologies including irrigation systems based on hydraulic and hydrostatic principles, machines such as norias, water-raising machines, dams, and reservoirs. This combined with the invention of a three-field system of crop rotation and the moldboard plow greatly improved agricultural efficiency.

In the European medieval period, agriculture was considered part of the set of *seven mechanical arts*.

Modern Era

After 1492, a global exchange of previously local crops and livestock breeds occurred. Key crops involved in this exchange included the tomato, maize, potato, manioc, cocoa bean and tobacco going from the New World to the Old, and several varieties of wheat, spices, coffee, and sugar cane going from the Old World to the New.

The most important animal exportation from the Old World to the New were those of the horse and dog (dogs were already present in the pre-Columbian Americas but not in the numbers and breeds suited to farm work). Although not usually food animals, the horse (including donkeys and ponies) and dog quickly filled essential production roles on western-hemisphere farms.

The potato became an important staple crop in northern Europe. Since being introduced by Portuguese in the 16th century, maize and manioc have replaced traditional African crops as the continent's most important staple food crops.

By the early 19th century, agricultural techniques, implements, seed stocks and cultivated plants selected and given a unique name because of its decorative or useful characteristics had so improved that yield per land unit was many times that seen in the Middle Ages. Although there is a vast and interesting history of crop cultivation before the dawn of the 20th century, there is little question that the work of Charles Darwin and Gregor Mendel created the scientific foundation for plant breeding that led to its explosive impact over the past 150 years.

With the rapid rise of mechanization in the late 19th century and the 20th century, particularly in the form of the tractor, farming tasks could be done with a speed and on a scale previously impossible. These advances have led to efficiencies enabling certain modern farms in the United States, Argentina, Israel, Germany, and a few other nations to output volumes of high-quality produce per land unit at what may be the practical limit.

The Haber-Bosch method for synthesizing ammonium nitrate represented a major breakthrough and allowed crop yields to overcome previous constraints. In the past century agriculture has been characterized by enhanced productivity, the substitution of labor for synthetic fertilizers and pesticides, water pollution, and farm subsidies. In recent years there has been a backlash against the external environmental effects of conventional agriculture, resulting in the organic movement.

The cereals rice, corn, and wheat provide 60% of human food supply. Between 1700 and 1980, "the total area of cultivated land worldwide increased 466%" and yields increased dramatically, particularly because of selectively bred high-yielding varieties, fertilizers, pesticides, irrigation, and machinery. For example, irrigation increased corn yields in eastern Colorado by 400 to 500% from 1940 to 1997.

However, concerns have been raised over the sustainability of intensive agriculture. Intensive agriculture has become associated with decreased soil quality in India and Asia, and there has been increased concern over the effects of fertilizers and pesticides on the environment, particularly as population increases and food demand expands. The monocultures typically used in intensive agriculture increase the number of pests, which are controlled through pesticides. Integrated pest management (IPM), which "has been promoted for decades and has had some notable successes" has not significantly affected the use of pesticides because policies encourage the use of pesticides and IPM is knowledge-intensive.

Although the "Green Revolution" significantly increased rice yields in Asia, yield increases have not occurred in the past 15–20 years. The genetic "yield potential" has increased for wheat, but the yield potential for rice has not increased since 1966, and the yield potential for maize has "barely increased in 35 years". It takes a decade or two for herbicide-resistant weeds to emerge, and insects become resistant to insecticides within about a decade. Crop rotation helps to prevent resistances.

Agricultural exploration expeditions, since the late 19th century, have been mounted to find new species and new agricultural practices in different areas of the world. Two early examples of expeditions include Frank N. Meyer's fruit-and nut-collecting trip to China and Japan from 1916-1918 and the Dorsett-Morse Oriental Agricultural Exploration Expedition to China, Japan, and Korea from 1929-1931 to collect soybean germplasm to support the rise in soybean agriculture in the United States.

In 2009, the agricultural output of China was the largest in the world, followed by the European Union, India and the United States, according to the International Monetary Fund. Economists measure the total factor productivity of agriculture and by this measure agriculture in the United States is roughly 2.6 times more productive than it was in 1948.

Six countries-the US, Canada, France, Australia, Argentina and Thailand-supply 90% of grain exports. The United States controls almost half of world grain exports. Water deficits, which are already spurring heavy grain imports in numerous middle-sized countries, including Algeria, Iran, Egypt, and Mexico, may soon do the same in larger countries, such as China or India.

Crop Production Systems

Cropping systems vary among farms depending on the available resources and constraints; geography and climate of the farm; government policy; economic, social and political pressures; and the philosophy and culture of the farmer. Shifting cultivation (or slash and burn) is a system in which forests are burnt, releasing nutrients to support cultivation of annual and then perennial crops for a period of several years.

Then the plot is left fallow to regrow forest, and the farmer moves to a new plot, returning after many more years (10-20). This fallow period is shortened if population density grows, requiring the input of nutrients (fertilizer or manure) and some manual pest control. Annual cultivation is the next phase of intensity in which there is no fallow period. This requires even greater nutrient and pest control inputs. Further industrialization lead to the use of monocultures, when one cultivar is planted on a large acreage.

Because of the low biodiversity, nutrient use is uniform and pests tend to build up, necessitating the greater use of pesticides and fertilizers. Multiple cropping, in which several crops are grown sequentially in one year, and intercropping, when several crops are grown at the same time are other kinds of annual cropping systems known as polycultures.

In tropical environments, all of these cropping systems are practiced. In subtropical and arid environments, the timing and extent of agriculture may be limited by rainfall, either not allowing multiple annual crops in a year, or requiring irrigation. In all of these environments perennial crops are grown (coffee, chocolate) and systems are practiced such as agroforestry. In temperate environments, where ecosystems were predominantly grassland or prairie, highly productive annual cropping is the dominant farming system.

The last century has seen the intensification, concentration and specialization of agriculture, relying upon new technologies of agricultural chemicals (fertilizers and pesticides), mechanization, and plant breeding (hybrids and GMO's).

In the past few decades, a move towards sustainability in agriculture has also developed, integrating ideas of socio-economic justice and conservation of resources and the environment within a farming system.

This has led to the development of many responses to the conventional agriculture approach, including organic agriculture, urban agriculture, community supported agriculture, ecological or biological agriculture, integrated farming and holistic management, as well as an increased trend towards agricultural diversification.

Crop Statistics

Important categories of crops include grains and pseudograins, pulses (legumes), forage, and fruits and vegetables. Specific crops are cultivated in distinct growing regions throughout the world. In millions of metric tons, based on FAO estimate.

Table: *Top Agricultural Products, by crop types*

(million tonnes) 2004 data

Cereals	2,263
Vegetables and melons	866
Roots and Tubers	715
Milk	619
Fruit	503
Meat	259
Oilcrops	133
Fish (2001 estimate)	130
Eggs	63
Pulses	60
Vegetable Fiber	30

Source: *Food and Agriculture Organization (FAO)*

Table: *Top agricultural products, by individual crops*

(million tonnes) 2004 data

Sugar Cane	1,324
Maize	721
Wheat	627
Rice	605
Potatoes	328
Sugar Beet	249
Soybean	204
Oil Palm Fruit	162
Barley	154
Tomato	120

Source: *Food and Agriculture Organization (FAO)*

Livestock Production Systems

Animals, including horses, mules, oxen, camels, llamas, alpacas, and dogs, are often used to help cultivate fields, harvest crops, wrangle other animals, and transport farm products to buyers. Animal husbandry not only refers to the breeding and raising of animals for meat or to harvest animal products (like milk, eggs, or wool) on a continual basis, but also to the breeding and care of species for work and companionship. Livestock production systems can be defined based on feed source, as grassland-based, mixed, and landless.

Grassland based livestock production relies upon plant material such as shrubland, rangeland, and pastures for feeding ruminant animals. Outside nutrient inputs may be used, however manure is returned directly to the grassland as a major nutrient source. This system is particularly important in areas where crop production is not feasible because of climate or soil, representing 30-40 million pastoralists.

Mixed production systems use grassland, fodder crops and grain feed crops as feed for ruminant and monogastic (one stomach; mainly chickens and pigs) livestock. Manure is typically recycled in mixed systems as a fertilizer for crops. Approximately 68% of all agricultural land is permanent pastures used in the production of livestock.

Landless systems rely upon feed from outside the farm, representing the de-linking of crop and livestock production found more prevalently in OECD member countries. In the U.S., 70% of the grain grown is fed to animals on feedlots. Synthetic fertilizers are more heavily relied upon for crop production and manure utilization becomes a challenge as well as a source for pollution.

Production Practices

Tillage is the practice of plowing soil to prepare for planting or for nutrient incorporation or for pest control. Tillage varies in intensity from conventional to no-till. It may improve productivity by warming the soil, incorporating fertilizer and controlling weeds, but also renders soil more prone to erosion, triggers the decomposition of organic matter releasing CO_2, and reduces the abundance and diversity of soil organisms.

Pest control includes the management of weeds, insects/mites, and diseases. Chemical (pesticides), biological (biocontrol), mechanical (tillage), and cultural practices are used. Cultural practices include crop rotation, culling, cover crops, intercropping, composting, avoidance, and resistance. Integrated pest management attempts to use all of these methods to keep pest populations below the number which would cause economic loss, and recommends pesticides as a last resort.

Nutrient management includes both the source of nutrient inputs for crop and livestock production, and the method of utilization of manure produced by livestock.

Nutrient inputs can be chemical inorganic fertilizers, manure, green manure, compost and mined minerals. Crop nutrient use may also be managed using cultural techniques such as crop rotation or a fallow period. Manure is used either by holding livestock where the feed crop is growing, such as in managed intensive rotational grazing, or by spreading either dry or liquid formulations of manure on cropland or pastures.

Water management is where rainfall is insufficient or variable, which occurs to some degree in most regions of the world. Some farmers use irrigation to supplement rainfall. In other areas such as the Great Plains in the U.S. and Canada, farmers use a fallow year to conserve soil moisture to use for growing a crop in the following year. Agriculture represents 70% of freshwater use worldwide.

Processing, Distribution, and Marketing

In the United States, food costs attributed to processing, distribution, and marketing have risen while the costs attributed to farming have declined. This is related to the greater efficiency of farming, combined with the increased level of value addition (e.g. more highly processed products) provided by the supply chain. From 1960 to 1980 the farm share was around 40%, but by 1990 it had declined to 30% and by 1998, 22.2%.

Market concentration has increased in the sector as well, with the top 20 food manufacturers accounting for half the food-processing value in 1995, over double that produced in 1954. As of 2000 the top six US supermarket groups had 50% of sales compared to 32% in 1992. Although the total effect of the increased market concentration is likely increased efficiency, the changes redistribute economic surplus from producers (farmers) and consumers, and may have negative implications for rural communities.

Crop Alteration and Biotechnology

Crop alteration has been practiced by humankind for thousands of years, since the beginning of civilization. Altering crops through breeding practices changes the genetic make-up of a plant to develop crops with more beneficial characteristics for humans, for example, larger fruits or seeds, drought-tolerance, or resistance to pests. Significant advances in plant breeding ensued after the work of geneticist Gregor Mendel. His work on dominant and recessive alleles gave plant breeders a better understanding of genetics and brought great insights to the techniques utilized by plant breeders. Crop breeding includes techniques such as plant selection with desirable traits, self-pollination and cross-pollination, and molecular techniques that genetically modify the organism.

Domestication of plants has, over the centuries increased yield, improved disease resistance and drought tolerance, eased harvest and improved the taste and nutritional value of crop plants. Careful selection and breeding have had enormous effects on the characteristics of crop plants.

Plant selection and breeding in the 1920s and 1930s improved pasture (grasses and clover) in New Zealand. Extensive X-ray an ultraviolet induced mutagenesis efforts (i.e. primitive genetic engineering) during the 1950s produced the modern commercial varieties of grains such as wheat, corn (maize) and barley.

The green revolution popularized the use of conventional hybridization to increase yield many folds by creating "high-yielding varieties". For example, average yields of corn (maize) in the USA have increased from around 2.5 tons per hectare (t/ha) (40 bushels per acre) in 1900 to about 9.4 t/ha (150 bushels per acre) in 2001.

Similarly, worldwide average wheat yields have increased from less than 1 t/ha in 1900 to more than 2.5 t/ha in 1990. South American average wheat yields are around 2 t/ha, African under 1 t/ha, Egypt and Arabia up to 3.5 to 4 t/ha with irrigation. In contrast, the average wheat yield in countries such as France is over 8 t/ha. Variations in yields are due mainly to variation in climate, genetics, and the level of intensive farming techniques (use of fertilizers, chemical pest control, growth control to avoid lodging).

Genetic Engineering

Genetically Modified Organisms (GMO) are organisms whose genetic material has been altered by genetic engineering techniques generally known as recombinant DNA technology. Genetic engineering has expanded the genes available to breeders to utilize in creating desired germlines for new crops. After mechanical tomato-harvesters were developed in the early 1960s, agricultural scientists genetically modified tomatoes to be more resistant to mechanical handling. More recently, genetic engineering is being employed in various parts of the world, to create crops with other beneficial traits.

Herbicide-tolerant GMO Crops

Roundup Ready seed has a herbicide resistant gene implanted into its genome that allows the plants to tolerate exposure to glyphosate. *Roundup* is a trade name for a glyphosate-based product, which is a systemic, nonselective herbicide used to kill weeds. *Roundup Ready* seeds allow the farmer to grow a crop that can be sprayed with glyphosate to control weeds without harming the resistant crop. Herbicide-tolerant crops are used by farmers worldwide. Today, 92% of soybean acreage in the US is planted with genetically modified herbicide-tolerant plants.

With the increasing use of herbicide-tolerant crops, comes an increase in the use of glyphosate-based herbicide sprays. In some areas glyphosate resistant weeds have developed, causing farmers to switch to other herbicides. Some studies also link widespread glyphosate usage to iron deficiencies in some crops, which is both a crop production and a nutritional quality concern, with potential economic and health implications.

Insect-resistant GMO Crops

Other GMO crops used by growers include insect-resistant crops, which have a gene from the soil bacterium *Bacillus thuringiensis* (Bt), which produces a toxin specific to insects. These crops protect plants from damage by insects; one such crop is Starlink. Another is cotton, which accounts for 63% of US cotton acreage.

Some believe that similar or better pest-resistance traits can be acquired through traditional breeding practices, and resistance to various pests can be gained through hybridization or cross-pollination with wild species. In some cases, wild species are the primary source of resistance traits; some tomato cultivars that have gained resistance to at least nineteen diseases did so through crossing with wild populations of tomatoes.

Costs and benefits of GMOs

Genetic engineers may someday develop transgenic plants which would allow for irrigation, drainage, conservation, sanitary engineering, and maintaining or increasing yields while requiring fewer fossil fuel derived inputs than conventional crops. Such developments would be particularly important in areas which are normally arid and rely upon constant irrigation, and on large scale farms.

However, genetic engineering of plants has proven to be controversial. Many issues surrounding food security and environmental impacts have risen regarding GMO practices.

For example, GMOs are questioned by some ecologists and economists concerned with GMO practices such as terminator seeds, which is a genetic modification that creates sterile seeds. Terminator seeds are currently under strong international opposition and face continual efforts of global bans. Another controversial issue is the patent protection given to companies that develop new types of seed using genetic engineering. Since companies have intellectual ownership of their seeds, they have the power to dictate terms and conditions of their patented product.

Currently, ten seed companies control over two-thirds of the global seed sales. Vandana Shiva argues that these companies are guilty of biopiracy by patenting life and exploiting organisms for profit Farmers using patented seed are restricted from saving seed for subsequent plantings, which forces farmers to buy new seed every year. Since seed saving is a traditional practice for many farmers in both developing and developed countries, GMO seeds legally bind farmers to change their seed saving practices to buying new seed every year.

Locally adapted seeds are an essential hertitage that has the potential to be lost with current hybridized crops and GMOs. Locally adapted seeds, also called land races or crop eco-types, are important because they have adapted over time to the specific microclimates, soils, other environmental conditions, field designs, and ethnic preference indigenous to the exact area of cultivation. Introducing GMOs and hybridized commercial seed to an area brings the risk of cross-pollination with local land races

Therefore, GMOs pose a threat to the sustainability of land races and the ethnic heritage of cultures. Once seed contains transgenic material, it becomes subject to the conditions of the seed company that owns the patent of the transgenic material. There is also concern that GMOs will cross-pollinate with wild species and permanently alter native populations' genetic integrity; there are already identified populations of wild plants with transgenic genes.

GMO gene flow to related weed species is a concern, as well as cross-pollination with non-transgenic crops. Since many GMO crops are harvested for their seed, such as rapeseed, seed spillage in is problematic for volunteer plants in rotated fields, as well as seed-spillage during transportation.

Modern Agriculture

Modern agriculture is a term used to describe the wide majority of production practices employed by America's farmers. The term depicts the push for innovation, stewardship and advancements continually made by growers to sustainably produce higher-quality products with a reduced environmental impact. Intensive scientific research and robust investment in modern agriculture during the past 50 years has helped farmers double food production while essentially freezing the footprint of total cultivated farmland.

Safety

The agriculture industry works with government agencies and other organizations to ensure that farmers have access to the technologies required to support modern agriculture practices. Farmers are supported by education and certification programs that ensure they apply agricultural with care and only when required.

Sustainability

Technological advancements help provide farmers with tools and resources to help reduce their environmental footprint and to make farming more sustainable.

New technologies have given rise to innovations like conservation tillage, a farming process which helps prevent land loss to erosion, water pollution and enhances carbon sequestration.

The World Bank, the Bill & Melinda Gates Foundation and others have noted that integrated crop management is based on agro-ecological principles and can increase yields while reducing environmental damage.

Affordability

Modern agriculture practices help farmers to provide an affordable supply of nutritious food to meet the demands of a growing population. With modern agriculture, more crops can be grown on less land allowing farmers to provide an increased supply of food at an affordable price.

Food Safety, Labeling and Regulation

Food security issues also coincide with food safety and food labeling concerns. Currently a global treaty, the BioSafety Protocol, regulates the trade of GMOs. The EU currently requires all GMO foods to be labeled, whereas the US does not require transparent labeling of GMO foods. Since there are still questions regarding the safety and risks associated with GMO foods, some believe the public should have the freedom to choose and know what they are eating and require all GMO products to be labeled.

The Food and Agriculture Organization of the United Nations (FAO) leads international efforts to defeat hunger and provides a neutral forum where nations meet as equals to negotiate agreements and debate food policy and the regulation of agriculture. According to

Dr. Samuel Jutzi, director of FAO's animal production and health division, lobbying by "powerful" big food corporations has stopped reforms that would improve human health and the environment.

The "real, true issues are not being addressed by the political process because of the influence of lobbyists, of the true powerful entities," he said, speaking at the Compassion in World Farming annual forum. For example, recent proposals for a voluntary code of conduct for the livestock industry that would have provided incentives for improving standards for health, and environmental regulations, such as the number of animals an area of land can support without long-term damage, were successfully defeated due to large food company pressure.

Environmental Impact

Agriculture imposes external costs upon society through pesticides, nutrient runoff, excessive water usage, and assorted other problems. A 2000 assessment of agriculture in the UK determined total external costs for 1996 of £2,343 million, or £208 per hectare. A 2005 analysis of these costs in the USA concluded that cropland imposes approximately $5 to 16 billion ($30 to $96 per hectare), while livestock production imposes $714 million.

Both studies concluded that more should be done to internalize external costs, and neither included subsidies in their analysis, but noted that subsidies also influence the cost of agriculture to society. Both focused on purely fiscal impacts. The 2000 review included reported pesticide poisonings but did not include speculative chronic effects of pesticides, and the 2004 review relied on a 1992 estimate of the total impact of pesticides.

A key player who is credited to saving billions of lives because of his revolutionary work in developing new agricultural techniques is Norman Borlaug. His transformative work brought high-yield crop varieties to developing countries and earned him an unofficial title as the father of the Green Revolution.

Livestock Issues

A senior UN official and co-author of a UN report detailing this problem, Henning Steinfeld, said "Livestock are one of the most significant contributors to today's most serious environmental problems". Livestock production occupies 70% of all land used for agriculture, or 30% of the land surface of the planet. It is one of the largest sources of greenhouse gases, responsible for 18% of the world's greenhouse gas emissions as measured in CO_2 equivalents. By comparison, all transportation emits 13.5% of the CO_2. It produces 65% of human-related nitrous oxide (which has 296 times the global warming potential of CO_2) and 37% of all human-induced methane (which is 23 times as warming as CO_2. It also generates 64% of the ammonia, which contributes to acid rain and acidification of ecosystems. Livestock expansion is cited as a key factor driving deforestation, in the Amazon basin 70% of previously forested area is now occupied by pastures and the remainder used for feedcrops. Through deforestation and land degradation, livestock is also driving reductions in biodiversity.

Land Transformation and Degradation

Land transformation, the use of land to yield goods and services, is the most substantial way humans alter the Earth's ecosystems, and is considered the driving force in the loss of biodiversity. Estimates of the amount of land transformed by humans vary from 39–50%. Land degradation, the long-term decline in ecosystem function and productivity, is estimated to be occurring on 24% of land worldwide, with cropland overrepresented. The UN-FAO report cites land management as the driving factor behind degradation and reports that 1.5 billion people rely upon the degrading land. Degradation can be deforestation, desertification, soil erosion, mineral depletion, or chemical degradation (acidification and salinization).

Eutrophication

Eutrophication, excessive nutrients in aquatic ecosystems resulting in algal blooms and anoxia, leads to fish kills, loss of biodiversity, and renders water unfit for drinking and other industrial uses. Excessive fertilization and manure application to cropland, as well as high livestock stocking densities cause nutrient (mainly nitrogen and phosphorus) runoff and leaching from agricultural land. These nutrients are major nonpoint pollutants contributing to eutrophication of aquatic ecosystems.

Pesticides

Pesticide use has increased since 1950 to 2.5 million tons annually worldwide, yet crop loss from pests has remained relatively constant. The World Health Organization estimated in 1992 that 3 million pesticide poisonings occur annually, causing 220,000 deaths. Pesticides select for pesticide resistance in the pest population, leading to a condition termed the 'pesticide treadmill' in which pest resistance warrants the development of a new pesticide.

An alternative argument is that the way to 'save the environment' and prevent famine is by using pesticides and intensive high yield farming, a view exemplified by a quote heading the Center for Global Food Issues website:

'Growing more per acre leaves more land for nature'. However, critics argue that a trade-off between the environment and a need for food is not inevitable, and that pesticides simply replace good agronomic practices such as crop rotation.

Climate Change

Climate change has the potential to affect agriculture through changes in temperature, rainfall (timing and quantity), CO_2, solar radiation and the interaction of these elements. Agriculture can both mitigate or worsen global warming. Some of the increase in CO_2 in the atmosphere comes from the decomposition of organic matter in the soil, and much of the methane emitted into the atmosphere is caused by the decomposition of organic matter in wet soils such as rice paddies.

Further, wet or anaerobic soils also lose nitrogen through denitrification, releasing the greenhouse gas nitric oxide. Changes in management can reduce the release of these greenhouse gases, and soil can further be used to sequester some of the CO_2 in the atmosphere.

International Economics and Agriculture

Differences in economic development, population density and culture mean that the farmers of the world operate under very different conditions.

A US cotton farmer may receive US$230 in government subsidies per acre planted (in 2003), while farmers in Mali and other third-world countries do without. When prices decline, the heavily subsidized US farmer is not forced to reduce his output, making it difficult for cotton prices to rebound, but his Mali counterpart may go broke in the meantime.

A livestock farmer in South Korea can calculate with a (highly subsidized) sales price of US$1300 for a calf produced. A South American Mercosur country rancher calculates with a calf's sales price of US$120–200 (both 2008 figures). With the former, scarcity and high cost of land is compensated with public subsidies, the latter compensates absence of subsidies with economics of scale and low cost of land.

In the Peoples Republic of China, a rural household's productive asset may be one hectare of farmland. In Brazil, Paraguay and other countries where local legislature allows such purchases, international investors buy thousands of hectares of farmland or raw land at prices of a few hundred US$ per hectare.

Energy and Agriculture

Since the 1940s, agricultural productivity has increased dramatically, due largely to the increased use of energy-intensive mechanization, fertilizers and pesticides. The vast majority of this energy input comes from fossil fuel sources.

Between 1950 and 1984, the Green Revolution transformed agriculture around the globe, with world grain production increasing by 250% as world population doubled. Modern agriculture's heavy reliance on petrochemicals and mechanization has raised concerns that oil shortages could increase costs and reduce agricultural output, causing food shortages.

Modern or industrialized agriculture is dependent on fossil fuels in two fundamental ways:

1) direct consumption on the farm and
2) indirect consumption to manufacture inputs used on the farm.

Direct consumption includes the use of lubricants and fuels to operate farm vehicles and machinery; and use of gas, liquid propane, and electricity to power dryers, pumps, lights, heaters, and coolers. American farms directly consumed about 1.2 exajoules (1.1 quadrillion BTU) in 2002, or just over 1 percent of the nation's total energy.

Indirect consumption is mainly oil and natural gas used to manufacture fertilizers and pesticides, which accounted for 0.6 exajoules (0.6 quadrillion BTU) in 2002. The energy used to manufacture farm machinery is also a form of indirect agricultural energy consumption, but it is not included in USDA estimates of U.S. agricultural energy use. Together, direct and indirect consumption by U.S. farms accounts for about 2 percent of the nation's energy use. Direct and indirect energy consumption by U.S. farms peaked in 1979, and has gradually declined over the past 30 years.

Food systems encompass not just agricultural production, but also off-farm processing, packaging, transporting, marketing, consumption, and disposal of food and food-related items. Agriculture accounts for less than one-fifth of food system energy use in the United States.

Oil shortages could impact this food supply. Some farmers using modern organic-farming methods have reported yields as high as those available from conventional farming without the use of synthetic fertilizers and pesticides. However, the reconditioning of soil to restore nutrients lost during the use of monoculture agriculture techniques made possible by petroleum-based technology takes time.

In 2007, higher incentives for farmers to grow non-food biofuel crops combined with other factors (such as over-development of former farm lands, rising transportation costs, climate change, growing consumer demand in China and India, and population growth) to cause food shortages in Asia, the Middle East, Africa, and Mexico, as well as rising food prices around the globe.

As of December 2007, 37 countries faced food crises, and 20 had imposed some sort of food-price controls. Some of these shortages resulted in food riots and even deadly stampedes.

The biggest fossil fuel input to agriculture is the use of natural gas as a hydrogen source for the Haber-Bosch fertilizer-creation process. Natural gas is used because it is the cheapest currently available source of hydrogen.

When oil production becomes so scarce that natural gas is used as a partial stopgap replacement, and hydrogen use in transportation increases, natural gas will become much more expensive.

If the Haber Process is unable to be commercialized using renewable energy (such as by electrolysis) or if other sources of hydrogen are not available to replace the Haber Process, in amounts sufficient to supply transportation and agricultural needs, this major source of fertilizer would either become extremely expensive or unavailable. This would either cause food shortages or dramatic rises in food prices.

Mitigation of Effects of Petroleum Shortages

One effect oil shortages could have on agriculture is a full return to organic agriculture. In light of peak-oil concerns, organic methods are more sustainable than contemporary practices because they use no petroleum-based pesticides, herbicides, or fertilizers. Some farmers using modern organic-farming methods have reported yields as high as those available from conventional farming. Organic farming may however be more labor-intensive and would require a shift of the workforce from urban to rural areas.

It has been suggested that rural communities might obtain fuel from the biochar and synfuel process, which uses agricultural *waste* to provide charcoal fertilizer, some fuel *and* food, instead of the normal food vs fuel debate.

As the synfuel would be used on-site, the process would be more efficient and might just provide enough fuel for a new organic-agriculture fusion.

It has been suggested that some transgenic plants may some day be developed which would allow for maintaining or increasing yields while requiring fewer fossil-fuel-derived inputs than conventional crops. The possibility of success of these programs is questioned by ecologists and economists concerned with unsustainable GMO practices such as terminator seeds, and a January 2008 report shows that GMO practices "fail to deliver environmental, social and economic benefits." While there has been some research on sustainability using GMO crops, at least one hyped and prominent multi-year attempt by Monsanto Company has been unsuccessful, though during the same period traditional breeding techniques yielded a more sustainable variety of the same crop.

Additionally, a survey by the bio-tech industry of subsistence farmers in Africa to discover what GMO research would most benefit sustainable agriculture only identified non-transgenic issues as areas needing to be addressed. Nevertheless, some governments in Africa continue to view investments in new transgenic technologies as an essential component of efforts to improve sustainability.

Position of Farmers

A farmer is a person, engaged in agriculture, who raises living organisms for food or raw materials, generally including livestock husbandry and growing crops such as produce and grain. A farmer might own the farmed land or might work as a labourer on land owned by others; but in advanced economies, a farmer is usually a farm owner, while employees of the farm are farm workers, farmhands, etc.

India is an agricultural country. India lives in villages. The villagers depend on agriculture. They are either farmers or workers on the agricultural fields. Ours industries and urban business also depend on agriculture. Thus, an Indian farmer truly represents India. He can be called the son of the soil. It is on his sweet and labour that our progress and prosperity depend.

It is he who feeds and clothes the people. An Indian farmer is very hard working. He is very busy throughout the year. For him there is no rest. He is engaged in tilling the soil, sowing the seeds, watering the fields, reaping and harvesting the crop and then taking it to the market to sell it.

And yet he is very poor. He is being exploited by the money-lenders, the middlemen and the government servants.

His needs are few and simple and yet they are not met. Most of the Indian farmers or tenants. Their exploitation should be stopped. They should be distributed agricultural land. They should be given cheap loans and other facilities. They should be given better seeds, fertilizers and return for their produce. The irrigation facilities should be improved.

India cannot prosper until Indian farmer is poor and miserable. He is the very soul of the country. He is as important as a soldier, a doctor or an engineer. That is why the then Prime Minister Lal Bahadur Shastri gave us the slogan: "Jai Jawan, Jai Kisan." But it should not remain only a slogan. The Indian farmer should be given his due regard and status. Every effort should be made to make him happy, rich and comfortable. His labours and sweat should not go unrewarded.

He should be taught how to read and write. Education should be taken to his door-steps so that his children do not remain illiterate. He should be provided with better medical and health facilities. He is the bread-earner of the country and should be treated accordingly. If he himself remains hungry, illcad or ignorant how India can make progress? Some schemes have been started to improve his economic and social condition. But many more such schemes need to be started.

Indian Farmers Position on WTO

The farmers of India are very much concerned with the recent developments in the WTO negotiations on agriculture. In the current negotiations to conclude the modalities on agriculture before the General Council in end July, it is becoming clearer that once again the interest of India and other developing countries and their farmers are in danger. And we fear that the Indian government, driven by its offensive interest in services, would try to push through a deal for conclusion of the Doha round even at the cost of its million of farmers and industry workers. We had witnessed this in Hong Kong where India betrayed other developing countries in joining hands with US and EU to protect services text in exchange of minor gains in agriculture.

Today it is clear that the Indian position in WTO is driven by its offensive interest in services negotiations. India has no stake in agricultural negotiations and we are quite apprehensive that any tradeoff in services negotiations can change Indian position in agriculture.

When UPA government came in power largely with the support of farmers and rural India, Indian farmers were quite hopeful that their interest would be paramount in its agenda. But last two years of UPA rule has brought misery and destitution for the rural community and never before there were such severe agrarian crisis as it is today. Every day dozens of farmers are committing suicide yet Mr. Sharad Pawar, Union Minister for Agriculture, in a live television interview (CNN-IBN-June 4) said that "100,000 farmers suicide per year is a normal thing that we have been seeing for a number of years".

This is the height of government's apathy towards farmers. And ironically even the relief packages announced by this government to deal with agrarian crisis are corporate driven and only promote the interest of the US biotech industries like Monsanto and their agribusiness like Cargill and ADM.

And quite obviously three giant US corporations (Monsanto, Wal-Mart and Archer Daniels Midland) along with an Indian agribusiness ITC have got formal entry in the Indian government system as board members of the "Indo-US Knowledge Initiative on Agricultural Research and Education", launched during the US President's recent visit to India.

In last two years the UPA government has done a lot to protect interest of the corporate India at the cost of the poor and marginal class. Most of the agricultural related policy introduced by the UPA government has been to further the agenda of corporate globalization.

The introduction of seed bills 2004; changes in the agriculture produce marketing act (APMC Act); the food safety and standards bill; withdrawal of food subsides for the poor under BPL programme; the contract farming; liberalization of imports for seeds and planting material; increased commercialization of GM cotton and field trials for GM food crops; providing data exclusivity to MNCs in agro-chemicals; and completely liberalizing imports of food grains are some of those decisions which favours only the corporations.

Recently we witnessed a classic example of anti farmer and pro corporate policy of the UPA government when it signed a deal with AWB Ltd of Australia for import of 5 lakh tonne of wheat, at the time of harvest in India and at a price much above the MSP price for procurement of wheat from farmers. Though the government refused to pay an MSP of above Rs. 7000/-per tonne to Indian farmers but it is paying Rs. 10500 per tonne to AWB, which is procuring wheat from Indian mandies at a little extra price than the MSP and supplying the same Indian wheat to the government. In view of the above, we fear that in the ongoing negotiations on agriculture as well, the UPA government will jeopardize the interest of Indian farmers by accepting whatever scrap being offered by US and EU. And this will be done on the name of protecting the export interest of an small section of big "farmers" and corporations like ITC.

In the current negotiations on agriculture, the main issue is about deciding the formulae for tariff cuts and subsidy cuts. In view of the impact of removal of quantitative restrictions, Indian farmer stand to lose from the proposed large tariff cuts under negotiations. Any further lowing of tariff on agricultural goods would be disastrous for small and marginal farmers of the country and would lead to an epidemic of farmers' suicide. It would jeopardize our self-sufficiency in food, increase our dependency on agricultural imports and reduce the margin between applied and bound rates, thereby restricting future governments from freely changing tariffs.

In return for the increased market access, the US and EU are offering artificial reduction in their domestic support and the proposed cut will not make any change in their applied level of support. Instead it allows them to raise their overall subsidies level. This was made clear in the recent Domestic Support Simulations conducted by Canada which proved that neither the U.S. nor the E.C. will have to make reductions in their domestic support payments (as per their current proposals) and the U.S. in particular, will be able to increase overall spending in the amber and blue boxes and the de minimis. It found that under the U.S. proposal, U.S. agriculture spending could legally increase to $22.5 billion a year, from last year's estimated $19.6 billion, simply by re-categorizing existing payments.

The US trade official also claim that they are under extreme pressure from number of leading U.S. agriculture organizations who demand lowering of U.S. ambitions on domestic support. That means there can't be any further increase in the current US offer for reduction in domestic support. Moreover, the US is not ready to concede an effective protection for the developing countries through SPs and allows only five tariff lines (against a demand of 20% by the G20) to be self designated as SPs (US framework paper on SP of 6th April 2006) which is less than 1% of India's total tariff line (680) in agriculture. Even on Special Safeguard Mechanism (SSM), US intentions are not very clear and it is trying to limit the scope of this safeguard to an extent that recourse to such mechanism becomes useless (US proposal of 24th April 2006).

In fact all the so-called gains from the Hong Kong Declaration are proving to be illusionary. Even though SP and SSM are not effective safeguard mechanisms to deal with cheap subsidized imports, but these are the only safeguard available to the developing nations given the proposed deepest cut in import tariff. But US and EU does not want to offer even these minimal safeguard to the developing countries to protect their farmers from cheap subsidized imports. Therefore there going to be a complete disaster for the farmers and agriculture of the developing countries if this present offers on the table goes through.

It is now clear how tough it is to get so little from the developed countries on any issues which is of the interest of the developing countries and LDCs in the agricultural negotiations. We therefore reassert our demand that agriculture must be kept out of the perview of the WTO.

Several recent studies have also indicated the same and predicted loses for developing countries including India from the Doha Development Round, in the agriculture as well as industrial sectors. Contrary to commonly held view, research from the World Bank, the Carnegie Endowment and the European Commission reveal that the majority in Asia and Africa will be faced with losses in both agriculture and industrial goods liberalisation. Even EU's own impact assessment of the Doha Round foresee that many of the world's developing economies will lose out from the Round, including parts of South Asia and much of Sub-Saharan Africa.

Chapter 4

Rural Housing

Economics

Affordable Housing

Affordable housing is a term used to describe dwelling units whose total housing costs are deemed "affordable" to those that have a median income. Although the term is often applied to rental housing that is within the financial means of those in the lower income ranges of a geographical area, the concept is applicable to both renters and purchasers in all income ranges.

This article focuses on the affordability of owner-occupied and private rental housing as social housing is a specialised tenure.

In the United States and Canada, a commonly accepted guideline for housing affordability is a housing cost that does not exceed 30% of a household's gross income. Housing costs considered in this guideline generally include taxes and insurance for owners, and usually include utility costs. When the monthly carrying costs of a home exceed 30–35% of household income, then the housing is considered unaffordable for that household.

Supply and Demand

In the United States, a key element in determining affordable housing is acceptable commuting time/distance.

In Southern California, for example, a household's inhabitants must decide whether to pay more for housing to keep commuting time and expense low, or to accept a long and/or expensive commute in order to obtain "better" housing.

Household Income

A primary factor in housing affordability is household income. The most common approach is to consider the percentage of income that a household is spending on housing costs.

Another method of studying affordability looks at the regular hourly wage of full-time workers who are paid only the minimum wage (as set by their local, regional, or national government). The hope is that a full-time worker will be able to afford at least a small apartment in the area that he or she works in.

Other countries look at those living in relative poverty, which is usually defined as making less than 60% of the median household income. In their policy reports, they consider the presence or absence of housing for people making 60% of the median income.

Housing Costs

The other major factor is the measurement of housing costs.

Some organization and agencies consider the cost of purchasing a single-family home; others look exclusively at the cost of renting an apartment.

Many U.S. studies, for example, focus primarily on the median cost of renting a two-bedroom apartment in a large apartment complex for a new tenant. These studies often lump together luxury apartments and slums, as well as desirable and undesirable neighborhoods. While this practice is known to distort the true costs, it is difficult to provide accurate information for the wide variety of situations without the report being unwieldy.

Normally, only legal, permitted, separate housing is considered when calculating the cost of housing. The low rent costs for a room in a single family home, or an illegal garage conversion, or a college dormitory are generally excluded from the calculation, no matter how many people in an area live in such situations. Because of this study methodology, median housing costs tend to be slightly inflated.

Costs are generally considered on a cash (not accrual) basis. Thus a person making the last payment on a large home mortgage might live in officially unaffordable housing one month, and very affordable housing the following month, when the mortgage is paid off. This distortion can be significant in areas where real estate costs are high, even if incomes are similarly high, because a high income allows a higher proportion of the income to be dedicated towards buying an expensive home without endangering the household's ability to buy food or other basic necessities. Furthermore, the absolute availability of housing is not generally considered in the calculation of affordable housing. In a depressed or sparsely settled rural area, for example, the predicted price of the canonical median two-bedroom apartment may be quite easily affordable even to a minimum-wage worker– if only any apartments had ever been built.

Cost of the "Right to Build"

An article in the November 2007 issue of Atlantic Monthly reported on a study of the cost of obtaining the "right to build" (i.e. a building permit, red tape, bureaucracy, etc.) in different U.S. cities. The "right to build" cost does not include the cost of the land or the cost of constructing the house.

The study was conducted by Harvard economists Edward Glaeser and Kristina Tobio. According to the chart accompanying the article, the cost of obtaining the "right to build" adds approximately $600,000 to the cost of each new house that is built in San Francisco.

Consequences of Affordable Housing Shortages

A common measure of community-wide affordability is the number of homes that a household with a certain percentage of median income can afford.

For example, in a perfectly balanced housing market, the median household (and the half of the households which are wealthier) could officially afford the median housing option, while those poorer than the median home could not afford the median home. 50% affordability for the median home indicates a balanced market.

A community might track the percentage of its housing that is affordable to households earning 60% of median income. In addition to the distress it causes families who cannot easily find a place to live, lack of affordable housing is considered by many urban planners to have negative effects on a community's overall health. For example, lack of affordable housing can make low-cost labour more scarce, and increase demands on transportation systems (as workers travel longer distances between jobs and affordable housing). Housing cost increases in U.S. cities have been linked to declines in enrollment at local schools.

Policy Tools

Numerous policies in the U.S. and abroad have been designed to address the problem of inadequate supplies of affordable housing. Sophisticated secondary market mechanisms, inclusionary zoning, and land banking are three prominent tools, as well as tax and fiscal policies that result in reducing the cost of mortgages and the cost of borrowing. Other more recently promoted policy tools include relaxation of prohibitions against accessory dwelling units, and reduction of the amount of parking that must be built for a new structure.

Affordable housing is a controversial reality of contemporary life, for gains in affordability often result from expanding land available for housing or increasing the density of housing units in a given area. Ensuring a steady supply of affordable housing means ensuring that communities weigh real and perceived livability impacts against the sheer necessity of affordability. The process of weighing the impacts of locating affordable housing is quite contentious, and is laden with race and class implications.

Affordability by Country

United States

Comprehensive data for the most affordable and least affordable places in the U.S. is published each year by an affordable housing non-profit organization, the National Low Income Housing Coalition. The NLIHC promotes a guideline of 30% of household income as the upper limit of affordability.

Under this definition, most people in the United States have secured affordable housing arrangements. In 2001, the median household paid $658 per month in total housing costs. A total of 20% of households are deemed to be living in unaffordable housing: Nine percent of all households are renters in unaffordable housing, and eleven percent of all households are homeowners with high housing costs.

In the 2000 U.S. Census, the median homeowner with a mortgage (70% of homeowners and 48% of census respondents) spent $1,088 each month, or 21.7% of household income, on housing costs. The median homeowner without a mortgage (30% of all homeowners (80% of elderly homeowners) and 20% of respondents) spent $295 per month, or 10.5% of household income, on housing costs. Renters in 2001 (32% of respondents) spent $633 each month, or 29% of household income, on housing costs.

Housing Subsidies by Country

Australia

Australians in receipt of many social security benefits from Centrelink who rent housing from a private landlord are eligible for rent assistance. Rent assistance is a subsidy paid directly to the tenant in addition to the basic Centrelink benefit such as the Age Pension or the Disability Pension. The amount of rent assistance paid depends on the amount of rent payable, whether the tenant has dependents and how many dependents there are. Tenants who live in public housing in Australia are not eligible for rent assistance.

Australians buying a home for the first time are eligible for a first home owner grant. These grants were introduced on 1 July 2000 and are jointly funded by the Commonwealth government and the state and territory governments. First home buyers are currently eligible for grants of $14,000 (for established dwellings) or $21,000 (for newly constructed dwellings) to alleviate the costs of entering the housing market.

The Commonwealth government in 2008 introduced first home saver accounts, whereby those saving for a new home are eligible for government contributions to their savings account, subject to conditions.

United Kingdom

The United Kingdom has a long tradition of promoting affordable social rented housing. This may be owned by local councils or housing associations· There are also a range of affordable home ownership options, including shared ownership (where a tenant rents part share in the property from a social landlord, and owns the remainder). The government has also attempted to promote the supply of owner occupied affordable stock for purchase, principally by using the land-use planning system to require that housing developers provide a proportion of lower cost housing within new developments.

This approach is commonly known as inclusionary zoning and the current mechanism for securing the provision of affordable housing as part of a planning application for new housing development is through the use of a S.106 Agreement. In Scotland a Section 75 Agreement (Section 75 of the 1997 Act) is the equivalent of England's S.106 agreement.

A high proportion of homes in the UK were previously council-owned, but the numbers have been reduced since the early 1980s due to initiatives of the Thatcher government that restricted council housing construction and provided financial and policy support to other forms social housing.

In 1980, the Conservative government of Margaret Thatcher introduced the Right to Buy scheme, offering council tenants the opportunity to purchase their housing at a discount of up to 60% (70%

on leasehold homes such as flats)· Alongside Right to Buy, council-owned stock was further diminished as properties were transferred to housing associations. Council Tenants in some instances have chosen to transfer management of the properties to arms-length non-profit organisations·

The tenants still remained Council tenants, and the housing stock still remained the property of the Council. This change in management was encouraged by extra funding from central government to invest in the housing stock under the Decent Homes Programme·

The program required council housing to be brought up to a set standard was combined with restrictions on the amounts that councils could borrow and led to an increase in such arms length management organisations being set up. In some areas, significant numbers of council houses were demolished as part of urban regeneration programmes, due to the poor quality of stock, low levels of demand and social problems·

In rural areas where local wages are low and house prices are higher (especially in regions with holiday homes) there are especial problems. Planning restrictions severely limit rural development. but if there is evidence of need then Exception sites can be used for people with a local connection. This evidence is normally provided by a housing Needs survey carried out by a Rural Housing Enabler working for the local Rural Community Council.

Housing associations are not-for-profit organisations with a history that goes back before the start of the 20th century. The number of homes under their ownership grew significantly from the 1980s as successive governments sought to make them the principal form of social housing, in preference to local authorities. Many of the homes previously under the ownership of local authorities have been transferred newly established housing associations, including some of the largest in the country. Despite being not-for-profit organisations, housing association rents are typically higher than for council housing. Renting a home through a housing association can in some circumstances prove costlier than purchasing a similar property through a mortgage.

United States

The federal government in the U.S. provides subsidies to make housing more affordable. Financial assistance is provided for homeowners through the mortgage interest tax deduction and for lower income households through housing subsidy programs. In the 1970s the federal government spent similar amounts on tax reductions for homeowners as it did on subsidies for low-income housing. However, by 2005, tax reductions had risen to $120 billion per year, representing nearly 80 percent of all federal housing assistance. The Advisory Panel on Federal Tax Reform for President Bush proposed reducing the home mortgage interest deduction in a 2005 report.

Housing assistance from the federal government for lower income households can be divided into three parts:

- "Tenant based" subsidies given to an individual household, known as the Section 8 program
- "Project based" subsidies given to the owner of housing units that must be rented to lower income households at affordable rates, and
- Public Housing, which is usually owned and operated by the government. (Some public housing projects are managed by subcontracted private agencies.)

"Project based" subsidies are also known by their section of the U.S. Housing Act or the Housing Act of 1949, and include Section 8, Section 236, Section 221(d)(3), Section 202 for elderly households, Section 515 for rural renters, Section 514/516 for farmworkers and Section 811 for people with disabilities. There are also housing subsidies through the Section 8 program that are project based. The United States Department of Housing and Urban Development (HUD) and USDA Rural Development administer these programs, and have further information on the particular programs on the agencies' respective web sites: HUD and USDA, Rural Development. HUD and USDA Rural Development programs have ceased to produce large numbers of units since the 1980s. Since 1986, the Low-Income Housing Tax Credit program has been the primary federal program to produce affordable units; however, the housing produced in this program is less affordable than the former HUD programs.

One of the most unique US public housing initiatives was the development of subsidized middle-class housing during the late New Deal (1940-42) under the auspices of the Mutual Ownership Defence Housing Division of the Federal Works Agency under the direction of Colonel Lawrence Westbrook. These eight projects were purchased by the residents after the Second World War and as of 2009 seven of the projects continue to operate as mutual housing corporations owned by their residents. These projects are among the very few definitive success stories in the history of the US public housing effort.

In the U.S., households are commonly defined in terms of the amount of realized income they earn relative to the Area Median Income or AMI. Localized AMI figures are calculated annually based on a survey of comparably-sized households within geographic ranges known as metropolitan statistical areas, as defined by the US Office of Management and Budget. For U.S. housing subsidies, households are categorized by federal law as follows:

- Moderate income households earn between 80% and 120% of AMI.
- Low income households earn between 50% and 80% of AMI.
- Very low income households earn no more than 50% of AMI.

Some states and cities in the United States operate a variety of affordable housing programs, including supportive housing programs, transitional housing programs and rent subsidies as part of public assistance programs. Local and state governments can adapt these income limits when administering local affordable housing programs; however, U.S. federal programs must adhere to the definitions above. For the Section 8 voucher program, the maximum household contribution to rent can be as high as 40% gross income.

Additional Resources

Canada

In Canada, the Social Housing Services Corporation (SHSC) is a leader in providing group services for social housing providers. SHSC was created in the Province of Ontario in 2002 to provide group services for social housing providers (public, non-profit and co-op housing) following the downloading of responsibility for over 270,000 social housing units to local municipalities. It is a non-profit corporation governed by a board of municipal, non-profit and co-op housing representatives. Its mandate is to provide Ontario housing providers and service managers with bulk purchasing, insurance, investment and information services that add significant value to their operations.

With an annual budget of $4.5 million, SHSC and its two subsidiaries, SOHO and SHSC Financial Inc. offers a dedicated insurance program for social housing providers, bulk gas purchasing and an innovative energy efficiency retrofit program which coordinates energy audits, expertise, funding, bulk purchasing of energy-efficient goods, training and education, and data evaluation. SHSC manages and provides investment advice to housing providers on capital reserves valued at more than $390 million.

Working closely with other housing sector organizations and non-governmental organizations, SHSC also supports and develops independent housing-related research, including a new Housing Internship program for graduate-level researchers.

Recently there has been a move toward the integration of affordable social housing with market housing and other uses, such as the 2006-10 redevelopment of the Woodward's building site in Vancouver.

Zoning changes in some areas of Canada to permit laneway houses has been part of the EcoDensity movement to permit home owners to create small affordable rental units in their backyards.

United States

Governmental and quasi-governmental agencies that contribute to the work of ensuring the existence of a steady supply of affordable housing in the United States are the U.S. Department of Housing and Urban Development (HUD), USDA Rural Development, the Federal Home Loan Bank, Fannie Mae, and Freddie Mac.

Important private sector institutions worth consulting are the National Association of Home Builders and the National Association of Realtors. Valuable research institutions with staff dedicated to the analysis of "affordable housing" includes:

The Center for Housing Policy, Brookings Institution, the Urban Institute and the Joint Center for Housing Studies at Harvard University and the Furman Center for Real Estate and Urban Policy at New York University, and the Center on Budget and Policy Priorities. Several of these institutions (the Fannie Mae Foundation, Urban Institute, Brookings Institution Metropolitan Policy Program, Enterprise Community Partners, LISC, the Harvard Joint Center for Housing Studies, and others) partnered to create KnowledgePlex, an online information resource devoted to affordable housing and community development issues.

Additional alignments have been established with Starta Development Starta Development to ease the process of funding application with the use of technology.

United Kingdom

All major housing associations are registered with the Housing Corporation, which regulates them and provides grants for development. Housing associations that are registered with the Corporation are also known as Registered Social Landlords.

The Department for Communities and Local Government has responsibility for housing in England. In January 2007 it announced a planned merger between the Housing Corporation and regeneration body English Partnerships to create the Homes and Communities Agency (initially announced as "Communities England"). This new body is likely to have access to more than £4 billion in resources.

In contrast to the rest of the United Kingdom, social housing in Northern Ireland is regulated by the Northern Ireland Housing Executive, which was established to take on ownership of former council stock and prevent sectarian allocation of housing to people from one religion.

Housing Bubble

A real estate bubble or property bubble (or housing bubble for residential markets) is a type of economic bubble that occurs periodically in local or global real estate markets. It is characterized by rapid increases in valuations of real property such as housing until they reach unsustainable levels relative to incomes and other economic elements, followed by a reduction in price levels.

Whether real estate bubbles can or should be identified or prevented, and whether they have broader macroeconomic importance or not are debated within and between different schools of economic thought, as detailed below. The financial crisis of 2007–2010 was related to the collapse of real estate bubbles, notably in the United States.

Identification and Prevention

As with all types of economic bubbles, whether real estate bubbles can be identified or prevented is contentious. Bubbles are generally not contentious in hindsight, after a peak and crash. Within mainstream economics, some argue that real estate bubbles cannot be identified as they occur and cannot or should not be prevented, with government and central bank policy rather cleaning up after the bubble bursts.

Others within mainstream economics and in heterodox economics, such as American economist Robert Shiller and British magazine *The Economist,* argue that housing market indicators can be used to identify real estate bubbles. Some argue further that governments and central banks can and should take action to prevent bubbles from forming, or to deflate existing bubbles.

Macroeconomic Significance

Within mainstream economics, economic bubbles, and in particular real estate bubbles, are not considered major concerns. Within some schools of heterodox economics, by contrast, real estate bubbles are considered of critical importance and a fundamental cause of financial crises and ensuing economic crises.

The mainstream economic view is that economic bubbles primarily effect first a temporary boost in wealth, and secondly a redistribution of wealth. When prices go up, there is a positive wealth effect – property owners feel richer, and hence spend more, and when prices go down, there is a negative wealth effect – property owners feel poorer, and hence spend less. It is argued that these effects can be smoothed by counter-cyclical monetary and fiscal policy. Secondly, the ultimate effect on owners who bought before the bubble formed and did not sell is zero – throughout, they owned the property. Conversely, those who bought when low and sold high profited, while those who bought high and sold low or held until the price had fallen lost money, though this ultimately is simply redistribution of wealth and, it is argued, of little economic significance.

In some schools of heterodox economics, notably Austrian economics and Post-Keynesian economics, real estate bubbles are seen as an example of credit bubbles (pejoratively, speculative bubbles), because property owners generally use borrowed money to purchase property, in the form of mortgages. These are then argued to cause financial and hence economic crises. This is first argued empirically – numerous real estate bubbles have been followed by economic slumps, and it is argued that there is a cause-effect relationship between these.

Austrian business cycle theory takes a supply-side view, arguing that real estate bubbles cause misallocation of resources – too many houses and offices are built, and too many resources (materials and labour) are wasted in building unneeded buildings. Further, this distorts the industrial base, yielding an excess of homebuilders who must then retrain and retool when the bubble bursts, this transition between non-productive and productive uses of resources (and the malinvestment during the lead-up) being a proximate cause of the resulting economic slump.

Fred Foldvary, economist at Santa Clara University, has synthesized the Austrian-school theory of the cycle with the land-based theory of Henry George. His proposition is that this geo-Austrian theory fits the 18-year real estate cycle as discovered by real estate economist Homer Hoyt.

The Post-Keynesian theory of debt deflation takes a demand-side view, arguing that property owners not only *feel* richer, but *borrow* against the increased value of their property (as via a home equity line of credit), or borrow money to speculate in property, buying property with borrowed money in the expectation that it will rise in value – this last view is associated with Hyman Minsky and his Financial Instability Hypothesis. When the bubble bursts, the value of the property decreases but, crucially, the level of debt does not. The burden of repaying or defaulting on this debt is argued to depress aggregate demand and be the proximate cause of the ensuing economic slump.

Recent Real Estate Bubbles

The crash of the Japanese asset price bubble from 1990 on has been very damaging to the Japanese economy and the lives of many Japanese who have lived through it, as is also true of the crash in 2005 of the real estate bubble in China's largest city, Shanghai. Unlike a stock market crash following a bubble, a real-estate "crash" is usually a slower process, because the real estate market is less liquid than the stock market. Other sectors such as office, hotel and retail generally move along with the residential market, being affected by many of same variables (incomes, interest rates, etc.) and also sharing the "wealth effect" of booms. Therefore this article focuses on housing bubbles and mentions other sectors only when their situation differs from housing.

As of 2007, real estate bubbles had existed in the recent past or were widely believed to still exist in many parts of the world, especially in the United States, Argentina, Britain, Netherlands, Italy, Australia, New Zealand, Ireland, Spain, Lebanon, France, Poland, South Africa, Israel, Greece, Bulgaria, Croatia, Canada, Norway, Singapore, South Korea, Sweden, Baltic states, India, Romania, Russia, Ukraine and China· Then U.S.

Federal Reserve Chairman Alan Greenspan said in mid-2005 that "at a minimum, there's a little 'froth' (in the U.S. housing market) ... it's hard not to see that there are a lot of local bubbles." The *Economist* magazine, writing at the same time, went further, saying "the worldwide rise in house prices is the biggest bubble in history". Real estate bubbles are invariably followed by severe price decreases (also known as a house price crash) that can result in many owners holding negative equity (a mortgage debt higher than the current value of the property).

Housing Market Indicators

In attempting to identify bubbles before they burst, economists have developed a number of financial ratios and economic indicators that can be used to evaluate whether homes in a given area are fairly valued. By comparing current levels to previous levels that have proven unsustainable in the past (*i.e.* led to or at least accompanied crashes), one can make an educated guess as to whether a given real estate market is experiencing a bubble. Indicators describe two interwoven aspects of housing bubble: a valuation component and a debt (or leverage) component.

The valuation component measures how expensive houses are relative to what most people can afford, and the debt component measures how indebted households become in buying them for home or profit (and also how much exposure the banks accumulate by lending for them). A basic summary of the progress of housing indicators for U.S. cities is provided by *Business Week.*

Housing Affordability Measures

- The *price to income ratio* is the basic affordability measure for housing in a given area. It is generally the ratio of median house prices to median familial disposable incomes, expressed as a percentage or as years of income. It is sometimes compiled separately for first time buyers and termed *attainability*. This ratio, applied to individuals, is a basic component of mortgage lending decisions.

  According to a back-of-the-envelope calculation by Goldman Sachs, a comparison of median home prices to median household income suggests that U.S. housing in 2005 is overvalued by 10%. "However, this estimate is based on an average mortgage rate of about 6%, and we expect rates to rise," the firm's economics team wrote in a recent report· According to Goldman's figures, a one-percentage-point rise in mortgage rates would reduce the fair value of home prices by 8%.

- The *deposit to income ratio* is the minimum required downpayment for a typical mortgage, expressed in months or years of income. It is especially important for first-time buyers without existing home equity; if the downpayment becomes too high then those buyers may find themselves "priced out" of the market. For example, as of 2004 this ratio was equal to one year of income in the UK.

Another variant is what the National Association of Realtors calls the "housing affordability index" in its publications. (The NAR's methodology was criticized by some analysts as it does not account for inflation. Other analysts, however, consider the measure appropriate, because both the income and housing cost data is expressed in terms that include inflation and, all things being equal, the index implicitly includes inflation). In either case, the usefulness of this ratio in identifying a bubble is debatable; while downpayments normally increase with house valuations, bank lending becomes increasingly lax during a bubble and mortgages are offered to borrowers who would not normally qualify for them.

- The *Affordability Index* measures the ratio of the actual monthly cost of the mortgage to take-home income. It is used more in the United Kingdom where nearly all mortgages are variable and pegged to bank lending rates. It offers a much more realistic measure of the ability of households to afford housing than the crude price to income ratio. However it is more difficult to calculate, and hence the price to income ratio is still more commonly used by pundits.

  In recent years, lending practices have relaxed, allowing greater multiples of income to be borrowed. Some speculate that this practice in the longterm cannot be sustained and may ultimately lead to unaffordable mortgage payments, and repossession for many.
- The *Median Multiple* measures the ratio of the median house price to the median annual household income. This measure has historically hovered around a value of 3.0 or less, but in recent years has risen dramatically, especially in markets with severe public policy constraints on land and development. The Demographia International Housing Affordability Survey uses the Median Multiple in its 6-nation report.

Housing debt measures

- The *housing debt to income ratio* or *debt-service ratio* is the ratio of mortgage payments to disposable income. When the ratio gets too high, households become increasingly dependent on rising property values to service their debt. A variant of this indicator measures total home ownership costs, including mortgage payments, utilities and property taxes, as a percentage of a typical household's monthly pre-tax income; for example see RBC Economics' reports for the Canadian markets.
- The *housing debt to equity ratio* (not to be confused with the corporate debt to equity ratio), also called loan to value, is the ratio of the mortgage debt to the value of the underlying property; it measures financial leverage. This ratio increases

when homeowners refinance and tap into their home equity through a second mortgage or home equity loan. A ratio of 1 means 100% leverage; higher than 1 means negative equity.

Housing Ownership and Rent Measures

- The *ownership ratio* is the proportion of households who own their homes as opposed to renting. It tends to rise steadily with incomes. Also, governments often enact measures such as tax cuts or subsidized financing to encourage and facilitate home ownership. If a rise in ownership is not supported by a rise in incomes, it can mean either that buyers are taking advantage of low interest rates (which must eventually rise again as the economy heats up) or that home loans are awarded more liberally, to borrowers with poor credit.

  Therefore a high ownership ratio combined with an increased rate of subprime lending may signal higher debt levels associated with bubbles.

- The *price-to-earnings ratio* or *P/E ratio* is the common metric used to assess the relative valuation of equities. To compute the P/E ratio for the case of a rented house, divide the price of the house by its potential earnings or net income, which is the market annual rent of the house minus expenses, which include maintenance and property taxes. This formula is:

$$\text{House P / E ratio} = \frac{\text{House price}}{\text{Rent} - \text{Expenses}}$$

  The house price-to-earnings ratio provides a direct comparison to P/E ratios used to analyze other uses of the money tied up in a home. Compare this ratio to the simpler but less accurate *price-rent ratio* below.

- The *price-rent ratio* is the average cost of ownership divided by the received rent income (if buying to let) or the estimated rent that would be paid if renting (if buying to reside)

$$\text{House Price} - \text{Rent ratio} = \frac{\text{House price}}{\text{Monthly Rent} \times 12}$$

  The latter is often measured using the "owner's equivalent rent" numbers published by the Bureau of Labour Statistics. It can be viewed as the real estate equivalent of stocks' price-earnings ratio; in other terms it measures how much the buyer is paying for each dollar of received rent income (or dollar saved from rent spending). Rents, just like corporate and personal incomes, are generally tied very closely to supply and demand fundamentals; one rarely sees an unsustainable "rent bubble" (or "income bubble" for that matter).

Therefore a rapid increase of home prices combined with a flat renting market can signal the onset of a bubble. The U.S. price-rent ratio was 18% higher than its long-run average as of October 2004.

- The *gross rental yield*, a measure used in the United Kingdom, is the total yearly gross rent divided by the house price and expressed as a percentage:

$$\text{Gross Rental Yield} = \frac{\text{Monthly Rent} \times 12}{\text{House price}} \times 100\%$$

This is the reciprocal of the house price-rent ratio. The *net rental yield* deducts the landlord's expenses (and sometimes estimated rental voids) from the gross rent before doing the above calculation; this is the reciprocal of the house P/E ratio.

Because rents are received throughout the year rather than at its end, both the gross and net rental yields calculated by the above are somewhat less than the true rental yields obtained when taking into account the monthly nature of rental payments.

- The *occupancy rate* (opposite: *vacancy rate*) is essentially the number of occupied units divided by the total number of units in a given region (in commercial real estate, it is usually expressed in terms of area such as square meters for different grades of buildings). A low occupancy rate means that the market is in a state of oversupply brought about by speculative construction and purchase. In this context, supply-and-demand numbers can be misleading: sales demand exceeds supply, but rent demand does not.

Housing Price Indices

Measures of house *price* are also used in identifying housing bubbles; these are known as house price indices (HPIs).

A noted series of HPIs for the United States are the Case–Shiller indices, devised by American economists Karl Case, Robert Shiller, and Allan Weiss. As measured by the Case–Shiller index, the US experienced a housing bubble peaking in the second quarter of 2006 (2006 Q2).

Real Estate Bubbles in the 2000s

As of 2006, several areas of the world are thought by some to be in a bubble state, although the subject is highly controversial. This hypothesis is based on similar patterns in real estate markets of a wide variety of countries. This includes similar patterns of overvaluation and excessive borrowing based on those overvaluations. Some economists maintain that there is not enough similarity to assert a world trend. Others assert that there are enough common characteristics to call it a broad pattern; the reasons for such a pattern can be attributed to any of a number of macroeconomic trends. One such trend might be the rapid growth of developing economies such as the BRIC group. This has caused significant growth in monetary reserves and savings in those countries, which in turn has made possible extension of credit elsewhere.

The subprime mortgage crisis, with its accompanying impacts and effects on economies in various nations, has given some credence to the idea that these trends might have some common characteristics.

Chapter 5

Rural Community

Study of Rural Community in India

People in rural areas in India, have many problems such as :-

1) Electricity
2) Education
3) Health
4) Roads
5) Jobs
6) Scope for development
7) Lack of security
8) Illiterate administration
9) No modern facilities
10) No water supply.

The burden of indebtedness in rural India is great, and falls mainly on the households of rural working people. The exploitation of this group in the credit market is one of the most pervasive and persistent features of rural life in India, and despite major structural changes in credit institutions and forms of rural credit in the post-Independence period, Darling's statement (1925), that "the Indian peasant is born in debt, lives in debt and bequeaths debt," still remains true for the great majority of working households in the countryside. Rural households need credit for a variety of reasons.

They need it to meet short-term requirements for working capital and for long-term investment in agriculture and other income-bearing activities. Agricultural and non-agricultural activity in rural areas are typically seasonal, and households need credit to smooth out seasonal fluctuations in earnings and expenditure.

Rural households, particularly those vulnerable to what appear to others to be minor shocks with respect to income and expenditure, need credit as an insurance against risk. In a society that has no free, compulsory and universal education or health care, and very few general social security programmes, rural households need credit for different types of consumption.

These include expenditure on food, housing, health and education. In the Indian context, another important purpose of borrowing is to meet expenses for a variety of social obligations and rituals.

Introduction

About 75% of the Indian population lives in rural areas and about 80% of this population is dependent on agriculture for its livelihood. Agriculture accounts for about 37% of the national income. The development of the rural areas and of agriculture and its allied activities thus becomes vital for the rapid development of the economy as a whole.In this regard, India has succeeded in developing one of the largest rural banking systems in the world.

Various regulatory measures have been taken enabling the banking system to play an important role in the economic development of the rural areas. The two most prominent measures are rural commercial bank branch expansion, thus moving from class banking to mass banking and secondly, priority sector lending and the formulation of specific development programmes and action plans to facilitate credit flow to the rural sectors.

Despite these measures, as per the Debt and Investment Survey, Govt. of India (1992) about 36% of the rural households are found to be outside the fold of institutional credit.

Agricultural Productivity

Even though India occupies the first or second position in the world in several crops in terms of area and production, it's rank in terms of productivity per hectare in the world is 52 for rice, 38 for wheat and much low in several other crops.

The productivity of some crops is not only low but also remained stagnant over the years. The yield gap needs to be bridged through an integrated package of technology and agricultural policies to reap the untapped production potential, particularly, in rain-fed and other low productivity areas.

Causes for Backwardness in Villages

Zamindari System, the legacy of the British Rule

India was under British rule for 200 years. British policies were aimed in revenue collection and not rural development. They introduced the zamindari system. The zamindars were deemed the owners of all land and they collected as much revenue as they could from the peasants. The system left the peasants very poor and the zamindars did very little to improve the conditions of the villages. After the country attained independence this system was abolished, but the conditions of the peasants is yet to transform completely.

The Bonded Labour System

It is equivalent to near slavery. Bonded labour is an indebted agricultural worker, who had borrowed from the money lender at usurious rate of interest and had to work in his farm for low wages. The system was used to permanently enslave the worker, as the worker was only able to repay a part of interest and the loan with compounded residual interest went on swelling. The agricultural labour can free himself eventually only by giving his son in bondage as a substitute. Under the 20-point economic programme, the Government India under Prime Minister Mrs.Indira Gandhi abolished bonded labour system and brought legislation to this effect in 1975. Despite the legislation the system is known to persist here and there in select areas.

Other contributory reasons are the total lack of agricultural development under foreign rule, poor communication, roads and other infrastructure development in villages, lack of education and health facilities, and the destruction of the thriving Indian cottage industries on account of competition from the cheap machine made goods imported under British rule

Progress made after the Country attained Independence

1. After Independence the Country adopted planned development. The very first five year plan laid stress on agricultural development. It took a number of measures to bring more land under irrigation. Major irrigation Dams like Bakra Nangal, Hirakud, Nagarjunasagar, Tungabhadra were constructed which generated power for industrialisation of the country and water for irrigation. A number canals were build to distribute stored water over an extensive area. The Indian farmer, as a result, is now not exclusive depending on the monsoon.

2. Intensive cultivation of land is made possible through farm mechanisation. Tractors are being produced in the country and these are available to the farmers everywhere. Farmers are also using threshing machines, deep boring and irrigation pumps. They get supplies of high yielding improved seeds, fertilisers and other inputs.

   To enable them to purchase such inputs the rural credit system has been invigorated with Cooperatives, Regional Rural Banks, and Rural Branches of Commercial Banks. The recent boon to the poor Indian peasant is the micro finance system and Self Help Groups that have rendered financial support within the easy reach of all.

3. Land Reform legislation introduced in the country after independence include the abolition of the zamindari system, the abolition of bonded labour system, land ceiling legislation etc.. Legislation was also introduced to relieve rural indebtedness and the money lender could no longer legally collect more than reasonable interest. Untouchability was abolished and special legislation for the upliftment of scheduled cases and scheduled tribes were enacted.

4. Community Development Programmes, Integrated Rural Development Programme, bringing local self-government to the roots of the village through introduction of panchayat raj system ushered a new era of rural development.

   Development of public health care system, schemes undertaken for promoting literacy and adult education in the country, programmes for development of rural industries are other development programmes that have received the thrust of the Government's development approach.

Future Perspectives

Agriculture, with its large dependent population has to thrive and flourish, in order to secure rural prosperity. To ensure orderly and vigorous growth of agriculture policy and structural issues need to be addressed quickly. Some of the important issues that need to be addressed are-

1. Improving profitability of agriculture, through yield improvements, diversification and reform of agricultural marketing.
2. Strengthening backward linkages and expanding irrigation coverage.

3. Providing forward linkages especially for post harvest management, processing, transport, storage and market infrastructure.
4. Securing a stable long term policy on agricultural commodities trade, including the role of private sector.
5. Encouraging emergence of a market mechanism for agricultural commodities such as a commodities exchange.
6. Streamlining the cooperative credit structure for facilitating hassle free flow of credit.
7. Implementing watershed development projects in the rain-fed and dry-land areas.

Rural Banking Faces Twin Challenges

Banking in rural India is faced with the twin challenges of regulation and distribution. Regulation with respect to banking has been designed for delivery in urban India and distribution required more manpower to be deployed in rural areas. Initiatives like cheque transaction — where the electronic image and not the actual cheque is sent — have in mind the urban customer, he said. "About 500-600 million people in India still do not have bank accounts.

For the rural segment, one needs to design no-frills products and deliver hard core value". The other handicap was that while Rs 1-crore business in microfinance required 30 people in terms of manpower, the same volume of business in other portfolios required only one person. Also, contract farming and supply chain integration has not gone the way they should have. Power, telecommunications, banking and transportation had reduced the urban-rural divide, he said. Besides traditional banking services, people in the rural and semi-urban areas are expressing interest in liability and investment products. He said, "Rural India is fast transforming a nation of savers into a nation of investors".

No doubt, villages are in a state of neglect and under-development, with impoverished people, as result of past legacies and defects in our planning process and investment pattern. But the potential in rural India is immense. What if every village in the country is provided with basic amenities, like drinking water, electricity, health care, educational transport, communication and other facilities, with only a smaller population of the village engaged in agriculture and the remaining in other gainful occupations? When this happens India will turn into mighty country.

The purchasing power of the rural population throwing enormous demand for goods and services will boost the national economy tremendously. The day will see the reverse migration of people from the urban slums back to the villages. Rural Development is the subject to come to the forefront after the economic reforms and rural banking will serve the backbone of this development.

The Greatest Problem of Less Population

The Indian government has therefore given rise to some more administrations (but to no avail) to help the people.

Drinking water quality in rural India: Issues and approaches. The rural population of India comprises more than 700 million people residing in about 1.42 million habitations spread over 15 diverse ecological regions. It is true that providing drinking water to such a large population is an enormous challenge. Our country is also characterised by non-uniformity in level of awareness, socio-economic development, education, poverty, practices and rituals which add to the complexity of providing water.

The health burden of poor water quality is enormous. It is estimated that around 37.7 million Indians are affected by waterborne diseases annually, 1.5 million children are estimated to die of diarrhoea alone and 73 million working days are lost due to waterborne disease each year. The resulting economic burden is estimated at $600 million a year. The problems of chemical contamination is also prevalent in India with 1,95,813 habitations in the country are affected by poor water quality. The major chemical parameters of concern are fluoride and arsenic. Iron is also emerging as a major problem with many habitations showing excess iron in the water samples.

Water Crisis in India

The provision of clean drinking water has been given priority in the Constitution of India, with Article 47 conferring the duty of providing clean drinking water and improving public health standards to the State. The government has undertaken various programmes since independence to provide safe drinking water to the rural masses. Till the 10th plan, an estimated total of Rs.1,105 billion spent on providing safe drinking water. One would argue that the expenditure is huge but it is also true that despite such expenditure lack of safe and secure drinking water continues to be a major hurdle and a national economic burden.

On one hand the pressures of development is changing the distribution of water in the country, access to adequate water has been cited as the primary factor responsible for limiting development. The average availability of water is reducing steadily with the growing population and it is estimated that by 2020 India will become a water stressed nation.

Groundwater is the major source of water in our country with 85% of the population dependent on it.

The 2001 Census reported that 68.2 per cent of households in India have access to safe drinking water. According to latest estimates, 94 per cent of the rural population and 91 per cent of the people living in urban areas have access to safe drinking water.

Data available with the Department of Drinking Water Supply shows that of the 1.42 million rural habitations in the country, 1.27 million are fully covered (FC), 0.13 million are partially covered (PC) and 15,917 are not covered (NC).However, coverage refers to installed capacity, and not average actual supply over a sustained period or the quality of water being supplied which is the most essential part.

While accessing drinking water continues to be a problem, assuring that it is safe is a challenge by itself. Water quality problems are caused by pollution and over-exploitation. The rapid pace of industrialisation and greater emphasis on agricultural growth combined with financial and technological constraints and non-enforcement of laws have led to generation of large quantities

Little Community and its Characteristics

In sociology, the concept of community has led to significant debate, and sociologists are yet to reach agreement on a definition of the term. There were ninety-four discrete definitions of the term by the mid-1950s. Traditionally a "community" has been defined as a group of interacting people living in a common location.

The word is often used to refer to a group that is organized around common values and is attributed with social cohesion within a shared geographical location, generally in social units larger than a household. The word can also refer to the national community or global community.

The word "community" is derived from the Old French *communité* which is derived from the Latin *communitas* (*cum*, "with/together" + *munus*, "gift"), a broad term for fellowship or organized society.

Since the advent of the Internet, the concept of community no longer has geographical limitations, as people can now virtually gather in an online community and share common interests regardless of physical location.

Types of Community

A number of ways to categorize types of community have been proposed; one such breakdown is:

1. Geographic communities: range from the local neighbourhood, suburb, village, town or city, region, nation or even the planet as a whole. These refer to communities of *location*.
2. Communities of culture: range from the local clique, sub-culture, ethnic group, religious, multicultural or pluralistic civilisation, or the global community cultures of today. They may be included as *communities of need* or *identity*, such as disabled persons, or frail aged people.
3. Community organizations: range from informal family or kinship networks, to more formal incorporated associations, political decision making structures, economic enterprises, or professional associations at a small, national or international scale.

Communities are nested; one community can contain another—for example a geographic community may contain a number of ethnic communities.

Location

Possibly the most common usage of the word *"community"* indicates a large group living in close proximity. Examples of local community include:

- A municipality is an administrative local area generally composed of a clearly defined territory and commonly referring to a town or village. Although large cities are also municipalities, they are often thought of as a collection of communities, due to their diversity.
- A neighbourhood is a geographically localized community, often within a larger city or suburb.
- A planned community is one that was designed from scratch and grew up more or less following the plan. Several of the world's capital cities are planned cities, notably Washington, D.C., in the United States, Canberra in Australia, and Brasília in Brazil.

  It was also common during the European colonization of the Americas to build according to a plan either on fresh ground or on the ruins of earlier Amerindian cities.

Identity

In some contexts, *"community"* indicates a group of people with a common identity other than location. Members often interact regularly. Common examples in everyday usage include:

- A "professional community" is a group of people with the same or related occupations. Some of those members may join a professional society, making a more defined and formalized group. These are also sometimes known as communities of practice.
- A virtual community is a group of people primarily or initially communicating or interacting with each other by means of information technologies, typically over the Internet, rather than in person. These may be either communities of interest, practice or communion. Research interest is evolving in the motivations for contributing to online communities.

Overlaps

Some communities share both location and other attributes. Members choose to live near each other because of one or more common interests.

- A retirement community is designated and at least usually designed for retirees and seniors—often restricted to those over a certain age, such as 56. It differs from a retirement home, which is a single building or small complex, by having a number of autonomous households.
- An intentional community is a deliberate residential community with a much higher degree of social communication than other communities.

  The members of an intentional community typically hold a common social, political or spiritual vision and share responsibilities and resources. Intentional communities include Amish villages, ashrams, cohousing, communes, ecovillages, housing cooperatives, kibbutzim, and land trusts.

Internet Communities

To a growing part of people the meaning of the word *"community"* indicates a smaller or larger group of internet users signing up to become members of a community page/system on internet. Examples of internet communities include:

- A business community is often an administrative community with possibilities to add CV's and other business-related information.

- An interest community is a based on specialized areas such as art, golf or bird watching.
- A general community is wider in its range-opening for its users to create areas, pages and groups.

Special Nature of Human Community

Definitions of community as "organisms inhabiting a common environment and interacting with one another," while scientifically accurate, do not convey the richness, diversity and complexity of human communities. Their classification, likewise is almost never precise. Untidy as it may be, community is vital for humans. M. Scott Peck expresses this in the following way: "There can be no vulnerability without risk; there can be no community without vulnerability; there can be no peace, and ultimately no life, without community."

Characteristics of the Rural Landscape

A classification system of eleven characteristics has been developed for reading a rural landscape and for understanding the natural and cultural forces that have shaped it. Landscape characteristics are the tangible evidence of the activities and habits of the people who occupied, developed, used, and shaped the land to serve human needs; they may reflect the beliefs, attitudes, traditions, and values of these people.

The first four characteristics are processes that have been instrumental in shaping the land, such as the response of farmers to fertile soils. The remaining seven are physical components that are evident on the land, such as barns or orchards.

Many, but not all, rural properties contain all eleven characteristics. When historic processes are linked to existing components, the rural landscape can be viewed as a unified whole. The section "Documentation of Landscape Characteristics" shows the relationship of the eleven characteristics and the features represented by them.

This classification system is a tool for gathering and organizing information. First of all, it is used to develop historic contexts for rural areas. The processes define specific themes, such as dairy farming or Belgian settlement, that have influenced historic development. The physical components define historic features of the landscape that may be used to describe significant property types and to identify properties eligible for listing in the National Register.

Second, the system is used to identify and evaluate the significant properties of a rural area or to determine the eligibility of a particular rural landscape. Through field survey and historic research, characteristics are associated with specific features, such as field patterns or roadways, and provide an understanding of an area or property's historic land uses and physical evolution.

Third, as information about existing characteristics is related to the historic contexts for a geographical area, assessments of significance, integrity, and boundaries can be made for specific properties. Information is evaluated to determine whether, within a rural area or region, a large historic district or separate properties should be considered for listing in the National Register. A comparison of past and present characteristics within a single property helps determine whether the property retains historic integrity and what the National Register boundaries should be.

Finally, the classification system provides a format for documenting rural properties on National Register forms. It can be used to organize the description and statement of significance for a specific rural property on the registration form. It is also useful for organizing information about rural historic contexts and property types on the multiple property documentation form.

Processes

Land Uses and Activities: Land uses are the major human forces that shape and organize rural communities. Human activities, such as farming, mining, ranching, recreation, social events, commerce, or industry, have left an imprint on the landscape. An examination of changing and continuing land uses may lead to a general understanding of how people have interacted with their environment and provide clues about the kinds of physical features and historic properties that should be present.

Topographic variations, availability of transportation, the abundance or scarcity of natural resources (especially water), cultural traditions, and economic factors influenced the ways people use the land. Changing land uses may have resulted from improved technology, exhausted soils or mineral deposits, climatic changes, and new economic conditions, as well as previous successes or failures. Activities visible today may reflect traditional practices or be innovative, yet compatible, adaptations of historic ones.

Patterns of Spatial Organization: The organization of land on a large scale depends on the relationship among major physical components, predominant landforms, and natural features. Politics, economics, and technology, as well as the natural environment, have influenced the organization of communities by determining settlement patterns, proximity to markets, and the availability of transportation.

Organization is reflected in road systems, field patterns, distance between farmsteads, proximity to water sources, and orientation of structures to sun and wind. For example, spatial patterns can be seen in the grid of square mile townships and 160-acre farmsteads in the Midwest established by the land ordinances of 1785 and 1787; the distribution of towns every seven miles along a railroad corridor; and the division of land in Louisiana, by the French long-lot system, to ensure that every parcel has river frontage.

Large-scale patterns characterizing the settlement and early history of a rural area may remain constant, while individual features, such as buildings and vegetation, change over time. Changes in technology, for example, may have altered plowing practices, although the location of plowed fields, and, therefore, the overall historic pattern may remain the same.

Response to the Natural Environment: Major natural features, such as mountains, prairies, rivers, lakes, forests, and grasslands, influenced both the location and organization of rural communities. Climate, similarly, influenced the siting of buildings, construction materials, and the location of clusters of buildings and structures. Traditions in land use, construction methods, and social customs commonly evolved as people responded to the physiography and ecological systems of the area where they settled. Early settlements frequently depended upon available natural resources, such as water for transportation, irrigation, or mechanical power. Mineral or soil deposits, likewise, determined the suitability of a region for particular activities. Available materials, such as stone or wood, commonly influenced the construction of houses, barns, fences, bridges, roads, and community buildings.

Cultural Traditions: Cultural traditions affect the ways that land is used, occupied, and shaped. Religious beliefs, social customs, ethnic identity, and trades and skills may be evident today in both physical features and uses of the land. Ethnic customs, predating the origins of a community, were often transmitted by early settlers and perpetuated by successive generations.

Others originated during a community's early development and evolution. Cultural groups have interacted with the natural environment, manipulating and perhaps altering it, and sometimes modifying their traditions in response to it.

Cultural traditions determined the structure of communities by influencing the diversity of buildings, location of roads and village centres, and ways the land was worked. Social customs dictated the crops planted or livestock raised. Traditional building forms, methods of construction, stylistic finishes, and functional solutions evolved in the work of local artisans.

For example, rustic saunas appeared among the outbuildings of Finnish farmsteads in northwestern Michigan, while community churches occupied isolated crossroads in the High Plains. Taro, grown as a staple in the Hawaiian daily diet, also assumed an important role in the traditional luau. At the Amana Colonies in Iowa, large expanses of farmland and forest—based upon communal ownership, a village settlement pattern, and religious beliefs—varied from the rectangular grid typical of Midwestern family farms.

Components

Circulation Networks: Circulation networks are systems for transporting people, goods, and raw materials from one point to another. They range in scale from livestock trails and footpaths, to roads, canals, major highways, and even airstrips. Some, such as farm or lumbering roads, internally served a rural community, while others, such as railroads and waterways, connected it to the surrounding region.

Boundary Demarcations: Boundary demarcations delineate areas of ownership and land use, such as an entire farmstead or open range. They also separate smaller areas having special functions, such as a fenced field or enclosed corral. Fences, walls, tree lines, hedge rows, drainage or irrigation ditches, roadways, creeks, and rivers commonly marked historic boundaries.

Vegetation Related to Land Use: Various types of vegetation bear a direct relationship to long-established patterns of land use. Vegetation includes not only crops, trees, or shrubs planted for agricultural and ornamental purposes, but also trees that have grown up incidentally along fence lines, beside roads, or in abandoned fields. Vegetation may include indigenous, naturalized, and introduced species.

While many features change over time, vegetation is, perhaps, the most dynamic. It grows and changes with time, whether or not people care for it. Certain functional or ornamental plantings, such as wheat or peonies, may be evident only during selected seasons. Each species has a unique pattern of growth and life span, making the presence of historic specimens questionable or unlikely in many cases.

Current vegetation may differ from historic vegetation, suggesting past uses of the land. For example, Eastern red cedars or aspens indicate the natural succession of abandoned farmland in the Midwest.

Buildings, Structures, and Objects: Various types of buildings, structures, and objects serve human needs related to the occupation and use of the land. Their function, materials, date, condition, construction methods, and location reflect the historic activities, customs, tastes, and skills of the people who built and used them.

Buildings—designed to shelter human activity—include residences, schools, churches, outbuildings, barns, stores, community halls, and train depots. Structures—designed for functions other than shelter—include dams, canals, systems of fencing, systems of irrigation, tunnels, mining shafts, grain elevators, silos, bridges, earthworks, ships, and highways. Objects—relatively small but important stationary or movable constructions—include markers and monuments, small boats, machinery, and equipment. Rural buildings and structures often exhibit patterns of vernacular design that may be common in their region or unique to their community. Residences may suggest family size and relationships, population densities, and economic fluctuations. The repeated use of methods, forms, and materials of construction may indicate successful solutions to building needs or demonstrate the unique skills, workmanship, or talent of a local artisan.

Clusters: Groupings of buildings, fences, and other features, as seen in a farmstead, ranch, or mining complex, result from function, social tradition, climate, or other influences, cultural or natural. The arrangement of clusters may reveal information about historical and continuing activities, as well as the impact of varying technologies and the preferences of particular generations. The repetition of similar clusters throughout a landscape may indicate vernacular patterns of siting, spatial organization, and land use. Also, the location of clusters, such as the market towns that emerged at the crossroads of early highways, may reflect broad patterns of a region's cultural geography.

Archeological Sites: The sites of prehistoric or historic activities or occupation, may be marked by foundations, ruins, changes in vegetation, and surface remains. They may provide valuable information about the ways the land has been used, patterns of social history, or the methods and extent of activities such as shipping, milling, lumbering, or quarrying. The ruins of mills, charcoal kilns, canals, outbuildings, piers, quarries, and mines commonly indicate previous uses of the land. Changes in vegetation may indicate abandoned roadways, homesites, and fields.

The spatial distribution of features, surface disturbances, subsurface remains, patterns of soil erosion and deposition, and soil composition may also yield information about the evolution and past uses of the land.

Small-scale elements: Small-scale elements, such as a foot bridge or road sign, add to the historic setting of a rural landscape. These features may be characteristic of a region and occur repeatedly throughout an area, such as limestone fence posts in Kansas or cattle gates in the Buffalo River Valley of Arkansas.

While most small-scale elements are long-lasting, some, such as bales of hay, are temporal or seasonal. Collectively, they often form larger components, such as circulation networks or boundary demarcations. Small-scale elements also include minor remnants—such as canal stones, road traces, mill stones, individual fruit trees, abandoned machinery, or fence posts—that mark the location of historic activities, but lack significance or integrity as archeological sites.

Peasant Society and its Features

A peasant is an agricultural worker who generally owns or rents only a small plot of ground. The word is derived from 15th century French *païsant* meaning one from the *pays*, or countryside, ultimately from the Latin *pagus*, or outlying administrative district (when the Roman Empire became Christian, these outlying districts were the last to Christianise, and this gave rise to "pagan" as a religious term). The term peasant today is sometimes used in a pejorative sense for impoverished farmers.

Peasants typically make up the majority of the agricultural labour force in a Pre-industrial society, dependent on the cultivation of their land: without stockpiles of provisions they thrive or starve according to the most recent harvest. The majority of the people in the Middle Ages were peasants. Pre-industrial societies have diminished with the advent of globalization and as such there are considerably fewer peasants to be found in rural areas throughout the world (as a proportion of the total world population).

Though "peasant" is a word of loose application, once a market economy has taken root the term *peasant proprietors* is frequently used to describe the traditional rural population in countries where the land is chiefly held by smallholders. It is sometimes used by people who consider themselves of higher class as *slang* to refer pejoratively to those of poorer education who come from a lower income background.

In many pre-industrial societies, peasants comprised the bulk of the population. Peasant societies often had well developed social support networks. Especially in harder climates, members of the community who had a poor harvest or suffered other hardships were taken care of by the rest of the community. Peasants usually only had one set of clothing, two at most.

Also, a peasant usually owed their lord 20% of their earnings. They also owed the priest or bishop 10% of their ownings. Of course, knights could, and would usually demand tributes for keeping them alive. Overall, the peasant usually retained only 10-20% of their total work and earnings.

Peasant societies can often have very stratified social hierarchies within them. Rural people often have very different values and economic behaviour from urbanites, and tend to be more conservative. Peasants are often very loyal to inherited power structures that define their rights and privileges and protect them from interlopers, despite their low status within those power structures.

Fernand Braudel devoted the first volume–called *The Structures of Everyday Life*–of his major work, *Civilization and Capitalism 15th–18th Century* to the largely silent and invisible world that existed below the market economy.

Since it was the literate classes who left the most records, and these tended to dismiss peasants as figures of coarse appetite and rustic comedy, the term "peasant" may have a pejorative rather than descriptive connotation in historical memory. Society was theorized as being organized into three "estates": those who work, those who pray, and those who fight.

Medieval European Peasants

The relative position of peasants in Western Europe improved greatly after the Black Death unsettled the demography of medieval Europe.

In the wake of this disruption to the established order, later centuries saw the invention of the printing press, the development of widespread literacy and the enormous social and intellectual changes of the Enlightenment.

This evolution of ideas in an environment of relatively widespread literacy laid the groundwork for the Industrial Revolution, which enabled mechanically-and chemically-augmented agricultural production while simultaneously increasing the demand for factory workers in cities. Urban factory-workers, with their low skill and large numbers, quickly came to occupy the socio-economic stratum formerly the preserve of the medieval peasants.

This process happened in an especially pronounced and truncated way in Eastern Europe. Lacking any catalysts for change in the 14th century, Eastern European peasants largely continued upon the original medieval path until the 18th and 19th centuries. The Tsars then began to notice that though the West had made enormous strides, they had not; they responded by forcing the largely illiterate peasant populations under their control to embark upon a course of Westernization and industrialization.

Peasant Revolution and Peasant Studies

The field of peasant studies as such was rooted in the early work of scholars such as Florian Znaniecki and Fei Xiaotong, and post-war studies of the Great Tradition and Little Tradition in work of lRobert Redfield. In the 1960s, anthropologists and historians began to rethink the role of peasant revolt in world history and their own disciplines. This rethinking was partly in response to American involvement in the Vietnam War, which critics on the left regarded as an attempt to repress a peasant revolution. Peasant Revolution was seen as a Third World response to capitalism and imperialism.

The anthropologist Eric Wolf, for instance, drew on the work of earlier scholars in the Marxist tradition, such as Daniel Thorner, who saw the rural population as a key element in the transition from feudalism to capitalism. Wolf and a group of scholars criticized both Marx and the field of modernization theorists for treating peasants as lacking the ability to take action. James C. Scott's field observation in Malaysia convinced him that villagers were active participants in their local politics even though they were forced to use indirect methods. Many of these activist scholars looked back to the Peasant Movement in India and the theories of revolution in China led by Mao Zedong starting in the 1920s. The anthropologist Myron Cohen, however, asked why the rural population in China were called "peasants" rather than "farmers," a distinction he called political rather than scientific. One important outlet for their scholarly work and theory was the Journal of Peasant Studies.

Peasant Society and the Image of Limited Good

The members of every society share a common cognitive orientation which is, in effect, an unverbalized, implicit expression of their understanding of the "rules of the game" of living imposed upon them by their social, natural, and supernatural universes. A cognitive orientation provides the members of the society it characterizes with basic premises and sets of assumptions normally neither recognized nor questioned which structure and guide behaviour in much the same way grammatical rules unrecognized by most people structure and guide their linguistic forms. All normative behaviour of the members of a group is a function of their particular way of looking at their total environment, their unconscious acceptance of the "rules of the game" implicit in their cognitive orientation.

A particular cognitive orientation cannot be thought of as world view in a Redneldian sense, i.e., as something existing largely at a conscious level in the minds of the members of the group.' The average man of any society cannot describe the underlying premises of which his behaviour is a logical function any more than he can outline a phonemic statement which expresses the patterned regularities in his speech. As Kluckhohn has pointed out, cognitive orientations (he speaks of "configurations") are recognized by most members of a society only 3n the sense that they make choices "with the configurations as unconscious but determinative backgrounds" (1943:218),

In speaking of a cognitive orientation—the terms "cognitive view," "world view' "world view perspective," "basic assumptions," "implicit premises' and perhaps "ethos" may be used as synonyms—I am as an anthropologist concerned with two levels of problems: (1) the nature of the cognitive orientation itself which I see as something "psychologically real," and the ways in which and the degree to which it can be known; and (2) the economical representation of this cognitive orientation by means of models or integrating principles which account for observed behaviour, and which permit prediction of behaviour yet unnoted or unperformed.

Such a model or principle is, as Kluckhohn has often pointed out, an inferential construct or an analytic, abstraction derived from observed behaviour, A model or integrating principle is not the cognitive orientation itself, but for purposes of analysis the two cannot be separated, A well-constructed model is, of course, nut really descriptive of behaviour at all (as is, for example, the term "ethos as used by Gillin. [1955] to describe contemporary Latin American culture).

A good model is heuristic and explanatory, not descriptive, and it has predictive value. It encourages an analyst to search for behaviour patterns, and relationships between patterns, which he may not yet have recognised, simply because logically—if the model is sound—it is reasonable to expect to find them. By the same token, a sound model should make it pos-. Bible to predict how people are going to behave when faced with certain, alternatives-A model therefore has at least two important functions: it is conducive to better Held work, and it has practical utility as a guide to policy and action in developmental programs.

A perfect model or integrating principle of a particular world view should subsume *all* behaviour of the members of a group. In practice il is unreasonable to expect this. But the best model is the one that subsumes the greatest amount of behaviour in such fashion that there are no mutually incompatible parts in the model, i.e., forms of behaviour cast together in what is obviously a logically inconsistent relationship. Kluckhohn speculated about the possibility of a single model, a dominant "master configuration" characterizing an entire society, for which he suggested the terms "integration" (1941:128) and "ethos" (1943:221), but I believe he never attempted the task of describing a complete ethos. Opler, on the other hand, has described Lipan Apache culture in terms of twenty "themes" which are, however, to a considerable extent descriptive, and which in no way approximate a master model (1946).'

How does an anthropologist fathom the cognitive orientation of the group he studies, to find patterns that will permit building a model or stating an integrating principle? Componential analysis and other formal semantic methods have recently been much in vogue, and these techniques unquestionably can tell us a great deal. But the degree of dissention among anthropologists who use these methods suggests that they are not a single royal road to "God's truth" (cf. Burling 1964). I suspect there will always remain a considerable element of ethnological art in the processes whereby we come to have some understanding of a cognitive orientation. However we organize our thought processes, we are engaging in an exercise in structural analysis in which overt behaviour (and the simpler patterns into which this behaviour is readily seen to fall) is viewed somewhat as a reflection or representation of a wider reality which our sensory apparatus can never directly perceive.

Or, we can view the search for a cognitive view as an exercise in triangulation. Of each trait and pattern the question is asked, "Of what implicit assumption might this behaviour be a logical function?" When enough questions have been asked, the answers will be found to point in a common direction. The model emerges from the point where the lines of answers intersect. Obviously, an anthropologist well acquainted with a particular culture cannot merely apply simple rules of analysis and automatically produce a model for, or even a description oi, a world view. In effect, we are dealing with a pyramidal structure; low-level regularities and coherences relating overt behaviour forms are fitted into higher-level patterns which in turn may be found to fall into place at a still higher level of integration. Thus, a model of a social structure, sound in itself, will be found to be simply one expression of a structural regularity which will have analogues in religion and economic activities.

Since all normative behaviour of the members of a group is a function of its particular cognitive orientation, both in an abstract philosophical sense and in the view of an individual himself, all behaviour is "rational" and sense-making. "Irrational" behaviour can be spoken of only in the context of a cognitive view which did not give rise to that behaviour.

Thus, in a rapidly changing world, in which peasant and primitive peoples are pulled into the social and economic Context of whole nations, some of their behaviour may appear irrational to others because the social, economic, and natural universe that in fact controls the conditions of their life is other than that revealed to them—however subconsciously—by a traditional world view. That is, a peasant's cognitive view provides moral and other precepts that are guides to—in fact, may be said to produce—behaviour that may not be appropriate to the changing conditions of life he has not yet grasped. For this reason when the cognitive orientation of large numbers of a nation's people is out of tune with reality, these people will behave in a way that will appear irrational to those who are more nearly attuned to reality. Such peoples will be seen as constituting a drag (as indeed they may be) on a nation's development, and they will be cutting themselves off from the opportunity to participate in the benefits that economic progress can bring.

In this paper I am concerned with the nature of the cognitive orientation of peasants, and with interpreting and relating peasant behaviour as described by anthropologists to this orientation. I am also concerned with the implications of this orientation-and related behaviour to the problem of the peasant's participation in the economic growth of the country to which he may belong.

Specifically, I will outline what I believe to be the dominant theme in the cognitive orientation of classic peasant societies,* show how characteristic peasant behaviour seems to flow from this orientation, and attempt to show that this behaviour—however incompatible with national economic growth—is not only highly rational in the context of the cognition that determines it, but that for the maintenance of peasant society in its classic form, it is indispensable. The kinds of behaviour that have been suggested as adversely influencing economic growth are, among many, the "luck" syndrome, a "fatalistic" outlook, inter- and intra-familial quarrels, difficulties in cooperation, extraordinary ritual expenses by poor people and the problems these expenses pose for capital accumulation, and the apparent lack of what the psychologist McClelland (1961) has called "need for Achievement." I will suggest that peasant participation in national development can be hastened not by stimulating a psychological process, the need for achievement, but by creating economic and other opportunities that will encourage the peasant to abandon his traditional and increasingly unrealistic cognitive orientation for a new one that reflects the realities of the modern world.

The model of cognitive orientation that seems to me best to account for peasant behaviour is the "Image of Limited Good." By "Image of Limited Good" I mean that broad areas of peasant behaviour are patterned in such fashion as to suggest that peasants view their social, economic, and natural universes—their total environment—as one in which all of the desired things in life such as land, wealth, health, friendship and love, manliness and honor, respect and status, power and influence, security and safety, *exist in finite quantity* and *are always in short supply,* as far as the peasant is concerned. Not only do these and all other "good things" exist in finite and limited quantities, but in addition *there is no way directly within peasant power to increase the available quantities.* It is as if the obvious fact of land shortage in a densely populated area applied to all other desired things: not enough to go around. "Good," like land, is seen as inherent in nature, there to be divided and re-divided, if necessary, but not to be augmented.

For purposes of analysis, and at this stage of the argument, I am considering a peasant community to be a closed system. Except in a special—but extremely important—way, a peasant sees his existence as determined and limited by the natural and social resources of his village and his immediate area. Consequently, there is a primary corollary to The Image of Limited Good: if "Good" exists in limited amounts which cannot be expanded, and if the system is closed, it follows that *an individual or a family can improve a position only at the expense of others.* Hence an apparent relative improvement in someone's position with respect to any "Good" is viewed as a threat to the entire community. Someone is being despoiled, whether he sees it or not. And since there is often uncertainty as to who is losing—obviously it may be ego—*any* significant improvement is perceived, not as a threat to an individual or a family alone, but as a threat to *all* individuals and families.

This model was first worked out on the basis of a wide variety of field data from Tzintzuntzan, Michoacin, Mexico: family behaviour, exchange patterns, cooperation, religious activities, court claims, disputes, material culture, folklore, language, and many other bits and pieces. At no point has an informant even remotely suggested that this is his vision of his universe. Yet each Tzintzuntzeno organizes his behaviour in a fashion entirely rational when it is viewed as a function of this principle which he cannot enunciate.'

The model of Limited Good, when "fed back" to behaviour in Tzintzuntzan, proved remarkably productive in revealing' hitherto unsuspected structural regularities linking economic behaviour with social relations, friendship, love and jealousy patterns, health beliefs, concepts of honor and masculinity, *egoismo* manifestations—even folklore (Foster 1964a). Not only were structural regularities revealed in Tzintzuntzan, but much peasant behaviour known to me from other field work, and reported in the literature, seemed also to be a function of this cognitive orientation. This has led me to offer the kinds of data I have utilized in formulating this model, and to explain the interpretations that seem to me to follow from it, as characterizing in considerable degree classic peasant societies, in the hope that the model will be tested against other extensive bodies of data. I believe, obviously, that if the Image of Limited Good is examined as a high-level integrating principle characterizing ' peasant communities, we will find within our individual societies unsuspected structural regularities and, on a cross-cultural level, basic patterns that will be most helpful in constructing the typology of peasant society. The data I present in support of this thesis arc illustrative, and arc not based on an exhaustive survey of peasant literature.

In the following pages I will offer evidence under four headings that seems to me to conform to the model I have suggested. I will then discuss the implications of this evidence.

When the peasant views his economic world as one in which Limited Good prevails, and he can progress only at the expense of another, he is usually very near the truth. Peasant economies, as pointed out by many authors, are not productive. In the average village there *is* only a finite amount of wealth produced, and no amount of extra hard work will significantly change the figure. In most of the peasant world land has been limited for a long, long time, and only in a few places have young farmers in a growing community been able to hive off from the parent village to start on a level of equality with their parents and grandparents. Customarily land is not only limited, but it has become increasingly limited, by population expansion and soil; deterioration. Peasant production techniques remained largely; unchanged for hundreds, and even thousands of years; at best, in farming, this means the-Mediterranean plow drawn by oxen, supplemented by human* powered hand tools. Handicraft techniques in weaving, pottery-making, wood-s working and building likewise have changed little over the years.

In fact, it seems accurate to say that the average peasant sees little or no : relationship between work and production techniques on the one hand, and: the acquisition of wealth on the other. Rather, wealth is seen by villagers in the same light as land: present, circumscribed by absolute limits, and having no relationship to work. One works to eat, but not to create wealth. Wealth, like land, is someting that is inherent in nature. It can be divided up and passed around in various ways, but, within the framework of the villagers' traditional world, it does not grow. Time and tradition have determined the shares each family and individual hold; these shares are not static, since obviously they do shift. But the reason for the relative position of each villager is known at any given time, and any significant change calls for explanation.

The evidence that friendship, love, and affection are seen as strictly limited in peasant society is strong. Every anthropologist in a peasant village soon realizes the narrow path he must walk to avoid showing excessive favor or friendship toward some families, thereby alienating others who will feel deprived, and hence reluctant to help him in his work.

Once I brought a close friend from Tzintzuntzan, working as a bracero in a nearby town, to my Berkeley home. When safely away from the camp he told me his brother was also there. Why did he not tell me, so I could have invited him? My friend replied, in effect, that he was experiencing a coveted "good" and he did not want to risk diluting the satisfaction by sharing it with another.

Adams reports how a social worker in a Guatemalan village unwittingly prejudiced her work by making more friends in one barrio than in the other, thereby progressively alienating herself from potential friends whose help she needed (1955:442). In much of Latin America the institutionalized best friend, particularly among post-adolescents, variously known as the *amigo carnal,* or the *cucllo* or *camaraderia* (the latter two described by Reina for Guatemala [1959]) constitutes both recognition of the fact that true friendship is a scarce commodity, and serves as insurance against being left without any of it. The jealousies and feelings of deprivation felt by one partner when the other leaves or threatens to leave sometimes lead to violence.

Widespread peasant definitions of sibling rivalry suggest that a mother's ability to love her children is viewed as limited by the amount of love she possesses. In Mexico when a mother again becomes pregnant and weans her nursing child, the child often becomes *chipil.* It fusses, cries, clings to her skirt, and is inconsolable.

The child is said to be *celoso,* jealous of its unborn sibling whose presence it recognizes and whom it perceives as a threat, already depriving him of maternal love and affection. Chfpil is known as *chip* or *chipe* in Guatemala, where it is described in a classic article by Paul (1950), as *sipe* in Honduras, and simply as *celos* ("jealousy") in Costa Rica. *Chucaque* in southern Colombia, described as the jealousy of a child weaned because of its mother's pregnancy, appears to be the same thing (communicated by Dr. Virginia Gutierrez de Pineda).

A similar folk etiology is used among the semi-peasant peoples of Buganda to explain the onset of *kwashiorkor* in a child recently weaned. If the mother is again pregnant, the child is said to have *obwosi,* and shows symptoms of pale hair, sweating of hands and feet, fever, diarrhea, and vomiting. "The importance of pregnancy is such that if a woman takes a sick child to a native doctor the first question he asks is 'Are you pregnant?'".

The African logic is the reverse of, but complementary to, that of Latin America: it is the *unborn child* that is jealous of its older sibling, whom it tries to poison through the mother's milk, thereby forcing weaning. In both areas, insufficient quantities of love and affection are seen as precipitating the crisis. In Buganda, "In the local culture it is essential that the mother should devote herself to the unborn child or a child recently born, at the expense of any other children; *there does not seem to be an easy acceptance of the idea that there can be enough love for all".*

Similarly, in an Egyptian village, sibling rivalry is recognized at this period in a child's development. As in Latin America, jealousy is one way; it is always the older who is jealous of the younger. "It is also acknowledged that the youngest child becomes jealous immediately his mother's abdomen becomes enlarged on pregnancy and he is usually told of the forthcoming event." This jealousy, in excess, may have ill effects on the child, causing diarrhea, swellings, lack of appetite, temper tantrums, and sleeplessness.'

In parts of Guatemala chipe is a term used to express a husband's jealousy of his pregnant wife, for temporary loss of sexual services and for the attention to be given to the baby. Tepoztlán husbands also suffer from *chipilez,* becoming sleepy and not wanting to work. Oscar Lewis says a husband can be cured by wearing a strip of his wife's skirt around his neck (1951:378).

In Tonalá, Jalisco, Mexico, husbands often are jealous of their adolescent sons and angry with their wives because of the affection the latter show their offspring. A wife's love and affection are seen as limited; to the extent the son receives what appears to be an excessive amount, the husband is deprived. In the Egyptian village described by Ammar a new mother-in-law is very affectionate toward her son-in-law, thereby making her own unmarried sons and daughters jealous. By showing affection to the outsider, the woman obviously is seen as depriving her own offspring of something they wish.

It is a truism to peasants that health is a "good" that exists in limited quantities. Peasant folk medicine does not provide the protection that scientific medicine gives those who have access to it, and malnutrition frequently aggravates conditions stemming from lack of sanitation, hygiene, and immunization. In peasant societies preoccupation with health and illness is general, and constitutes a major topic of interest, speculation, and discussion. Perhaps the best objective evidence that health is viewed within the framework of Limited Good is the widespread attitude toward blood which is, to use Adams' expression, seen as "non-regenerative" .

For obvious reasons, blood is equated with life, and good blood, and lots of it, means health. Loss of blood—if it is seen as something that cannot be renewed—is thus seen as a threat to health, a permanent loss resulting in weakness for as long as an individual lives. Although best described for Guatemala, the belief that blood is non-regenerative is widespread in Latin America. This belief, frequently unverbalized, may be one of the reasons it is so difficult to persuade Latin Americans to give blood transfusions: by giving blood so that someone can have more, the donor will have less.

Similar beliefs are found in Nigeria (communicated by Dr. Adeniyi-Adeniji Jones) and they are well known in Indian peasant villages. Here the psychological problem is further compounded by the equation of blood with semen: one drop of semen to seven (or forty, depending on area) drops of blood. The exercise of masculine vitality is thus seen as a permanently debilitating act. Only so much sexual pleasure is allotted man, and nothing he can do will increase his measure. Sexual moderation and the avoidance of bloodletting are the course of the prudent man.

In parts of Mexico (e.g., the Michoacán villages of Tzintzuntzan and Erongaricuaro) the limits on health are reflected in views about long hair. A woman's long hair is much admired, but the price is high: a woman with long hair is thought always to be thin and wan, and she cannot expect to have vigor and strength. Sources of vitality are insufficient to grow long hair and still leave an individual with energy and a well-fleshed body.

Oft-noted peasant sensitiveness to real or imagined insults to personal honor, and violent reactions to challenges which cast doubt on a man's masculinity, appear to be a function of the belief that honor and manliness exist in limited quantities, and that consequently not everyone can enjoy a full measure. In rural Mexico, among braceros who have worked in the United States, American ethnologists have often been asked, "In the United States it's the wife who commands, no?" Masculinity and domestic control appear to be viewed much like other desirable things: there is only so much, and the person who has it deprives another.

Mexican men find it difficult to believe that a husband and wife can share domestic responsibilities and decision making, without the husband being deprived of his *machismo.* Many believe a wife,/however good, must be beaten from time to time, simply so she will not lose sight of a God-decreed familial hierarchy. They are astonished and shocked to learn that an American wife-beater can be jailed; this seems an incredibly unwarranted intrusion of the State into God's plans for the family.

The essence of machismo is valor, and *un hombre muy valienle,* i.e.j-a *macho,* is one who is strong and tough, generally fair, not a bully, but who never dodges a fight, and who always wins. Above all, a macho inspires *respeto* ("respect"). One achieves machismo, it is clear, by depriving others of access to it. In Greece *philotimo,* a "love of honor," equates closely with Mexican machismo. A man who is physically sound, lithe, strong, and agile has philotimo. If he can converse well, show wit, and act in other ways that facilitate sociability and establish ascendency, he enhances his philotimo.

One attacks another male through his philotimo, by shaming or ridiculing him, by showing how he lacks the necessary attributes for a man. Consequently, avoiding ridicule becomes a major concern, a primary defence mechanism among rural Greek males. In a culture shot through with envy and competitiveness, there is the ever-present danger of attack, so a man must be prepared to respond to a jeer or insult with a swift retort, an angry challenge, or a knife thrust. "Philotimo can be enhanced at the expense of another. It has a see-saw characteristic; one's own goes up as another's declines... the Greek, in order to maintain and increase his sense of worth, must be prepared each moment to assert his superiority over friend and foe alike. It is an interpersonal combat fraught with anxiety, uncertainty, and aggressive potentials. As one proverb describes it, 'When one Greek meets another, they immediately despise each other".

If, in fact, peasants see their universe as one in which the good things in life are in limited and unexpandable quantities, and hence personal gain must be at the expense of others, we must assume that social institutions, personal behaviour, values, and personality will all display patterns that can be viewed as functions of this cognitive orientation. Preferred behaviour, it may be argued, will be that which is seen by the peasant as maximizing his security, by preserving his relative position in the traditional order of things. People who see themselves in "threatened" circumstances, which the Image of Limited Good implies, react normally in one of two ways: maximum cooperation and sometimes communism, burying individual differences and placing sanctions against individualism; or extreme individualism. Peasant societies seem always to choose the second alternative.

The reasons are not clear, but two factors may bear on the problem. Cooperation requires leadership. This may be delegated democratically by the members of a group itself; it may be assumed by a strong man from within the group; or it may be imposed by forces lying outside the group. Peasant societies—for reasons that should be clear in the following analysis—are unable by their very nature to delegate authority, and assumption of authority by a strong man is, at best, temporary, and not a structural solution to a problem.

The truncated political nature of peasant societies, with real power lying outside the community, seems effectively to discourage local assumption and exercise of power, except as an agent of these outside forces. By the very nature of peasant society, seen as a structural part of a larger society, local development of leadership which might make possible cooperation is effectively prevented by the rulers of the political unit of which a particular peasant community is an element, who see such action as a potential threat to themselves.

Again, economic activities in peasant societies require only limited cooperation. Peasant families typically can, as family units, produce most of their food, farm without extra help, build their houses, weave cloth for their clothes', carry their own produce to market and sell it—in short, take care of themselves with a degree of independence impossible in an industrial society, and difficult in hunting-fishing-gathering societies. Peasants, of course, usually do not live with the degree of independence here suggested, but it is more clearly possible than in any other type of society.

Whatever the reasons, peasants are individualistic, and it logically follows from the Image of Limited Good that each minimal social unit (often the nuclear family and, in many situations, a single individual) sees itself in perpetual, unrelenting struggle with its fellows for possession of or control over what it considers to be its share of scarce values. This is a position that calls for extreme caution and reserve, a reluctance to reveal true strength or position.

It encourages suspicion and mutual distrust, since things will not necessarily be what they seem to be, and it also encourages a male self image as a valiant person, one who commands respect, since he will be less attractive as a target than a weakling. A great deal of peasant behaviour, I believe, is exactly what we would predict from these circumstances. The works of Lewis (1951), Banfield (1958), Simmons (1959), Carstairs (1958), Dube (1958), the Weisers (1963), and Blackman (1927) (summarized by Foster 1960-1961) and my others testify to the "mentality of mutual distrust" that is widespread in peasant societies.

Since an individual or family that makes significant economic progress or acquires a disproportionate amount of some other "good" is seen to do so at the expense of others, such a change is viewed as a threat to the stability of the community. Peasant culture is provided with two principal mechanisms with which to maintain the essential stability:

a) an agreed-upon, socially acceptable, preferred norm of behaviour for its people, and
b) a "club" and a "carrot," in the form of sanctions and rewards, to ensure that real behaviour approximates this norm.

The agreed-upon norm that promotes maximum community stability is behaviour that tends to maintain the status quo in relationships. The individual or family that acquires more than its share of a "good," and particularly an economic "good," is, as we have seen, viewed as a threat to the community at large. Individuals and families which are seen to or are thought to progress violate the preferred norm of behaviour, thereby stimulating cultural mechanisms that redress the imbalance. Individuals or families that lose something, that fall behind, are seen as a threat in a different fashion; their envy, jealousy, or anger may result in overt or hidden aggression toward more fortunate people. The self-correcting mechanisms that guard the community balance operate at three levels, viz:

1) Individual and family behaviour. At this level I am concerned with the steps taken by *individuals* to maintain their positions in the system, and the ways in which they try to avoid both sanctions and exploitation by fellow villagers.
2) Informal and usually unorganized group behaviour. At this level I am concerned with the steps taken by the *community,* the sanctions that are invoked when it is felt someone is violating the agreed-upon norm of behaviour. Negative sanctions are the "club."
3) Institutionalized behaviour. At this level I am concerned with the "carrot": major community expressions of cultural forms which neutralize achieved imbalances. Each of these forms will be examined in turn.

3.1) On the individual-family level, two rules give guidance to preferred behaviour. These can be stated as:
   a) Do not reveal evidence of material or other improvement in your relative position, lest you invite sanctions; should you display improvement, take action necessary to neutralize the consequences.
   b) Do not allow yourself to fall behind your rightful place, lest you and your family suffer.

A family deals with the problem of real or suspected improvement in its relative position by a combination of two devices.

First, it attempts to conceal evidence that might lead to this conclusion, and it denies the veracity of suggestions to this effect.

Second, it meets the charge head on, admits an improvement in relative position, but shows it has no intention of using this position to the detriment of the village by neutralizing it through ritual expenditures, thereby restoring the status quo.

Accounts of peasant communities stress that in traditional villages people do not compete for prestige with material symbols such as dress, housing, or food, nor do they compete for authority by seeking leadership roles. In peasant villages one notes a strong desire to look and act like everyone else, to be inconspicuous in position and behaviour. This theme is well summed up in the Wisers' paragraph on the importance of dilapidated walls suggesting poverty as a part of a family's defence (1963:120).

Also much remarked is the peasant's reluctance to accept leadership roles. He feels—for good reason—that his motives will be suspect and that he will be subject to the criticism of neighbors. By seeking, or even accepting, an authority position, the ideal man ceases to be ideal. A "good" man therefore usually shuns community responsibilities (other than of a ritual nature); by so doing he protects his reputation. Needless to say, this aspect of socially-approved behaviour heavily penalizes a peasant community in the modern world by depriving it of the leadership which is now essential to its development.

The mechanism invoked to minimize the danger of loss of relative position appears to center in the machismo-philotimo complex. A tough, strong man whose fearlessness in the face of danger, and whose skill in protecting himself and his family is recognized, does not invite exploitation. A "valiant" individual can command the "respect" so much sought after in many peasant societies, and he can strive toward security with the goal in mind (however illusory) of being able to live—as is said in Tzintzuntzan—*sin compromises* ("without obligations" to, or dependency on, others). A picture of the ideal peasant begins to emerge: a man who works to feed and clothe his family, who fulfills his community and ceremonial obligations, who minds his own business, who does not seek to be outstanding, but who knows how to protect his rights! Since a macho, a strong man, discourages exploitation, it is clear that personality characteristic has a basic function in peasant society. Not sur-f prisingly, defence of this valuable self-image may, by the standards of other societies, assume pathological proportions, for it is seen as a basic weapon in the struggle for life.

The ideal man must avoid the appearance of presumption, lest this be; interpreted as trying to take something that belongs to another. In tracing' the diffusion of new pottery-making techniques in Tzintzuntzan I found that no one would admit he had learned the technique from a neighbor. The inevitable reply to my question was *Me puse a pensar* ("I dreamed it up all by myself"), accompanied by a knowing look and a tapping of the temple with the; forefinger. Reluctance to give credit to others, common in Mexico, is often; described as due to *egoísmo,* an egotistical conceited quality. Yet if egofsmo, f as exemplified by unwillingness to admit profiting by a neighbour's new pottery knowledge, is seen as a function of an image of Limited Good, it is clear that a potter *must* deny that the idea is other than his own. To confess that he "borrowed" an idea is to confess that he has taken something not rightfully his, that he is consciously upsetting the community balance and the self image he tries so hard to maintain. Similarly, in trying to determine how compa-drazgo (godparenthood) ties are initiated, I found no informant who admitted he had asked a friend to serve; he always was asked by another. Informants | appear to fear that admission of asking may be interpreted as presuming or imposing on another, trying to get something to which they may not be entitled.

A complementary pattern is manifest in the general absence of compliments in peasant communities; rarely is a person heard to admire the performance of another, and when admiration is expressed by, say, an anthropologist, the person admired probably will try to deny there is any reason to compliment him. Reluctance of villagers to compliment each other again looks, at first glance, like egofsmo. But in the context of the Limited Good model, it is seen that such behaviour is proper. The person who compliments is, in fact, guilty of aggression; he is telling someone to his facc that hc is rising above the dead level that spells security for all, and he is suggesting that he may be confronted with sanctions.

Consider this interpretation as applied to an incident reported in southern Italy: "My attempt, in private, to praise a peasant friend for his large farm and able system of farming brought a prompt and vigorous denial that he did anything special. He said, 'There is no system, you just plant.' This attitude was expressed by others in forced discussions of farming" (Cancian 1961:8). Dr. Cancian offers this as illustrating the peasant's lack of confidence in his own ability to change his environment. Speaking specifically of agriculture, he writes that "All the examples indicate denial of the hope of progress in agriculture and alienation from the land". I believe the peasant viewed Dr. Cancian's praise as threatening, since it reminded him of his vulnerability because of his superior farming methods. His denial is not of hope of progress, but of cause for anyone to envy him.

The ideal man strives for moderation and equality in his behaviour. Should he attempt to better his comparative standing, thereby threatening village stability, the informal and usually unorganized sanctions appear. This is the "club," and it takes the form of gossip, slander, backbiting, character assassination, witchcraft or the threat of witchcraft, and sometimes actual physical aggression. These negative sanctions usually represent no formal community decision, but they are at least as effective as if authorized by law. Concern with public opinion is one of the most striking characteristics of peasant communities.

Negative sanctions, while usually informal, can be institutionalized. In peasant Spain, especially in the north, the charivari *(cencerrada)* represents such an instance. When an older man marries a much younger woman— usually a second marriage for the groom—marriageable youths serenade the couple with cowbells *(cencerros)* and other noisemakers, parade straw-stuffed manikins representing them through the streets, incense the manikins with foul-smelling substances, and shout obscenities. It seems clear that this symbolizes the resentment of youths, who have not yet had even one wife, against the inequalities represented by an older man who has already enjoyed marriage, who takes a young bride from the available pool, thereby further limiting the supply for the youths. By institutionalizing the sanctions the youths are permitted a degree of freedom and abuse not otherwise possible.

Attempted changes in the balance of a peasant village are discouraged by the methods just described; *achieved* imbalance is neutralized, and the balance restored, on an institutional level. A person who improves his position is encouraged—by use of the carrot—to restore the balance through conspicuous consumption in the form of ritual extravagance. In Latin America he is prcssured into sponsoring a costly fiesta by serving as *mayordomo.* His reward is prestige, which is viewed as harmless. Prestige cannot be dangerous since it is traded for dangerous wealth; the mayordomo has, in fact, been "disarmed," shorn of his weapons, and reduced to a state of impotence.

There is good reason why peasant fiestas consume so much wealth in fireworks, candles, music, and food; and why, in peasant communities the rites of baptism, marriage, and death may involve relatively huge expenditures. These practices are a redistributive mechanism which permits a person or family that potentially threatens community stability gracefully to restore the status quo, thereby returning itself to a state of acceptability. Wolf, speaking specifically of the "closed" Indian peasant community of Mexico as it emerged after the Conquest, puts it this way: "the system takes from those who have, in order to make all men have-nots. By liquidating the surpluses, it makes all men rich in sacred experience but poor in earthly goods. Since it levels differences of wealth, it also inhibits the growth of class distinctions based on wealth.... In engineering parlance, it acts as a feedback, returning a system that is beginning to oscillate to its original course" (1959:216).

I have said that in a society ruled by the Image of Limited Good there 'is no way, save at the expense of others, that an individual can get ahead. This is true in a closed system, which peasant communities approximate. But even a traditional peasant village, in another sense, has access to other systems, and an individual can achieve economic success by tapping sources of wealth that are recognized to exist outside the village system. Such success, though envjed, is not seen as a direct threat to community stability, for no one within the community has lost anything. Still, such success must be explained.

In today's transitional peasant communities, seasonal emigration for wage labor is the most available way in which one can tap outside wealth. Hundreds of thousands of Mexican peasants have come to the United States as braceros in recent years and many, through their earnings, have pumped significant amounts of capital into their communities. Braceros generally are not criticized or attacked for acquisition of this wealth; it is clear that their good fortune is not at the direct expense of others within the village. Fuller finds a similar realistic appraisal of the wealth situation in a Lebanese community: "they [the peasants] realize... that the only method of increasing their incomes on a large scale is to absent themselves from the village for an extended period of time and to find work in more lucrative areas" (1961:72).

These examples, however, are but modern variants of a much older pattern in which luck and fate—points of contact with an open systen—are viewed as the only socially acceptable ways in which an individual can acquire more "good" than he previously has had. In traditional (not transitional) peasant communities an otherwise inexplicable increase in wealth is often seen as due to the discovery of treasure which may be the result of fate or of such positive action as making a pact with the Devil.

Recently I have analysed treasure tales in Tzintzuntzan and have found without exception they are attached to named individuals who, within living memory, have suddenly begun to live beyond their means. The usual evidence is that they suddenly opened stores, in spite of their known previous poverty (Foster 1964a). Erasmus has recorded this interpretation among Sonora villagers (1961:251), Wagley finds it in an Amazon small town (1964:128), and Friedmann reports it in southern Italy (1958:21). Clearly, the role of treasure tales in communities like these is to account for wealth that can be explained in no other manner.

The common peasant concern with finding wealthy and powerful patrons who can help them is also pertinent in this context. Since such patrons usually are outside the village, they are. not part of the closed system. Their aid, and material help, like bracero earnings or buried treasure, are seen as coming from beyond the village. Hence, although the lucky villager with a helpful patron may be envied, the advantages he receives from his patron are not seen as depriving, other villagers of something rightfully theirs. In Tzintzuntzan a villager who obtains a "good" in this fashion makes it a first order of business to advertise his luck and the source thereof, so there can be no doubt as to his basic morality; this behaviour is just the opposite of usual behaviour, which is to conceal good fortune.

Treasure tales and concern with patrons, in turn, are but one expression of a wider view: that any kind of success and progress is due to fate, the favor of deities, to luck, but not to hard work, energy, and thrift. Banfield notes in a south Italian community, "In the TAT stories, dramatic success came only as a gift of fortune: a rich gentleman gave a poor boy a violin, a rich gentlewoman adopted an abandoned child, and so on" (1958:66).

Continuing, "Great success, then, is obtained by the favor of the saints or by luck, certainly not by thrift, work, and enterprise. These may be important if one is already lucky, but not otherwise, and few would invest large amounts of effort—any more than they would invest large amounts of fertilizer—on the rather remote possibility of good fortune". Friedmann also finds that the south Italian peasant "firmly believes that the few who have succeeded in making a career were able to do so for some mysterious reason: one hit upon a hidden treasure; another was lucky enough to win in the lottery; another was called to America by a successful uncle" (1958:21).

All such illustrations underlie a fundamental truth not always recognized in comparing value systems: in the traditional peasant society hard work and thrift are moral qualities of only the slightest functional value. Given the limitations on land and technology, additional hard work in village productive enterprises simply does not produce a significant increment in income. It is pointless to talk of thrift in a subsistence economy in which most producers are at the economic margin; there is usually nothing to be thrifty about. As Fei and Chang point out, "In a village where the farms are small and wealth is accumulated slowly, there are very few ways for a landless man to become a landowner, or for a petty owner to become a large landowner.... It is not going too far to say that in agriculture there is no way really to get ahead.... To become rich one must leave agriculture" (1945:227). And again, "The basic truth is that enrichment through the exploitation of land, using the traditional technology, is not a practical method for accumulating wealth" (Fei and Chang: 1945:302). And, as Ammar says about Egypt, "It would be very difficult with the fellah's simple tools and the sweat involved in his work, to convince him that his lot could be improved by more work" (1954:36).

It is apparent that a peasant's cognitive orientation, and the forms of behaviour that stem therefrom, are intimately related to the problems of economic growth in developing countries. Heavy ritual expenditures, for example, are essential to the maintenance of the equilibrium that spells safety in the minds of traditional villagers. Capital accumulation, which might be stimulated if costly ritual could be simplified, is just what the villager wants to prevent, since he sees it as a community threat rather than a precondition to economic improvement.

In national developmental programs much community-level action in agriculture, health and education is cast in the form of cooperative undertakings. Yet it is abundantly clear that traditional peasant societies are cooperative only in the sense of honoring reciprocal obligations, rather than in the sense of understanding total community welfare, and that mutual suspicion seriously limits cooperative approaches to village problems.' The image of Limited Good model makes clear the peasant logic underlying reluctance to participate in joint ventures. If the "good" in life is seen as finite and non-expandable, and if apart from luck an individual can progress only at the expense of others, what does one stand to gain from a cooperative project? At best an honorable man lays himself open to the charge—and well-known consequences—of utilizing the venture to exploit friends and neighbors; at worst he risks his own defenses, since someone more skilful or less ethical than he may take advantage of the situation.

The Anglo-Saxon virtues of hard work and thrift seen as leading to economic success are meaningless in peasant society. Horatio Alger not only is not praiseworthy, but he emerges as a positive fool, a clod who not knowing the score labors blindly against hopeless conditions. The gambler, instead, is more properly laudable, worthy of emulation and adulation. If fate is the only way in which success can be obtained, the prudent and thoughtful man is the one who seeks ways in which to maximize his luck-position. He looks for the places in which good fortune is most apt to strike, and. tries to be there. This, I think, explains the interest in lotteries in underdeveloped countries. They offer the only way in which the average man can place himself in a luck-position.

The man who goes without lunch, and fails to buy shoes for his children in order to buy a weekly ticket, is not a ne'er-do-well; he is the Horatio Alger of his society who is doing what he feels is most likely to advance his position. He is, in modern parlance, buying a "growth stock." The odds are against him, but it is the *only* way he knows in which to work toward success.

Modern lotteries are very much functional equivalents of buried treasure tales in peasant societies, and at least in Tzintzuntzan the correlation is clearly understood. One elderly informant, when asked why no one had found buried treasure in recent years, remarked that this was indeed true but that "Today we Mexicans have the lottery instead."

Hence, the "luck" syndrome in underdeveloped countries is not primarily a deterrent to economic progress, as it is sometimes seen from the vantage point of a developed country, but rather it represents a realistic approach to the near-hopeless problem of making significant individual progress.

David C. McClelland has argued persuasively that the presence of a human motivation which he calls "the need for Achievement" is a precursor to economic growth, and that it is probably a *causative* factor, that it is "a change in the minds of men which produces economic growth rather than being produced by it". McClelland further finds that in experimental situations children with high *n* Achievement avoid gambling situations because should they win there would be no sense of personal achievement, while children with low *n* Achievement do not perform in a way suggesting they calculate relative risks and behave accordingly. "They [low *n* Achievement children] thus manifest behaviour like that of many people in underdeveloped countries who, while they act very traditionally economically, at the same time love to indulge in lotteries—risking a little to make a great deal on a very long shot". McClelland sees this as showing an absence of a sense of realistic risk calculation.

If the arguments advanced in this paper are sound, it is clear that *n* Achievement is rare in traditional peasant societies, not because of psychological factors, but because display of Achievement is met by sanctions that a traditional villager does not wish to incur. The villager who feels the need for Achievement, and who does something about it, is violating the basic, un-verbalized rules of the society of which he is a member. Parents (or government school programs) that attempt to instill *n* Achievement in children are, in effect, training children to be misfits in their society *as long as it remains a relatively static system.*

As indicated above, I would argue in opposition to McClelland that the villager who buys a lottery ticket *is not* behaving in an inconsistent fashion— that is, rationally in traditional economic matters, irrationally in his pursuit of luck—but in the most consistent fashion possible. He *has* calculated the chances and risks, and in a most realistic manner *in the context of the way in which he sees his traditional environment.* The man who buys a lottery ticket in a peasant society, far from displaying lack of « Achievement, is in fact showing a maximum degree of it. It simply happens that this is about the only display of initiative that is permitted him by his society, since it is the only form not viewed as a threat to the community by his colleagues.

Banfield, and Fei and Chang, appear to see the economic factors in the presence or absence of initiative in much the same light. The former writes about the Italian peasant, "The idea that one's welfare depends crucially upon conditions beyond one's control—upon luck or the caprice of a saint—and that one can at best only improve upon good fortune, not create it—this idea must certainly be a check on initiative". The latter sec, in the Chinese data, evidence that a particular economic attitude is a function of a particular view of lifc.

The traditional economic attitude among Chinese peasants is that of "contentment... an acceptance of a low standard of material comfort", which is contrasted to "acquisitiveness" characteristic of "modern industry and commerce in an expanding universe". "Both attitudes—contentment and acquisitiveness—have their own social context. Contentment is adopted in a closed economy; acquisitiveness in an expanding economy. *Without economic opportunities the striving for material gain is a disturbance to the existing order, since it means plunder of wealth from others....* Therefore, to accept and be satisfied with the social role and material rewards given by the society is essential. But when economic opportunity develops through the development of technology and when wealth can be acquired through the exploitation of nature instead of through the exploitation of man, the doctrine of contentment becomes reactionary because it restricts individual initiative". In other words, change the economic rules of the game and change the cognitive orientation of a peasant society, and a fertile field for the propagation of *n* Achievement is created.

For the above-reasons, I believe most strongly that the primary task in development is not to attempt to create *n* Achievement at the mother's knee but to try to change the peasants' view of his social and economic universe, away from an Image of Limited Good toward that of expanding opportunity in an open system, *so that he can feel safe* in displaying initiative. The brakes on change are less psychological than social. Show the peasant that initiative is profitable, and that it will not be met by negative sanctions, and he acquires it in short order.

This is, of course, what is happening in the world today. Those who have known peasant villages over a period of years have seen how the old sanctions begin to lose their power. Local entrepreneurs arise in response to the increasing opportunities of expanding national economies, and emulative urges, with the city as the model, appear among these people. The successful small entrepreneurs begin to see that the ideal of equality is inimical to their personal interests, and presently they neither seek to conceal their well being nor to distribute their wealth through traditional patterns of ritual extravagance. *N* Achievement bursts forth in full vitality in a few new leaders, and others see the rewards and try to follow suit. The problem of the new countries is to create economic and social conditions in which this latent energy and talent is not quickly brought up against absolute limits, so that it is nipped in the bud. This is, of course, the danger of new expectations—released latent *n* Achievement—outrunning the creation of opportunities.

Viewed in the light of Limited Good peasant societies are not conservative and backward, brakes on national economic progress, because of economic irrationality nor because of the absence of psychological characteristics in adequate quantities. They are conservative because individual progress is seen as—and in the context of the traditional society in fact is—the supreme threat to community stability, and all cultural forms *must* conspire to discourage changes in the status quo. Only by being conservative can peasant societies continue to exist as peasant societies. But change cognitive orientation through changing access to opportunity, and the peasant will do very well indeed; and his *n* Achievement will take care of itself.

Chapter 6

Agriculture and Rural Development

History of Agriculture in India

Indian agriculture began by 9000 BCE as a result of early cultivation of plants, and domestication of crops and animals. Settled life soon followed with implements and techniques being developed for agriculture. Double monsoons led to two harvests being reaped in one year. Indian products soon reached the world via existing trading networks and foreign crops were introduced to India. Plants and animals—considered essential to their survival by the Indians—came to be worshipped and venerated.

The middle ages saw irrigation channels reach a new level of sophistication in India and Indian crops affecting the economies of other regions of the world under Islamic patronage. Land and water management systems were developed with an aim of providing uniform growth. Despite some stagnation during the later modern era the independent Republic of India was able to develop a comprehensive agricultural program.

Early History

Wheat, barley and jujube were domesticated in the Indian subcontinent by 9000 BCE. Domestication of sheep and goat soon followed. This period also saw the first domestication of the elephant. Barley and wheat cultivation—along with the domestication of cattle, primarily sheep and goat—was visible in Mehrgarh by 8000-6000 BCE. Agro pastoralism in India included threshing, planting crops in rows—either of two or of six—and storing grain in granaries. By the 5th millennium BCE agricultural communities became widespread in Kashmir. Zaheer Baber (1996) writes that 'the first evidence of cultivation of cotton had already developed'. Cotton was cultivated by the 5th millennium BCE-4th millennium BCE. The Indus cotton industry was well developed and some methods used in cotton spinning and fabrication continued to be practiced till the modern Industrialization of India.

A variety of tropical fruit such as mango and muskmelon are native to the Indian subcontinent. The Indians also domesticated hemp, which they used for a number of applications including making narcotics, fiber, and oil.

The farmers of the Indus Valley grew peas, sesame, and dates. Sugarcane was originally from tropical South Asia and Southeast Asia. Different species likely originated in different locations with *S. barberi* originating in India and *S. edule* and *S. officinarum* coming from New Guinea.

Wild Oryza rice appeared in the Belan and Ganges valley regions of northern India as early as 4530 BCE and 5440 BCE respectively. Rice was cultivated in the Indus Valley Civilization. Agricultural activity during the second millennium BC included rice cultivation in the Kashmir and Harrappan regions. Mixed farming was the basis of the Indus valley economy. Denis J. Murphy (2007) details the spread of cultivated rice from India into South-east Asia:

Several wild cereals, including rice, grew in the Vindhyan Hills, and rice cultivation, at sites such as Chopani-Mando and Mahagara, may have been underway as early as 7000 BP. The relative isolation of this area and the early development of rice farming imply that it was developed indigenously....Chopani-Mando and Mahagara are located on the upper reaches of the Ganges drainage system and it is likely that migrants from this area spread rice farming down the Ganges valley into the fertile plains of Bengal, and beyond into south-east Asia.

Irrigation was developed in the Indus Valley Civilization by around 4500 BCE. The size and prosperity of the Indus civilization grew as a result of this innovation, which eventually led to more planned settlements making use of drainage and sewers. Sophisticated irrigation and water storage systems were developed by the Indus Valley Civilization, including artificial reservoirs at Girnar dated to 3000 BCE, and an early canal irrigation system from circa 2600 BCE. Archeological evidence of an animal-drawn plough dates back to 2500 BC in the Indus Valley Civilization.

Vedic Period–Post Maha Janapadas Period (1500 BCE–200 CE)

Gupta (2004) finds it likely that summer monsoons may have been longer and may have contained moisture in excess than required for normal food production. One effect of this excessive moisture would have been to aid the winter monsoon rainfall required for winter crops. In India, both wheat and barley are held to be *Rabi* (winter) crops and—like other parts of the world—would have largely depended on winter monsoons before the irrigation became widespread.

The growth of the *Kharif* crops would have probably suffered as a result of excessive moisture. Jute was first cultivated in India, where it was used to make ropes and cordage. Some animals—thought by the Indians as being vital to their survival—came to be worshipped. Trees were also domesticated, worshipped, and venerated—*Pipal* and *Banyan* in particular. Others came to be known for their medicinal uses and found mention in the holistic medical system *Ayurveda*. The Encyclopædia Britannica—on the subject of agriculture of the later Vedic period—holds that:

In the later Vedic texts (c. 1000–500 BC), there are repeated references to iron. Cultivation of a wide range of cereals, vegetables, and fruits is described. Meat and milk products were part of the diet; animal husbandry was important. The soil was plowed several times. Seeds were broadcast. Fallowing and a certain sequence of cropping were recommended. Cow dung provided the manure. Irrigation was practiced.

The Mauryan Empire (322–185 BCE) categorized soils and made meteorological observations for agricultural use. Other Mauryan facilitation included construction and maintenance of dams, and provision of horse-drawn chariots—quicker than traditional bullock carts.

The Greek diplomat Megasthenes (c. 300 BC)—in his book *Indika*—provides a secular eyewitness account of Indian agriculture:

India has many huge mountains which abound in fruit-trees of every kind, and many vast plains of great fertility.... The greater part of the soil, moreover, is under irrigation, and consequently bears two crops in the course of the year.... In addition to cereals, there grows throughout India much millet... and much pulse of different sorts, and rice also, and what is called bosporum [Indian millet].... Since there is a double rainfall [i.e., the two monsoons] in the course of each year... the inhabitants of India almost always gather in two harvests annually.

Early Common Era – High Middle Ages (200–1200 CE)

The Tamil people cultivated a wide range of crops such as rice, sugarcane, millets, black pepper, various grains, coconuts, beans, cotton, plantain, tamarind and sandalwood. Jackfruit, coconut, palm, areca and plantain trees were also known. Systematic ploughing, manuring, weeding, irrigation and crop protection was practiced for sustained agriculture. Water storage systems were designed during this period. Kallanai (1st-2nd century CE), a dam built on river Kaveri during this period, is considered the as one of the oldest water-regulation structures in the world still in use.

Spice trade involving spices native to India—including cinnamon and black pepper—gained momentum as India starts shipping spices to the Mediterranean. Roman trade with India followed as detailed by the archaeological record and the *Periplus of the Erythraean Sea*. Chinese sericulture attracted Indian sailors during the early centuries of the common era. Crystallized sugar was discovered by the time of the Guptas (320-550 CE), and the earliest reference of candied sugar come from India. The process was soon transmitted to China with traveling Buddhist monks. Chinese documents confirm at least two missions to India, initiated in 647 CE, for obtaining technology for sugar-refining. Each mission returned with results on refining sugar. Indian spice exports find mention in the works of Ibn Khurdadhbeh (850), al-Ghafiqi (1150), Ishak bin Imaran (907) and Al Kalkashandi (fourteenth century).

Noboru Karashima's research of the agrarian society in South India during the Chola Empire (875-1279) reveals that during the Chola rule land was transferred and collective holding of land by a group of people slowly gave way to individual plots of land, each with their own irrigation system. The growth of individual disposition of farming property may have led to a decrease in areas of dry cultivation. The Cholas also had bureaucrats which oversaw the distribution of water—-particularly the distribution of water by tank-and-channel networks to the drier areas.

Late Middle Ages – Early Modern Era (1200–1757 CE)

The construction of water works and aspects of water technology in India is described in Arabic and Persian works. The diffusion of Indian and Persian irrigation technologies gave rise to an irrigation systems which bought about economic growth and growth of material culture. Agricultural 'zones' were broadly divided into those producing rice, wheat or millets. Rice production continued to dominate Gujarat and wheat dominated north and central India. The Encyclopædia Britannica details the many crops introduced to India during this period of extensive global discourse:

Introduced by the Portuguese, cultivation of tobacco spread rapidly. The Malabâr Coast was the home of spices, especially black pepper, that had stimulated the first European adventures in the East. Coffee had been imported from Abyssinia and became a popular beverage in aristocratic circles by the end of the century. Tea, which was to become the common man's drink and a major export, was yet undiscovered, though it was growing wild in the hills of Assam. Vegetables were cultivated mainly in the vicinity of towns.

New species of fruit, such as the pineapple, papaya, and cashew nut, also were introduced by the Portuguese. The quality of mango and citrus fruits was greatly improved. Land management was particularly strong during the regime of Akbar the Great (reign: 1556-1605), under whom scholar-bureaucrat Todarmal formulated and implemented elaborated methods for agricultural management on a rational basis. Indian crops—such as cotton, sugar, and citric fruits—spread visibly throughout North Africa, Islamic Spain, and the Middle East. Though they may have been in cultivation prior to the solidification of Islam in India, their production was further improved as a result of this recent wave, which led to far-reaching economic outcomes for the regions involved.

Colonial British Era (1757–1947 CE)

Few Indian commercial crops—such as Cotton, indigo, opium, and rice—made it to the global market under the British Raj in India. The second half of the 19th century saw some increase in land under cultivation and agricultural production expanded at an average rate of about 1 percent per year by the later 19th century. Due to extensive irrigation by canal networks Punjab, Narmada valley, and Andhra Pradesh became centers of agrarian reforms. Roy (2006) comments on the Influence of the world wars on the Indian agricultural system:

Agricultural performance in the interwar period (1918–1939) was dismal. From 1891 to 1946, the annual growth rate of all crop output was 0.4 percent, and food-grain output was practically stagnant. There were significant regional and intercrop differences, however, nonfood crops doing better than food crops. Among food crops, by far the most important source of stagnation was rice. Bengal had below-average growth rates in both food and nonfood crop output, whereas Punjab and Madras were the least stagnant regions.

In the interwar period, population growth accelerated while food output decelerated, leading to declining availability of food per head. The crisis was most acute in Bengal, where food output declined at an annual rate of about 0.7 percent from 1921 to 1946, when population grew at an annual rate of about 1 percent.

The British regime in India did supply the irrigation works but rarely on the scale required. Community effort and private investment soared as market for irrigation developed. Agricultural prices of some commodities rose to about three times between 1870-1920.

A rich source of the state of Indian agriculture in the early British era is a report prepared by a British engineer, Thomas Barnard, and his Indian guide, Raja Chengalvaraya Mudaliar, around 1774. This report contains data of agricultural production in about 800 villages in the area around Chennai in the years 1762 to 1766.

This report is available in Tamil in the form of palm leaf manuscripts at Thanjavur Tamil University, and in English in the Tamil Nadu State Archives. A series of articles in The Hindu newspaper in the early 1990s authored by researchers at The Center for Policy Studies led by Shri Dharampal highlight the impressive production statistics of Indian farmers of that era.

Republic of India (1947 CE Onwards)

Special programs were undertaken to improve food and cash crops supply. The Grow More Food Campaign (1940s) and the Integrated Production Programme (1950s) focused on food and cash crops supply respectively. Five-year plans of India—oriented towards agricultural development—soon followed. Land reclamation, land development, mechanization, electrification, use of chemicals—fertilizers in particular, and development of agriculture oriented 'package approach' of taking a set of actions instead of promoting single aspect soon followed under government supervision.

The many 'production revolutions' initiated from 1960s onwards included Green Revolution in India, Yellow Revolution (oilseed: 1986-1990), Operation Flood (dairy: 1970-1996), and Blue Revolution (fishing: 1973-2002) etc. Following the economic reforms of 1991, significant growth was registered in the agricultural sector, which was by now benefiting from the earlier reforms and the newer innovations of Agro-processing and Biotechnology.

Due to the growth and prosperity that followed India's economic reforms a strong middle class emerged as the main consumer of fruits, dairy, fish, meat and vegetables—a marked shift from the earlier staple based consumption. Since 1991, changing consumption patterns led to a 'revolution' in 'high value' agriculture while the need for cereals is experienced a decline.

The per capita consumption of cereals declined from 192 to 152 kilograms from 1977 to 1999 while the consumption of fruits increased by 553%, vegetables by 167%, dairy products by 105%, and non-vegetarian products by 85% in India's rural areas alone. Urban areas experienced a similar increase.

Agricultural exports continued to grow at well over 10.1% annually through the 1990s. Contract farming—which requires the farmers to produce crops for a company under contract—and high value agricultural product increased. Contract farming led to a decrease in transaction costs while the contract farmers made more profit compared to the non-contract workforce. However, small landholding continued to create problems for India's farmers as the limited land resulted in limited produce and limited profits.

Since independence, India has become one of the largest producers of wheat, edible oil, potato, spices, rubber, tea, fishing, fruits, and vegetables in the world. The Ministry of Agriculture oversees activities relating to agriculture in India. Various institutions for agriculture related research in India were organized under the Indian Council of Agricultural Research (est. 1929). Other organizations such as the National Dairy Development Board (est. 1965), and National Bank for Agriculture and Rural Development (est. 1982) aided the formation of cooperatives and improved financing.

The contribution of agriculture in employing India's male workforce declined from 75.9% in 1961 to 60% in 1999–2000. Dev (2006) holds that 'there were about 45 million agricultural labor households in the country in 1999–2000.' These households recorded the highest incidence of poverty in India from 1993 to 2000. The green revolution introduced high yielding varieties of crops which also increased the usage of fertilizers and pesticides.

About 90% of the pesticide usage in India is accounted for by DDT and Lindane (BHC/HCH). There has been a shift to organic agriculture particularly for exported commodities. During 2003-04, agriculture accounted for 22 % of India's GDP and employed 58 per cent of the country's workforce. India is the world's largest producer of milk, fruits, cashew nuts, coconuts, ginger, turmeric, banana, sapota, pulses, and black pepper.

India is the second largest producer of groundnut, wheat, vegetables, sugar and fish in the world. India is also the third largest producer of tobacco and rice, the fourth largest producer of coarse grains, the fifth largest producer of eggs, and the seventh largest producer of meat.

In Fertile India, Growth Outstrips Agriculture

India's supply of arable land is second only to that of the United States, its economy is one of the fastest growing in the world, and its industrial innovation is legendary. But when it comes to agriculture, its output lags far behind potential.

For some staples, India must turn to already stretched international markets, exacerbating a global food crisis.

It was not supposed to be this way.

Forty years ago, a giant development effort known as the Green Revolution drove hunger from an India synonymous with famine and want. Now, after a decade of neglect, this country is growing faster than its ability to produce more rice and wheat.

The problem has grown so dire that Prime Minister Manmohan Singh has called for a Second Green Revolution "so that the specter of food shortages is banished from the horizon once again."

And while Mr. Singh worries about feeding the poor, India's growing affluent population demands not only more food but also a greater variety.

Today Indian agriculture is a double tragedy. "Both in rice and wheat, India has a large untapped reservoir. It can make a major contribution to the world food crisis," said M. S. Swaminathan, a plant geneticist who helped bring the Green Revolution to India.

India's own people are paying as well. Farmers, most subsisting on small, rain-fed plots, are disproportionately poor, and inflation has soared past 11 percent, the highest in 13 years.

Experts blame the agriculture slowdown on a variety of factors.

The Green Revolution introduced high-yielding varieties of rice and wheat, expanded the use of irrigation, pesticides and fertilizers, and transformed the northwestern plains into India's breadbasket. Between 1968 and 1998, the production of cereals in India more than doubled.

But since the 1980s, the government has not expanded irrigation and access to loans for farmers, or to advance agricultural research. Groundwater has been depleted at alarming rates.

The Peterson Institute for International Economics in Washington says changes in temperature and rain patterns could diminish India's agricultural output by 30 percent by the 2080s.

Family farms have shrunk in size and quantity, and a few years ago mounting debt began to drive some farmers to suicide. Now many find it more profitable to sell their land to developers of industrial buildings.

Among farmers who stay on their land, many are experimenting with growing high-value fruits and vegetables that prosperous Indians are craving, but there are few refrigerated trucks to transport their produce to modern supermarkets.

A long and inefficient supply chain means that the average farmer receives less than a fifth of the price the consumer pays, a World Bank study found, far less than farmers in, say, Thailand or the United States.

Surinder Singh Chawla knows the system is broken. Mr. Chawla, 62, bore witness to the Green Revolution — and its demise.

Once, his family grew wheat and potatoes on 20 acres. They looked to the sky for rains. They used cow manure for fertilizer. Then came the Mexican semi-dwarf wheat seedlings that the revolution helped introduce to India. Mr. Chawla's wheat yields soared. A few years later, the same happened with new high-yield rice seeds.

Increasingly prosperous, Mr. Chawla finally bought his first tractor in 1980.

But he has since witnessed with horror the ills the revolution wrought: in a common occurrence here, the water table under his land has sunk by 100 feet over three decades as he and other farmers irrigated their fields.

By the 1980s, government investment in canals fed by rivers had tapered off, and wells became the principal source of irrigation, helped by a shortsighted government policy of free electricity to pump water.

Here in Punjab, more than three-fourths of the districts extract more groundwater than is replenished by nature.

Between 1980 and 2002, the government continued to heavily subsidize fertilizers and food grains for the poor, but reduced its total investment in agriculture.

Public spending on farming shrank by roughly a third, according to an analysis of government data by the Center for Policy Alternatives in New Delhi.

Today only 40 percent of Indian farms are irrigated. "When there is no water, there is nothing," Mr. Chawla said.

And he sees more trouble on the way. The summers are hotter than he remembers. The rains are more fickle. Last summer, he wanted to ease out of growing rice, a water-intensive crop.

Agricultural marketing involves in its simplest form the buying and selling of agricultural produce. In olden days when the village economy was more or less self-sufficient the marketing of agricultural produce presented no difficulty as the farmer sold his produce to the consumer on a cash or barter basis.

Marketing functions. In modern marketing the agricultural produce has to undergo a series of transfers or exchanges from one hand to another before it finally reaches the consumer. This is achieved through three marketing functions (a)assembling,(b)preparation for consumption and (c) distribution. Concentration pertains to the operations concerned with the assembly and transport from the field to a common assembly field or market.

The produce may be taken direct to the market or it may be stored on the farm or in the village for varying periods before its transport. It may be sold as obtained from the field or may be cleaned, graded, processed and packed either by the farmer or village merchant before it is taken to the market. Some of the processing is done not because consumers desire it, but because it is necessary for the conservation of quality.

At the market the produce may be sold by the farmer direct to the consumer or more usually through a commission agent or a broker.

It may also be purchased by traders, wholesalers or retailers. The transactions may be carried out by direct negotiation or through middlemen, by barter or cash, by open or under cover auction, on the spot or in future markets.

The transactions take place at one or more levels in the primary, secondary or terminal markets or all three. Distribution (dispersion) involves the operations of wholesaling and retailing at various points. By a series of indispensable adjustments and equalising functions, it is the task of the distribution system to match the available supplies with the existing demand.

Marketing Functionaries (Agencies)

The transfer of produce or goods takes place through a chain of middlemen or agencies. In the primary market the main functionaries are the producer, the village or itinerary merchant, pre-harvest contractors, commission agents, transport agents etc.

In the secondary market the processing and manufacturing agents are the additional functionaries. Financing agents such as shroffs, banks and co-operatives may also take part. In the terminal or export market the commercial analyst and shipping agent also gets involved in the transfer of goods.

The functionaries have their own set up. They may be individuals, partners or co-operatives who may buy and sell on ready and future basis at a price determined by forces of supply and demand. Each functionary renders some service in the process of marketing and also earns a varying margin of profit for himself.

This procedure makes marketing rather complicated and inflates the price of the produce. The nature of some of the agricultural products for eg. their bulk form and perishability and their seasonal availability further add to the complexity of agricultural marketing.

Marketing Improvements

India being a primary producing country, agriculture plays a vital role, both as an essential infrastructure and a development component in generating and sustaining a higher national income. Out of a natonal income of about Rs 38,921 crores in 1972-73 as much as Rs 17,500 crores or about 44.9% is contributed by agriculture and allied sectors. It is estimated that about 50% of the agricultural produce is available as marketable surplus. The marketing system in India provides sustenance for abour 3 million persons who are engaged in performing various marketing function. In the field of exports too, the agricultural sector accounts for about 50% of the total value.

The process involved in the disposal of such a substantial produce of great economic importance are significant not only for the farmer but also for the country as a whole. The unreasonably low return that the farmer gets for his produce and the excessive margin of profit retained by the intermediaries attracted the Govt's attention and it was felt that the economic condition of the agriculturists could not be improved unless determined steps were taken to establish an orderly system of marketing in the country.

Government Regulatory Programmes

With this object in view, a number of marketing surveys were conducted by the Directorate of Marketing and Inspection which revealed the shortcomings in the country's marketing system. A rectification of these deficiencies was sought to be achieved by rationalizing various activities and standardizing various practices in the markets through legislation or otherwise.

The primary objective of improving the system of agricultural marketing was not only to remove the handicaps from which the producer-seller was suffering but also to increase his income by ensuring him a fair price.

Regulation of markets. Prevailing market practices and market charges made a deep cut in the share of the producer in the price paid by the consumer. Some of the market charges were authorized whereas others were more than what the service rendered warranted. It was felt that a remunerative price to the producer could only be ensured if the market practices and market charges were regulated and rationalised. And thus the regulation of the markets has been given a high priority in the various Five Year Plans. The markets are sought to be regulated through an Act of each legislature.

The Act is generally known as the Agricultural Produce Markets Act and it is provided for the removal of various malpractices widely prevalent in the markets for the settlement of disputes between sellers and buyers and for the promoting of orderly marketing of farm produce in general. Various state govts have made considerable progress in this field by bringing in the necessary legislation. The Acts enabling the respective states to regulate the markets generally provide for the notification of market areas and the commodities to be covered in the act in different areas.

A 'Marketing Committee' consisting of the representatives of growers, traders, merchants, local bodies and govt nominees administers the working of each market. The functions of the market committee are to frame bye-laws, define local market prices, fix market prices payable to various functionaries, licence the functionaries, settle disputes, supervise weightment and promote the development of orderly marketing in general. The committee is generally empowered to raise funds for its working by levying a small fee on the produce bought and sold in the market in addition to the licence fees received from the functionaries.

Market surveys. A survey conducted in 496 markets in 1961-62 has shown that after the regulation the market charges have been reduced by 48%. Another survey of selected commodities revealed that for some commodities market charges have been reduced by as much as 98%.

Although the first market to be regulated was Karanja in 1886 the regulation of markets did not make headway till the first Five Year plan. It got a fillup in the second and third five year plan.

The states and union territories which have regulated the markets are: Andhra Pradesh(335), Bihar(62), Chandigarh(1), Delhi(3), Gujarat(212), Mysore(102), Madhya Pradesh(233), Haryana(80), Kerela(6), Maharashtra(212), Orissa(34), Punjab(95), Rajasthan(90), Tamil Nadu(136), Tripura(1), Uttar Pradesh(264), Goa, Daman and Diu(1), West Bengal(15), and Himachal Pradesh(5). The states and union territories which are yet to regulate markets are Assam, Andaman and Nicobar islands, Arunachal Pradesh, Dadra and Nagar Haveli, Jammu and Kashmir, Laccadive and Minicoy islands, Meghalaya, Mizoram, Nagaland, and Pondicherry. Necessary measures to regulate markets in these states and union territories are at various stages of progress. It is expected that these states and union territories will regulate the markets by the end of the Fifth plan.

All the states where necessary legislation has since been passed, have formulated phased programs for the regulation of markets. By the end od the fifth plan it is expected that all the wholesale assembling markets would be brought within the regulatory orbit.

As a result of this scheme, excessive commissions and other market charges have been substantially rationalized. Unauthorized and arbitrary deductions have been prohibited and malpractices stopped. The issue of sale slips by licensed commission agents to the sellers, indicating the details of sale proceeds, deductions effected etc has been made obligatory. Weightment is also done by licensed weightmen of the market committee.

The dissemination of marketing information and news is one of the functions of the market committees. This is done through the displaying of the prices prevailing in the market and also in the neighbouring markets on the notice boards and announcements through loud speakers at regular intervals. This information is also supplied to the Central Govt and the State Govt and also to other market committees. Arrangements have been made for the maintainence of reliable statistics arrivals, sales, stocks, prices etc which are maintained by the market committees. It is also obligatory on the part of the market committee to provide the market yards with the necessary amenities. In some of the markets that have been regulated amenities like rest houses, cattle sheds and water troughs have been provided by the market committees for the convenience of the producer sellers. Facilities for grading before sale and storage have also been provided.

A survey of 500 regulated markets was undertaken by the Directorate of Marketing and Inspection in the Ministry of Agriculture in 1970-71 and 1971-72, with a view to assessing the adequacy and efficiency of the existing regulated markets and highlighting their drawbacks and deficiencies and suggesting measures to develop them. One of the most important drawbacks has been the inadequate financial resources of some of the market committees. During the fourth plan, a central sector scheme was drawn up by the Ministry of Agriculture to provide a grant at 20% of the cost of development of market, subject to a maximum of Rs 2 lakhs. The balance will have to be provided by the commercial banks.

An important development in the field of regulated markets is the keen interest taken by the International Development Agency (IDA) in the development of the infrastructure in regulated markets. The IDA is financing the development of infrastructure in 50 markets of Bihar.

The World Bank has approved a loan assistance of 6.5 crores to Karnataka also for the development of markets.

Contract terms. Under the existing trade practices, the sale of produce in a primary market takes place on the basis of the visual inspection of the goods, and in the secondary and terminal markets on the inspection of the samples. Thereafter the buyer and the seller decide upon the terms either orally or through written contracts. The contract terms specify the quality and quantity of the produce, the time and place of delivery, the price and terms of payment, handling and incidental charges, the procedure for settlement of disputes and penalties. The terms of contract were not standardized and thus varied for every individual transaction, and were more favourable to the buyer.

With a view to improving trade practices, All-India standard contract terms have been drawn up for a number of commodities. In standard contract terms the definition of quality and allowances in respect of refraction, damaged goods have been specifically standardized. though the adoption of these standard contract terms by traders is voluntary they have to a large extent strengthened the position of the producer-seller and have improved the quality of the product marketed.

Standardisation and grading. In order to gain the confidence and establish a rational relationship between the quality of a produce and its price, it is necessary to devote some attention to the proper preparation sifting and sorting of a material according to certain attributes before it is taken to the market. This is sought to be achieved by grading the produce in conformity with certain accepted quality standards viz. shape, size, form, weight, and other physical and technical characteristics. The produce brought to the market is very often contaminated with dust, stones and other foreign matter added either deliberately or by accident. Sometimes the produce is immature or not properly dried or contains shrivelled grains or damaged and rotten material. Such a produce brings a lower price to the farmers. Care should be exercised while assembling the produce of different farmers so that the good material is not mixed with the inferior material brought in by some farmers.

The Govt. of India had recognized the need to introduce the standardization of agricultural produce which would enable the farmers to derive the benefits of grading in terms of fair practices according to the prescribed standards and enacted the Agricultural Produce Grading and Marking Act in 1937. The Act empowers the central govt to prescribe grade standards indicating the quality of articles included in the schedule and specify grade designation marks to represent particular grades or qualities.

The Act provides for the grading and marketing of agricultural produce. The grade standards prescribed under this act are based on both physical and chemical characteristics and are formulated after analysing representative samples of each commodity collected from different regions and different seasons. Besides the international standards and special requirements of overseas consumers are also taken into account while formulating these standards for the commodities which are exported.

The grade standards are reviewed and amended from time to time in the light of the shift of the pattern of production and trade and changes in the consumer's preferences. The grades are designated as the 'Agmark' grades.

A central Agmark Laboratory at Nagpur with sixteen regional laboratories at Guntur, Madras, Bombay, Kanpur, Cochin, Rajkot, Calcutta, Sahidabad, Jamnagar, Bangalore, Patna, Tuticorin, Virudhunagar, Mangalore, Alleppey and Kozhikode are assisting to provide adequate laboratory facilities for fixing grade standards for new commodities, for revising old grade standards and for routine quality control work. Grade for export. Grading of agricultural produce under the A.P.(G and M) Act is voluntary. Exports of certain agricultural commodities have however been prohibited unless duly graded and marked in accordance with the grade standards laid down under the A.P. Act 1937. The power to so prohibit exports was derived under the provisions of the sea-customs act.

The Directorate of Marketing and Inspection under the Ministry of Agriculture exercises a three tier control on the quality of agricultural commodities that are graded under 'Agmark' before they are exported. This is done through inspection. Grading for internal trade. Commodities such as cotton, ghee, butter, rice, wheat, atta, gur, eggs, arecanut, potatoes, fruits, bura, pulses, vegetable oils and ground spices are being presently graded under; Agmark' on voluntary basis.

Grading at farmers level. The grading of agricultural commodities under 'Agmark' has been consumer oriented. Generally the grading was done at the level of the traders. At this stage the producer was not a direct beneficiary of the grading scheme. It was felt the need to introduce grading at the producers' level. Thus the Directorate of marketing and inspection introduced a scheme for setting up commercial grading units.

Grading of fruits and vegetable products. With a view to exercising quality control over fruits and vegetables the govt promulgated the Fruits Product Order under the essential Commodities Act. The preservatives and colors to be used are also clearly laid down. The order also stipulates the hygeinic and sanitary methods which must be adopted by the manufacturers. The licence for all this is issued by the executive Director, food and Nutrition board.

The total number of licensed factories was 1194. The total average production of fruits and vegetable products in the country during 1970 has been estimated as 156 thousand tonnes valued at Rs 32.66 crores. Some of the products are very popular in foreign markets and are a good source of foreign exchange. In 1970 alone fruit products worth Rs 2.92 crores were exported from India.

Regulation of Cold Stores

Most of the problems relating to the marketing of fruits and vegetables can be traced to their perishability. Perishability is responsible for high marketing costs, market gluts, price fluctuations and other similar problems. At low temperature, perishability is considerably reduced and the shelf life is increased and thus the importance of cold storage or refrigeration.

The first cold store in India was reported to have been established in Calcutta in 1892. However significant progress in the expansion of the cold storage industry in the country has been made only after independence.

An ad-hoc survey of the cold stores carried out by the directorate of marketing and inspection in 1955 showed that the total available cold storage in the country was only 77 thousand tonnes. The survey also highlighted the need to regulate the cold storage industry in a planned manner.

With a view to ensuring the observance of proper conditions in the cold stores and to providing for development of the industry in a scientific manner, the govt of India and the ministry of agriculture promulgated an order known as "cold storage order, 1964" under Section 3 of the Essential Commodities Act,1955. The order is applicable in respect of every cold store with a capacity more than 8.4 cu m. The jurisdiction of this Order extends to the whole of India except West Bengal. Under this order, it is obligatory on every operator of the cold store to obtain a licence from the Licensing Officer before using the installation for storing any food stuffs eg. fruit, vegetables, meat, fish, dairy products. The Agricultural Marketing Advisor to the govt of India is the Licensing Officer.

The directorate of marketing and inspection is enforcing the cold storage order. The field staff posted in the regional and sub offices located in different states regularly inspects the cold stores and offers necessary guidance for better and scientific preservation of foodstuffs. Besides the directorate of marketing and inspection gives general guidance on all technical matters concerning the setting up of cold stores to the intending entrepreneurs. The govt of India constituted a Central Cold Storage Advisory Committee consisting of official and non official members, representing the growers, owners, machinery manufacturers, research organizations etc. The Committee advises the govt on all matters pertaining to the enforcement of Cold Storage Order and the future development of the industry.

At the end of 1973-74 there were 1503 cold stores in the country with a capacity of 18.70 lakh tonnes. Uttar Pradesh had the maximum number of cold stores of 9.37 lakh tonnes followed by Bihar with 169 cold stores with 2.10 lakh tonnes capacity and West Bengal with 133 cold stores with 3.15 lakh tonnes capacity.

Out of 1217 cold stores licensed during 1970, 1021 representing 84% of the total were owned by the private sector, whereas 121 and 75 were owned by the public and co-operative sector respectively. The respective capacity are 13.88 lakh tonnes, 0.25 lakh tonnes and 0.73 lakh tonnes. Though numerically the cold stores in the co-operative sector were less than those in the public sector the capacity was more. The National Co-operative Development Corporation(NCDC) has formulated a scheme for financial assistance for setting up new cold stores in the co-operative sector. Potato is the most important commodity which is presently placed in the cold stores accounting for as much as 92 % of the total capacity in the country. The remaining 8% is being utilized for other perishables viz. fruits, vegetables, meat, sea-foods, dairy and poultry products.

With the attainment of self-sufficiency in the production of food grains, greater attention is being paid to the increased production of protective foods such as fruits, vegetables, fish, poultry and dairy products. These products being highly perishable are required to be kept in cold stores. Owing to the inadequate cold storage facilities at present considerable losses occur in the case of these commodities. There is enough scope for expanding the cold-storage industry with a view to providing facilities for preserving and prolonging the shelf life of these protective foods which are essential for human health.

Consumer protection. In the marketing process the producers and consumers are the two weak ends of the chain. It is incumbent on the part of the govt to protect the interests of both of them. Producers are are sought to be protected through the regulation of the markets, grading at the producers level and other similiar measures. Consumer's interests on the other hand are safeguarded by grading under 'Agmark' at the level of traders. The progress towards making the consumer quality conscious is slow. With the growing popularity of semi-processed foods the danger of sub-standard food articles being marketed has become manifold.

With this in view steps have been taken in many directions. eg. Acts relating to grading and standardisation of agricultural commodities, certification marks in respect of manufactured goods, pure food laws, laws relating to weights and measures, and laws relating to the manufacture of fruits and vegetable products have been passed and enforced. Commodities such as ghee, vegetable oils, butter, honey and powdered spices are being graded and marked under 'Agmark' under the provisions of the Agricultural Produce (Grading and Marking) Act 1937. The Agmark attempts to provide a third party guarantee for the consumer. It not only certifies the purity of the product but also gives an indication of their quality by the grade-designating mark. The economic incentive to the producer-manufacturer is reflected in the premium the Agmarked product fetches in the market over the ungraded products.

Running parallel to the enforcement of laws, certain measures to complement the effort of achieving the overall objective of consumer protection are also being adopted. Monopoly procurement of foodgrains being operated by the Food corporation of India and other state departments achieves the two objectives of ensuring a remunerative price to the farmers and a uniform and reasonable price commensurate with the quality of the produce to the consumers.

The task of consumer education and protection is formidable and the govt machinery alone will be inadequate to accomplish this task. There is a need of active consumers' movement as in other countries. The Consumers' Guidance Society has been established with the objective of educating the consumers about their rights and responsibilities and advising them on the quality of products available in the market. Similiarly it has advised the producers and manufacturers to abide by such standards as are nècessary for the health and safety of the users.

Co-operative Marketing

The existing institutional structure of co-operative marketing is such that the co-operatives are functioning at the primary level, at the secondary level (taluka or district) and at the state level. In pursuance of a recommendation of the Dantwala Committee, efforts have been made to persuade the state govts to divert the middle tier viz. the district marketing federations, of the functions legitimately falling within the purview of the state or primary marketing societies, so that a two-tier system can be brought into operation. The co-operatives in different states have been federated into a central level federation viz. the National Agricultural Co-operative Marketing Federation (NAFED). At the end of 1960-70 as many as 3335 primary cooperative marketing societies were operating. Of these more than 500 were specialized commodity marketing societies for special crops, cotton, fruits and vegetables.

In certain states intermediate organizations at district and state levels have also been established. At the end of 1960-70, 232 such societies were functioning. They included some commodity federations also. At the state level 28 apex co-operative marketing federations are functioning. They are normally handling all the commodities. There are a few apex cooperative societies which are handling exclusively a particular commodity eg. two apex societies in Gujarat are handling cotton, one is handling fruits and vegetables and one in Uttar Pradesh is handling sugarcane only. In order to strengthen and develop co-operative marketing to an extent where it may have an impact on the marketing of agricultural produce, several measures have been initiated. Steps are also being taken to see that there is an effective co-ordination between the state cooperative departments and their counterparts dealing with agricultural marketing. Consequently there has been a significant expansion in the operations of marketing co-operatives. This is exclusive of the value of agricultural requisites and consumer articles handled by the marketing cooperatives. The main commodities marketed by the cooperatives were sugarcane, cotton, oilseeds, fruits, vegetables and plantation crops.

In pursuance of the decision of the govt, a scheme of outright purchases of agricultural produce by the co-operative marketing societies was launched in 1964-65 in 200 selected marketing societies. The basic theme of this scheme has been to bring the small producers within the fold of co-operative marketing together for such farmers. To provide the necessary financial backing the scheme envisaged the creation of a price-fluctuation fund. The fund envisages to meet losses if suffered by the co-operative marketing societies at different levels as a result of outright purchases of agricultural produce.

The scheme has been operative in several states. During 1969-70 the value of the agricultural produce purchased under the outright purchase scheme was about 34 crores. As a result of this scheme there has been a greater involvement of cooperative societies in the marketing of agricultural produce.

Besides this scheme has given impetus to inter-state trade by the cooperatives. They transacted about Rs 66.55 crores worth of agricultural produce during 1969-70.

Inter state trade. The co-operative marketing societies are devoting increasing attention to inter state trade in agricultural produce. The main commodities are wheat, pulses, plantation crops, copra, spices, fruits and vegetables. The bulk of the transactions were made by the Punjab Apex Federation. During 1970-71 the NAFED acted as the agency of the co-operatives of Jammu and Kashmir for marketing their apples outside the state.

Co-operative export of agricultural produce. The export of agricultural produce by the co-operative sector continues to be a growing activity. The bulk of the exports are made by National Agricultural Cooperative Marketing Federation Ltd., which accounted for exports worth Rs 5.64 crores. Besides, the Gujurat State Cooperative Marketing Federation Ltd., the Khanna Cooperative Marketing Federation Ltd., the Kerela state Cooperative Marketing Federation Ltd., the Jalgaon district fruit sales societies and the coconut oil millers society also cooperated to exports to countries like Kuwait, Malaysia, Ceylon, Singapore, Bahrain, Doha, Dubai, Iran,Muscat. The Khanna Solvent Extraction Plant in the Punjab State exported de-oiled cake worth Rs 35 lakhs during 1969-70. The main commodities exported by the cooperatives were pulses, chillies, onions, pepper, de-oiled cake, potatoes and kardi extraction meal.

The exports were mainly made to Ceylon and other important markets were Mauritius, Kuwait, Doha, Bahrain, Hong Kong, the USSR, the UK, Iran, Czechoslovakia and France. Some of the traditional items of export have been marketed in non traditional areas. Pulses were exported to Cuba and onions to Malaysia and Singapore. The cooperatives also assisted various agencies to export agricultural commodities. In this connection exports of coffee and raw sugar were made.

During 1970-71, NAFED exported agricultural produce worth Rs 5.26 crores. The Jalgaon District Fruit Sale Societies Cooperative Marketing Federation Ltd., directly exported bananas worth Rs. 34 lakhs to Kuwait and Bahrain Islands.

Co-operative cold stores. Co-operatives are also to facilitate the storage and marketing of perishable commodities especially seed potatoes. By the end of the Third plan the cooperatives had established 87 cold stores and the target for the fourth plan was set at 45 more. At the end of December 1971 there were as many as 96 cooperative cold stores with a capacity of 1.42 lakhs tonnes.

Training of Marketing Personnel

Several training courses, viz. (a)11 months Diploma Course in Agricultural Marketing in Nagpur, (b)4 months Market Secretaries Course at Chandigarh, Lucknow and Hyderabad, (c)6 months Diploma in Livestock Marketing at Nagpur, (d) 3 months training for grading supervisors at Nagpur (e) 3 months Graders Course at Hubli, Lucknow, and Chandigarh, (f)4 months Training Course in Cotton Classing Centre at Surat, (g)6 months Training Course in Tobacco Grading at Guntur, and (h)3 weeks course at Demonstration cum training centre in animal casing at Bombay and New Delhi are being run by the directorate of marketing and inspection.

In addition short term condensed training courses of one week duration organized for the state govt personnel in Kapas grading. As many as 407 candidates in the 11 months Diploma course, 1596 in 4 mths course; 212 in 3 mths course; and 76 in 3 mths grading course were trained by the end of 1972-73.

Market extension. The directorate of marketing and inspection has set up a seperate extension wing for the dissemination of information valuable to producers as well as to consumers. The primary aim of the scheme is to enlighten the producer seller on consumer preference and to advise him on the proper methods of preparation for marketing, grading, storing, packaging, handling and transporting and to improve the quality of the produce and to secure a better return to the growers.

Since 1969, the Directorate of marketing and inspection has in collaboration with the directorate of extension launched a series of 'Agmark' exhibitions known as 'vital link between farm and home'. These have been held in New Delhi, Lucknow, Chandigarh, Trivandrum, Bombay, Calcutta, Bangalore, Nagpur, Ahmedabad, Madras and Hyderabad. These have designed to educate the general public in the field of agricultural marketing to promote quality consciousness among producers.

Marketing intelligence. With a view to disseminating the marketing intelligence to the interested parties the directorate of marketing and inspection publishes the following journals:

1. Agricultural Marketing—a quarterly journal
2. Marketing Newsletter— a monthly letter
3. Agmark Statistics— yearly
4. Commodity Intelligence Bulletins for tobacco, wool, bristles, potatoes etc.

Marketing Research and Investigation

The role of market research in the establishment of an efficient system of marketing cannot be overemphasized. In order to be able to introduce reforms one should know the defects and shortcomings of the prevailing system. This calls for and justifies the necessity of intensive research and investigation. Under the third five-year plan an elaborate scheme for conducting survey, and research in the various facets of agricultural marketing has been undertaken by the Directorate of marketing and inspection. Particular attention is being paid to the collection of market information, with regard to price spreads, shifts in marketing practices, consumption pattern, consumer preferences, directional movements, packaging, assembling, transportation, distribution etc. Authentic statisics and data are being collected so that up-to date information may be maintained in respect of all important agricultural commodities. Besides the market surveys cover studies on the organisational aspect of the mktg. system, problem orinted studies etc. Under the fourth five year plan a specialized study to estimate the post harvest losses and marketable surpluses of agricultural produce have been taken up on an all-India level.

The Research Wing of the Directorate of marketing and inspection has been further strengthened by creating the Market Research and Planning Cell. The cell has a big component of exports in the field of agricultural marketing research and is expected to increase the tempo of development in this field.

Conclusion. Marketing is a multistage process. For the improvement and development of marketing structure, a co-ordinate approach aiming at removing all the weak links of the marketing chain is essential. A package of improved marketing services in the form of regulated markets, grading, weighing, storing, transporting, handling services and marketing finance need to be made available to ensure the producer a fair return from his production efforts and a better share in the price paid by the consumer.

At the same time, market research programs should be oriented to the developing of an orderly and efficient marketing system. This is a crucial time in the development of agricultural marketing when the country is poised to enter an ers of production surpluses. A piecemeal approach at this stage can be disastrous and can nullify the advantages gained by the farmer on the production front.

Chapter 7

Small Holdings in Agriculture

Small Holdings in India

It may be said that some countries are predominantly countries of small holdings while in others it is the large holdings that prevail. According to Adam Smith it is the adoption of the law of primogeniture chiefly due to the exigencies of a military life that leads to the creation and preservation of large holdings. While it is the adoption of the law of equal sub-division necessitated by the comparatively peaceful career of a nation that gives rise to small holdings. He says :

> *"When land like moveables is considered as the means only of subsistence and enjoyment, the natural law of succession divides it like them among all the children of the family; of all of whom the subsistence and enjoyment may be supposed equally dear to the father, [thus tending to have small holdings. But when land was considered as the means, not of subsistence merely, but of power and protection it was thought better that it should descend undivided to one. In those disorderly times.......to divide it was to ruin it, and to expose every part of it to be opposed and swallowed up by its neighbours. The law of primogeniture, therefore came to take place in the succession of landed estates [thus tending to preserve large holdings]."*

Consolidation

Consolidation of holdings is a practical problem while the enlargement of them is a theoretical one, demanding a discussion of the principle which can be said to govern their size. Postponing the consideration of the theoretical question of enlargement, we find that the problem of consolidation raises the following two issues:—(1) how to unite such small and scattered holdings as the existing ones, and (2) once consolidated how to perpetuate them at that size. Let us consider them each in turn. Sub-division of land need not involve what is called the fragmentation of land.

But unfortunately it does, for, every heir desires to secure a share from each of the survey numbers composing the entire lands of the deceased instead of so arranging the distribution that each may get as many whole numbers as possible, i.e. the heirs instead of sharing the lands by survey numbers, claim to share in each survey number, thus causing fragmentation. Though fragmentation does subserve the ends of distributive justice it renders farming in India considerably inefficient as it once did in Europe.

It involves waste of labour and cattle power, waste in hedges and boundary marks, and waste of manure. It renders impracticable the watching of crops, sinking of wells and the use of labour saving implements. It makes difficult changes in cultivation, the making of roads, water channels, etc., and it increases the cost of production. These disadvantages of fragmentation arc I to be recounted only to lend their support to the process of restripping or \ consolidation.

The methods of "restripping" are many, though all are not equally efficacious. Voluntary exchanges can hardly be relied upon for much. But a restricted sale of the right of occupancy may be expected to go a good deal. For, under it, when survey numbers are put to auction on account of their being relinquished by the holders or taken in attachment for arrears of assessments, only those may be allowed lo bid in the auction for the sale of the right of occupancy whose lands are contiguous to the land hammered out. Again as further helping the process of reunion, the right of pre-emption may be given to farmers whose neighbour wishes to sell his land.

These methods, it must be admitted, can achieve the desired result in a very small measure. The evils of fragmentation are very great and must be met by a comprehensive scheme of consolidation. It is, therefore, advocated that if two-thirds of the Khatedars, dealing more than half of the village lands, apply, Government, should undertake compulsorily to restrip the scattered fields of the village. This compulsory restripping is to be executed on two principles, (1) of "Economic Unit" and (2) of "Original Ownership". Regarding the merits of these two principles the Baroda Committee observes.

"In the first the value of each holding is ascertained, then the original boundaries are removed, roads are marked out, lands required for public purposes are set apart, and the rest of the land is parcelled out into new plots. Each of these new plots must be of such a size as, having regard to the local conditions of soil, tillage etc. to form an economic field, i.e., a parcel of land necessary to keep fully engaged and support one family. These new plots may be sold by auction among the old occupants, restriction being placed on purchase so as to prevent a large number of cultivators from being ousted.

The purchase money may then be divided in a certain proportion among the original owners of pieces, a portion being reserved for expenses, in which Government would also contribute a share. Another mode would be to acquire all the land of the village then to sell it in newly constituted plots by auction as is done by City Improvement Trusts or by Government when laying out new roads in Cities or when extending a town. But we do not recommend its adoption in the improvement of agricultural land. It may result in land speculation and the small holders may be ousted in such numbers as to cause a real hardship.

"According to the second method when the restripping has been decided, a list of Khatedars and their holdings is made and the latter are valued at their market price by Panchas. Then the land is redistributed and each Khatedar is given new land in proportion to his original holding and as far as possible of the same value, difference to be adjusted by cash payment. In this method no Khatedar is deprived of his land. Each is accommodated and in the place of his original small and scattered fields gets one plot of almost their aggregate size. It is only a few people whose holding may be very small and whom it would not be expedient to keep on as farmers, that may have to lose their small pieces. But they too would benefit as they would get their full value in money."

The Baroda Committee prefers the second method because:

> *"It takes as its starting principle, that nobody (except perhaps a few, holding plots of insignificant sizes) is going to be driven off the land. It will give even the smallest man, chance to better his condition. Each land holder receives a new compact piece of land proportionate to the value of his old small and scattered field. In this way the previous sub-divisions together with their attendant evils totally disappear."*

Regarding consolidation Prof. H. S. Jevons says:

> *"The principles which should guide the choice of a method of carrying out the re-organization of villages on the lines above described are the following. In the first place compulsion should be avoided as far as possible and the principle adopted that no charge should be imposed upon any area unless the owners of more than one-half of that area desire the change.*
>
> *Should this condition be satisfied for an area......... it would seem expedient that legal power should be taken to compel the minority to accept the redistribution of holdings under the supervision of Government. In the second place............the expense of the operation should be kept as low as possible.........In the third place considerable elasticity should be permitted in the methods of carrying through the re-organization in the different places during the first few years, as the whole undertaking would be in an experimental stage so that different methods might be tried, and the best be ultimately selected for a permanent set of regulations. Fourthly, the possible necessity for a considerable change of the existing tenancy law in the re-organised villages must be faced............ For the sake of completeness I may add as a fifth principle the obvious condition that redistribution of land must be made upon the most equitable basis possible, and that liberal compensation should be given to those, if any, who may be excluded from a former cultivating ownership."*

As for procedure in the compulsory consolidation of holdings both Prof. Jevons and the Baroda Committee propose the appointment of Commissioners to hear applications for consolidation and to carry it out, leaving to any objector the right to petition the Court to stay the proceedings in case he felt that an injustice was being done to him.

The problem of perpetuating such a consolidated holding will next demand the care of the legislator. It is accepted without question by many that the law of inheritance that prevails among the Hindus and the Mohomedans is responsible for the sub-division of land. On the death of a Hindu or a Mahomedan his heirs are entitled without let or hindrance to equal shares in the property of the deceased. Now a consolidated holding subject to the operation of such a law of inheritance will certainly not endure for long. It will be the task of Sisyphus over again if, after consolidation, the law of inheritance were to remain unaltered. But how is the existing law of inheritance to be changed? If it is not to be the law of equal sub-division shall we have the law of primogeniture.

The Baroda Committee thanks that

> *"It is not necessary that it should be introduced. All that it wanted is, that there should not be sub-divisions of land beyond a certain limit, which may be fixed for the sake of good agriculture. There is no objection to a holding being sub-divided, so long as by so doing each of the parts does not become less than the limit fixed for the sub-division of land. But when a holding reaches a stage to render further sub-division uneconomic, the other members of the family may not be allowed to force further sub-division of the holding. Instead of being sub-divided, it may be either cultivated in common or be given to one of the members of the family as a whole, and that member made to pay amounts equal to the value of their shares as compensation to the other members."*

The principle of not dividing immovable property among the heirs, when division would result in inconveniently small shares, but of giving to the highest bidder among the sharers or in case none of them is willing to have it, to outside bidders, and dividing the money realized in proportion to the recognized shares, has been accepted in the Indian Partition Act, No. 4 of 1893, section 2 of which runs thus:

> *"Whenever in any suit for partition, in which, if instituted prior to the commencement of this Act, a decree for partition might have been made, it appears to the Court that, by reason of the nature of the property to which the suit relates, or of the number of the shareholders therein or of any other special circumstance, a division of the property cannot reasonably or conveniently be made and that a sale of the property and distribution of proceeds would be more beneficial for all the share-holders, the Court may, if it thinks fit, on the request of any such share-holder interested individually or collectively to the extent of one moiety or upwards direct a sale of the property and a distribution of the proceeds."*

Granting the advisability of thus changing the law of inheritance it only requires to amend the Civil Procedure Code so as to make it obligatory on the Courts to refuse partition whenever it would reduce a field beyond the economic limit fixed in advance. Another method of dealing with the problem is advocated by the Hon. Mr. G. F. Keatinge, Director of Agriculture, Bombay Presidency. In the Statement of Objects and Reasons appended to his draft bill he says:

> "................ *The object of this bill is to enable such landowners as may wish to do so to check: the further sub-division of their lands and to enable them, when it is otherwise possible, to effect a permanent consolidation of their holdings; and also to enable the executive government to secure the same results in respect of unoccupied land. The legislation proposed is purely enabling, and it will be operative in the case of any holding only upon the expressed wish of any person possessing an interest in that holding.*
>
> ". *The scheme embodied in this bill for securing these objects is briefly as follows. In order to be constituted an economic holding a plot of land must be entered as such in a register prescribed by rules. If the land is occupied, it will rest with some person having an interest in the land to make an application to the Collector to have the land registered as an economic holding........... Unless the Collector considers that there are sufficient grounds for rejecting the application, he holds a careful enquiry in which he follows a procedure similar to that prescribed in the Land Acquisition Act, 1894. If the proceedings show that all persons interested agree, the land is registered. Land vesting absolutely in Government may be registered without inquiry.*

The holding must in any case be registered in one name only, and the act of registration annuls all the interest of all other persons, except the registered owner, in the holding. Thereafter the owner cannot divide the plot but must so long as he owns it, keep it entire. He may sell, mortgage or otherwise dispose of it as an entire unit, but not dispose of part of it or do anything that might result in splitting up the holding. On the death of the holder, if he has not disposed of the land by will it will devolve upon a single heir. If the provisions of the bill are contravened (for instance if the holder mortgages a part of his Holding and the mortgagee obtains a decree for possession), the Collector is empowered to send a certificate to the Court, and the Court will set aside its decree or order.

The Collector may also evict a person in wrongful possession. When a plot has been once constituted an economic holding, the registration cannot be cancelled except with the consent of the Collector; the grounds on which cancellation will be allowed, will be laid down by rule and it is proposed that it shall be permitted chiefly in cases where economic considerations indicate that it is expedient."

Summing up this discussion of the two issues of consolidation, it must be said that the problem has not been viewed as a whole by all its advocates. The Baroda Committee alone endeavours to consolidate as well as to preserve the consolidated holding. Prof. Jevons makes no provision to conserve the results of consolidation. Mr. Keatinge does not deal with consolidation at all. He is concerned only with the prevention of further fragmentation. But fragmentation, there will be in a holding even after it is entered as an economic holding. By his measure he will only succeed in preserving the holdings, as they will be found at the time of registration, i.e., he will not allow them to be reduced in size. But they will be small and scattered all the same. Mr. Keatinge, notwithstanding his legislation, leaves the situation more or less as it exists. Real consolidation is, however, aimed at by Prof. Jevons and the Baroda Committee. The principles they advocate for the purpose are almost the same; and so are their procedures for carrying it out.

As for the preservation of consolidated holdings Mr. Keatinge as well as the Baroda Committee establish the one-man rule of succession. The Baroda Committee would adopt this rule only when division of land would result in uneconomic holdings and then too would compel the successor to buy off the claims of the other dispossessed heirs. Mr. Keatinge would let the dispossessed heirs off without compensation.

A more serious criticism against these projects of consolidation consists in the fact they have failed to recognize that a consolidated holding must be an enlarged holding as well. If it is said that Indian agiculture suffers from small and scattered holdings we must not only consolidate, but also enlarge them. It must be borne in mind that consolidation may obviate the evils of scattered holdings, but it will not obviate the evils of small holdings unless the consolidated holding is an economic, i.e. an enlarged holding. The Committee as well as Mr. Keatinge have entirely lost sight of this aspect of the question. Prof. Jevons, alone of the advocates, keeps it constantly before his mind that consolidation must bring about in its train the enlargement of holdings.

Enlargement

Granted that enlargement of holdings is as important as their consolidation we will now turn to the discussion of regulating their size. It is desired by all interested in our agriculture that our holdings should be economic holdings. We would have been more thankful to the inventors of this new, precise and scientific terminology had they given us a precise and scientific definition of an economic holding. On the other hand, it is believed that a large holding is somehow an economic holding. It may be said that even Prof. Jevons has fallen a victim to this notion.

For when discussing what the size of a holding should be he dogmatically states that in the consolidated village the mode should be between 29 and 30 acres. But why should the mode be at this point and not at 100 or say 200? We might imagine Pro. Jevons to reply that his model point is placed at that particular acreage because it would produce enough for a farmer to sustain a higher standard of living. Raising the general standard of living in India is the one string on which Prof. Jevons harps even to weariness throughout his pamphlet. The error underlying this doctrine we shall consider later on. It is enough to say that he does not give any sound economic reason for his model farm.

The case with the Baroda Committee is much worse, Prof. Jevons at least sticks to one definition of an ideal economic holding; but the Report of the Baroda Committee suffers from a plurality of definitions. While cementing on the size of an average holding in the state as is summarized in the above table, it should be noted that the Committee, though it desired consolidation, was perfectly satisfied with the existing size of the holding as is clear, from the following:

> *" If the average holding of a Khatedar was a compact field of those figures, the situation would be an ideal one and would not leave much to be desired."*

But absent-minded as it were, the Committee, without any searching analysis of the question it was appointed to investigate and report upon, lays down that:

> *" An ideal economic holding would consist of 30 to 50 bighas of fair land in one block with at least one good irrigation well and a house situated in the holding."*

If the size of existing holdings is an ideal size why should they be enlarged? To this, the Committee gives no answer. But this is not all. The Committee does not even adhere to the quantitative limit it has already set down to its ideal economic holding. When it comes to discuss the project of re-arrangement of the scattered fields of the village on the principle of " Economic unit " it presents a third ideal of an economic holding. To realize this ideal it says :

> *"Each of these new plots must be of such a size, as having regard to the local conditions of soil, tillage, etc., to form an Economic field, i.e., a parcel of land necessary to keep fully engaged and support one family."*

Thus with perfect equanimity (1) the Baroda Committee holds, not too fast, to three notions of an ideal economic holding. No wonder then that the Report of the Committee is a model of confused reasoning though it is a valuable repository of facts bearing on the subject.

According to the Hon. Mr. Keatinge an economic holding is:— " a holding which allows a man chance of producing sufficient to support himself and his family in reasonable comfort, after paying his necessary expenses." His definition of an economic holding will be accepted, we may expect, by the Baroda Committee; for, it does not differ from its own, given above as third in order.

It is plain that these definitions including that of Professor Jevons view an economic holding from the standpoint of consumption rather than of production. In this lies their error; for consumption is not the correct standard by which to judge the economic character of a holding. It would be perverse accounting to condemn a farm as not paying because its total output does not support the family of the farmer though as a pro-rata return for each of his investments it is the highest. The family of a farmer can only be looked upon in the light of so much labour corps at his disposal. It may well be that some portion of this labour corps is superfluous, though it has to be supported merely in obedience to social custom as is the case in India. But if our social custom compels a farmer to support some of his family members even when he cannot effectively make any use of them on his farm we must be careful not to find fault with the produce of the farm because it does not suffice to provide for the workers as well as the dependants that may happen to compose the family.

The adoption of such an accounting system will declare many enterprises as failures when they will be the most successful. There can be no true economic relation between the family of the entrepreneur and the total out-turn of his farm or industry. True economic relation can subsist only between the total out-turn and the investments. If the total out-turn pays for all the investments no producer in his senses will ever contemplate closing his industry because the total out-turn does not support his family.

This is evident; for though production is for the purpose of consumption it is for the consumption only of those who help to produce. It follows, then, that if the relation between out-turn and investments is a true economic relation, we can only speak of a farm as economic, i.e., paying in the sense of production and not in the sense of consumption. Any definition, therefore, that leans on consumption mistakes the nature of an economic holding which is essentially an enterprise in production.

Before going further, we must clear the ground by a few preliminary remarks to facilitate the understanding of an economic holding from the standpoint of production.

It must be premised at the outset that in a competitive society the daily transactions of its members, as consumers or producers, are controlled by a price regime. It is production, then, in a price regime that we have to analyse here for our purpose. In the main the modern process of production is captained by the entrepreneur, is guided and supervised by him and is worked out through him. All employers of labour or hirers of instrumental goods are entrepreneurs. His computations run, as they must, in a pecuniary society, in terms of price-outlay as over against price-product, no matter whether the prospective product is offered for sale or not. The entrepreneur, in producing for gain, apportions his outlays in varieties of investments, These investments, the same as factors of production or costs to the entrepreneur, have by tradition been confined to wages (labour) profits, rent (land) and interest (capital). Industrial facts do not support this classification. There are many other factors, it is contended, which as they share in the distributive process must have functioned in the productive process, in some way immediate or remote.

But it is immaterial how many factors there are and whether they differ in kind or degree. What is important for the purpose of production is the process of combining them. This combination of necessary factors of production is governed by a law called the law of proportion. It lays down that disadvantage is bound to attend upon a wrong proportion among the various factors of production employed in a concern. Enlarged, the principle means that as a certain volume of one factor has the capacity to work only with a certain volume of another to give maximum efficiency to both, an excess or defect in the volume of one in comparison with those of the others will tell on the total output by curtailing the efficiency of all. Having regard then to this interdependence of factors, an economically efficient combination of them compels the producer if he were to vary the one to vary the rest correspondingly. Neither can it be otherwise.

For, the chief object of an efficient production consists in making every factor in the concern contribute its highest; and it can do that only when it can co-operate with its fellow of the required capacity. Thus, there is an ideal of proportions that ought to subsist among the various factors combined, though the ideal will vary with the changes in the proportions.

These proportions it must be acknowledged are affected by the principle of substitution chiefly brought into play owing to variations in the prices of the factors. But this principle of substitution is too limited in its application to invalidate the law of proportion which is the law governing all economic production and which no producer can hope to ignore with impunity. Bringing to bear the above remarks regarding production on the definition of an economic holding, we can postulate that if agriculture is to be treated as an economic enterprise, then, by itself, there could be no such thing as a large or a small holding.

To a farmer a holding is too small or too large for the other factors of production at his disposal necessary for carrying on the cultivation of his holding as an economic enterprise. Mere size of land is empty of all economic connotation. Consequently, it cannot possibly be the language of economic science to say that a large holding is economic while a smallholding is uneconomic. It is the right or wrong proportion of other factors of production to a unit of land that renders the latter economic or uneconomic. Thus a small farm may be economic as well as a large farm; for, economic or uneconomic does not depend upon the size of land but upon the due proportion among all the factors including land.

An economic holding, therefore, if it is not to be a hollow concept, consists in a combination of land, capital and labour, etc., in a proportion such that the pro rata contribution of each in conjunction with the rest is the highest. In other words to create an economic holding it will not do for a farmer solely to manipulate his piece of land. He must also have the other instruments of production required for the efficient cultivation of his holding and must maintain a due proportion of all the factors for, without it, there can be no efficient production. If his equipment shrinks, his holding must also shrink. If his equipment augments, his holding must also augment. The point is that his equipment and his holding must not be out of proportion to each other. They must be in proportion and must vary, if need be, in proportion.

The line of argument followed above is not without support from actual practice. It is happy from an economist's point of view, to find it recognized and adopted in India itself by the fathers of the Survey and Settlement System in the Bombay Presidency. The famous Joint Report (1840) contains an illuminating discussion of the problem. The question before the officers deputed to introduce the Survey System in the Deccan was how to levy the assessment. Was it to be a field assessment or an assessment to be placed on the whole lands of the village or on the entire holdings of individuals or co-parceners, whether proprietors or occupants. That after much deliberation the system of field assessment was finally adopted is known to many. But as the reasons that led to its adoption are known only to a few the following explanatory parts from the Joint report will be found to be both interesting and instructive:

That one manifest advantage of breaking up the assessment of a village into portions so minute [as indicated by a survey number] is the facility it affords to the cultivators of contracting or enlarging his farm from year to year, according to the fluctuating amount of agricultural capital at their disposal which is of incalculable importance to farmers possessed of so limited resources as those of the cultivating classes throughout India. The loss of a few bullocks by disease or other causes may quite incapacitate a ryot from cultivating profitably the extent of land he had previously in village and, without the privilege of contracting his farm, and consequent liabilities on occasion of such loss, his ruin would be very shortly consummated."

Judging in the light of this conclusion the proposal to regulate the size of holdings appears ill considered and futile. For as Prof. Richard T. Ely observes: Obviously no simple answer can be given to the question [as to what should be the size of a farm]. The value of land or the rent it will bring is perhaps the most important factor........................In addition to the factor of rent the amount of capital that he can command, the kind of farming in which he is most skilled, the character of the labour he can secure, the proximity of markets, and the adequacy of transportation facilities, all must be taken into account by the farmer in determining how large a farm he will attempt to manage and how intensively he will farm it.

This question is primarily one of private profit which the individual must decide far himself, but the legislator and the scientific student can be of some assistance in helping to develop that most difficult branch of commercial science—farm accounting—and in keeping the farmer alive to those charges in prices, wages, and transportation charges to which the farm organization must adjust itself."

To those who have the temerity to fix the size of a holding Prof. Ely's well-considered opinion will bring home that in spite of good intentions their vicarious mission will end in disaster; for none but the cultivator can decide what should be the size of his holding. They would do well to remember that the size of his holdings will vary in time.

Consequent to the changes in his equipment with which he has to adjust the size of his farm, at one point in time he will decide in favour of a small, as at another he will decide in favour of a large holding. He would therefore be a poor economist who would legally fix the size of the holding which in the interest of economic production must be left to vary when variation is demanded. By fixing the size of a holding he can only make it a large holding but not an economic holding. For an economic holding is not a matter of the size of land alone but is a matter of the adjustment of a piece of land to the necessary equipment for its efficient cultivation.

Critique of the Remedies

The proposal to enlarge the existing holdings which is brought forward as a cure to the ills of our agriculture can be entertained only if it is shown that farms have diminished in size while the agricultural stock has increased in amount. Facts regarding the size of farms have already been recorded. It only remains to see if the agricultural stock has increased. Mr. K. L. Datta in his exhaustive survey says:

Most of the Indian witnesses, whom we examined, appeared to be under the belief that there has been a decrease in the supply of agricultural products, owing to the inefficient tillage of land. It was said that land is not now cultivated as carefully and efficiently as before, owing to the scarcity and dearness of plough, cattle and labour. In order to effect, a saving in the cost of cultivation, cultivators do not also plough their lands as often as they did before, and manuring and weeding, as also the amount of irrigating where wells are used for the purpose, have all been reduced."

As regards the scarcity of plough cattle... (the) figures bear testimony to the deplorable effects of famine, the inevitable result of which has always been to reduce the number of cattle, though the deficiency is generally made good in a few years if otherwise favourable. The number of plough cattle in the latest year (1908-09) included in the statement was lower than in the commencement (1893-94), in some of the circles namely Assam, Bundelkhund, Agra Provinces—North and West, Gujarat, Deccan, Berar, Madras-North and Madras-West. Although great reliance cannot be placed on these statistics, they can be accepted as showing that in some areas at any rate there has been a dearth of plough cattle."

Regarding the existence of capital Mr. Elliot James says:

> *"The ryots have a keen eye to the results of a good system of farming as exhibited on model farms, but they cannot derive much good from the knowledge though they may take it in and thoroughly understand that superior tillage and proper manuring mean a greater outturn in crops. "*

The farmer knows, says the same author, that his agricultural equipment is inefficient and antiquated but he cannot substitute better ones in its place for:

> *"A superior class of cattle and superior farm implements mean to him so much outlay of what he has not—Money."*

Similar facts for the Baroda State have been collected in another connection by Mr. M. B. Nanavati, Director of Commerce and Indus. But unfortunately he did not bring his knowledge of such facts to bear upon the conclusions of the Committee for the consolidation of holdings in the State of which he was also a member, apparently thinking that the size of a holding bore no relation to the instruments of production. He bemoans that:

> *"The farmers are not fully equipped with draught-cattle. They have today (1913) 8,34,901 bullocks, etc., for use on farms, that is one pair for 36 bighas of land. On an average a pair of good bullocks can cultivate 25 bighas of land. But the present breed has much deteriorated and one pair is supposed to cultivate 20 bighas at the most, while the present actual averages comes to about 36 bighas. Under the circumstances it is not likely that ploughing can be deep. It must be like scratching the surface. The small cultivators do not possess any draught-cattle or at the most a single one and cultivate land in co-operation with their friends similarly situated. As for farm implements there are 1,54,364 ploughs in the State, i.e., one for two Khatedars. It must be understood here that the number of cultivators and tenants is much more than three lakhs-Every one of them needs full equipment. Therefore actually the average must be much smaller than shown above."*

In fact the equipment for agricultural production in the State has considerably deteriorated since 1898 as shown by the table below :

Year	*Plough*	*Carts*	*Plough Cattle*	*Other Domestics*
1898	1,75,989	—	4,15,089	5,70,517
1910	1,51,664	68,946	3,34,801	5,09,416

Given, this state of affairs can we not say with more propriety that not only the existing equipment is inadequate for the enlarged holdings but that the existing holdings, small as they are, are too big for the available instruments of production other than land? Facts such as these interpreted in the light of our theory force upon us the conclusion that the existing holdings are uneconomic, not, however, in the sense that they are too small but that they are too large. Shall we therefore argue that the existing holdings should be further reduced in size with a view to render them economic in the sense in which we have used the term? Unwary readers might suppose that this is the only logical and inevitable conclusion— a conclusion that is in strange contrast with the main trend of opinion in) this country. Contrary, no doubt, the conclusion is; but it is by no means inevitable.

For, from our premises we can with perfect logic and even with more cogency argue for increase in agricultural stock and implements which in turn will necessitate enlarged holdings which will be economic holdings as well. Consequently the remedy for the ills of agriculture in India does not lie primarily in the matter of enlarging holdings but in the matter of increasing capital and capital goods. That capital arises from saving and that saving is possible where there is surplus is a commonplace of political economy.

Does our agriculture—the main stay of our population—-give us any surplus? We agree with the answer which is unanimously in the negative. We also approve of the remedies that are advocated for turning the deficit economy into a surplus economy, namely by enlarging and consolidating the holdings. What we demur to is the method of realizing this object. For we most strongly hold that the evil of small holdings in India is not fundamental but is derived from the parent evil of the mal-adjustment in her social economy. Consequently if we wish to effect a permanent cure we must go to the parent malady.

But before doing that we will show how we suffer by a bad social economy. It has become a tried statement that India is largely an agricultural country. But what is scarcely known is that notwithstanding the vastness of land under tillage, so little land is cultivated in proportion to her population.

Mulhall's figures for the year 1895 clearly demonstrate the point. Acres per inhabitant in 1895:

Great Britain	Ireland	France	Germany	Russia	Austria	Italy	Spain And Portugal	USA	India
0.91	3.30	2.30	1.70	5.60	2.05	1.75	2.90	8.90	1.0

That since 1895 the situation, however, has gone from bad to worse figures eloquently bear out :

	1881	1891	1901	1911
Bengal	1.5	0.8	1.12	
Bombay	1.7	1.6	1.41	1.3
Madras	1.3	0.3	.68	.79
Assam		0.5	.78	.85
Punjab	1.2	1.3	1.05	1.11
Oudh	0.81	0.7}		.75
N. W. P.	-	0.8}	.73	
Burmah	-	1.5	1	1.09
Central P	1.67	2.4	1.8	1.79
B. India	1.04	1.0	0.86	0.88

Now, what does this extraordinary phenomenon mean? A large agricultural population with the lowest proportion of land in actual cultivation means that a large part of the agricultural population is superfluous and idle. How much idle labour there is on, Indian farms it is not possible to know accurately. Sir James Caird who was the first to notice the existence of this idle labour estimated in 1884 that,

> *"A square mile of land in England cultivated highly gives employment to 50 persons, in the proportion 25 men, young and old, and 25 women and boys. If four times that number, or 200, were allowed for each square mile of cultivated land in India, it would take up only one-third of the population."*

Out of the total population of 254 millions in 1881 nearly two-thirds were returned as agricultural. Allowing, as per estimate, one-third to be taken up, we can safely say that a population of equal magnitude was lying idle instead of performing any sort of productive labour. With the increasing ruralization of India and a continually decreasing proportion of land under cultivation, the volume of idle labour must have increased to an enormous extent. The economic effects of this idle labour are twofold. Firstly, it adds to the tremendous amount of pressure that our agricultural population exerts on land. A quantitative statement will serve to bring home to our mind how high the pressure is:

Mean density per square mile in 1911:

	Oudh and N.W.P.	Bengal	Madras	Punjab	Bombay	Assam	Berar and C.P	Coorg	British Burma
of Total Area of Cultivated Area	427 829	551 1162	291 785	177 453	145 444	115 766	122 360	111 792	53 575

Such high pressure of population on land is probably unknown in any other part of the world. The effect of it is, of course, obvious.

Notwithstanding what others have said, this enormous pressure is the chief cause of the subdivision of land. It is the failure to grasp the working of this pressure on land that makes the law of inheritance such a great grievance. To say that the law of inheritance causes sub-division of land is to give a false view by inverting the real situation. The mere existence of the law cannot be complained of as a grievance. The grievance consists in the fact that it is invoked. But why is it invoked even when it is injurious? Simply because it is profitable. There is nothing strange in this. When farming is the only occupation, to get a small piece of land is better than to have none. Thus the grievance lies in the circumstances which put a premium on these small pieces of land.

The premium, is no doubt, due to the large population depending solely on agriculture to eke out its living. Naturally a population that has little else lo prefer to agriculture will try lo invoke every possible cause to get a piece of land however small. It is not therefore the law of inheritance that is the evil, but it is the high pressure on land which brings it into operation.

People cultivate the small piece not because their standard of living is low as Prof. Jevons seems to think but because it is the only profitable thing for them to do at present. If they had something more profitable to do they would never prefer the small piece. It is therefore easy to understand how the universal prevalence of the small farms or petit culture is due to this enormous pressure on land.

In spite of the vehement struggle that our agricultural population maintains in trying to engage itself productively as cultivators of a farm however small, it is true that judged by the standard of Sir James Caird a large portion of it is bound to remain idle. Idle labour and idle capital differ in a very important particular.

Capital exists, but labour lives. That is to say capital when idle does not earn, but does not also consume much to keep itself. But labour, earning or not consumes in order to live. Idle labour is, therefore, a calamity; for if it cannot live by production as it should, it will live by predation as it must. This idle labour has been the canker of India gnawing at its vitals. Instead of contributing to our national dividend it is eating up what little there is of it.

Thus the depression of our national dividend is another important effect of this idle labour. The income of a society as of an individual proceeds (1) from the efforts made, and (2) from possessions used. It may be safely asserted that the aggregate income of any individual or society must be derived either from the proceeds of the current labour or from productive possession already acquired. All that society can have today it must acquire today or must take out of its past product. Judging by this criterion a large portion of our society makes very little current effort; nor does it have any very extensive possessions from which to derive its sustenance.

No doubt then that our economic organization is conspicuous by want of capital. Capital is but crystallized surplus; and surplus depends upon the proceeds of effort. But where there is no effort there is no earning, no surplus, and no capital.

We have thus shown how our bad social economy is responsible for the ills of our agriculture. We have also proved how our entire dependence on agriculture leads to small and scattered farms. How a large portion of our population which our agriculture cannot productively employ is obliged to remain idle has been made clear. We have also shown how the existence of this idle labour makes ours a country without capital. This being our analysis of the problem, it will be easy to see why the remedies for consolidation and enlargement under the existing social economy arc bound to fail.

Those who look on small holdings as the fundamental evil naturally advocate their enlargement. This, however, is a faulty political economy and as Thomas Arnold once said "a faulty political economy is the fruitful parent of crime". Apart from the fact that merely to enlarge the holding is not to make it economic, this project of artificial enlargement is fraught with many social ills. The future in the shape of an army of landless and dispossessed men that it is bound to give rise to is neither cheerful from the individual, nor agreeable from the national, point of view. But even if we enlarged the existing holdings and procured enough capital and capital goods to make them economic, we will not only be not advocating the proper remedy but will end in aggravating the evils by adding to our stock of idle labour; for capitalistic agriculture will not need as many hands as are now required by our present day methods of cultivation.

But if enlargement is not possible, can we not have consolidation? It can be shown that under the existing social economy even consolidation is not possible. The remedy for preventing sub-division and fragmentation of consolidated holdings cannot be expected to bring real relief. Instead it will only serve to be a legal eyewash. This becomes easy of comprehension if we realize at the start what the one man rule of succession means in actual practice. For this we shall have to note the changes it will introduce in the survey records. At present according to the Bombay Land Revenue Code Chapter I, Section 3, clause (6).

"Survey Number" means a portion of land of which the area and other particulars are separately entered, under an indicative number in the survey records of the village, town or city in which it is situated, and includes a recognized share of a survey number. Again by clause (7).

"Recognized share of a survey number" means a sub-division of a survey number separately assessed and registered. After the adoption of the one man rule of succession a survey number will be made to cover a piece of land which will be of the size fixed for an ideal economic holding. Secondly, it will be necessary to refuse separate registration to any sub-division of such a survey number; i.e., in order that a piece of land should be registered with a separate and a distinct survey number it must not be below the economic limit. Then too this survey number covering a piece of land large enough to be styled economic will be registered in the name of one person. This is precisely what will happen if we put into practice the project of the Baroda Committee. Mr. Keatinge instead of having one survey number covering a large and compact holding will have in the name of one person many survey numbers covering a unit of land composed of small and scattered fields.

Abandoning Mr. Keatinge's scheme as serving no practical purpose the one man rule of succession lo a consolidated holding means in practice refusal to recognize legally a piece of land if it were below a certain size. Now this refusal to recognize smaller pieces of land, it is claimed, will prevent the sub-division of a consolidated holding: Sub-division of land may be due to many causes the operation of which is rendered economic or uneconomic by the nature of the occasion which evokes it. Not to allow sub-division on any ground, as does Mr. Keatinge, is to cause a serious depreciation of the value of land. But if sub-division is needed as when the stock has depleted, not to grant it is to create an uneconomic situation—a result just opposite of what is intended to be achieved, apart from this to prevent sub-division legally is not to prevent it actually, if necessitated by the weight of economic circumstances.

Granting the pressure of population on land and the scanty agricultural equipment—evils to which the authors of consolidation and enlargement have paid no attention—we must look forward to the sub-division of holdings. If we legislate in the face of this inevitable tendency and refuse to record on our survey roll holdings below a certain limit required for a separate survey number we will not only fail to cure what we must know we cannot, at least by this means, but will help to create a register that will be false to the true situation.

This being our criticism of the means for preventing sub-division and fragmentation it will not take us long to state our view as regards the project of consolidation. Consolidation and its conservation are so intimately connected that the one cannot be thought of without the other. Now if we cannot conserve a consolidated holding, is it worth our while to consolidate, however feasible the project may be? This work of Sysiphus will not fail to fall to our lot unless we make effective changes in our social economy. As the evils of this surplus and idle labour which will be added on to by the consolidation and enlargement of holdings are likely to outweigh their advantages, the proposals do not find much favour at the hands of Prof. Gilbert Slater.

As against Prof. Slater we hold that the evils are avoidable and it is because we are anxious to avoid them that we wish to advocate different remedies for bringing about the enlargement of holdings. Consequently, we maintain that our efforts should be primarily directed towards this idle labour.

If we succeed in sponging off this labour in non-agricultural channels of production we will at one stroke lessen the pressure and destroy the premium that at present weighs heavily on land in India. Besides, this labour when productively employed will cease to live by predation as it does today, and will not only earn its keep but will give us surplus: and more surplus is more capital. In short, strange though it may seem, industrialization of India is the soundest remedy for the agricultural problems of India. The cumulative effects of industralization, namely, a lessening pressure and an increasing amount of capital and capital goods will forcibly create the economic necessity of enlarging the holding. Not only this, but industralization by destroying the premium on land will give rise to few occasions for its sub-division and fragmentation. Industrialization is a natural and powerful remedy and is to be preferred to such ill-conceived projects as we have considered above. By legislation we will get a sham economic holding at the cost of many social ills. But by industrialization a large economic holding will force itself upon us as a pure gain.

Our remedy for the enlargement as for the consolidation of holdings as well as the preservation of consolidated holdings reduces itself to this: We prefer to cure agriculture by the reflex effects of industrialization. Lest this might be deemed visionary we proceed to give evidence in support of our view. How agriculture improves by the reflex effects of industrialization has been studied in the United States in the year 1883. We shall quote in extenso the summary given by the London Times:

> *"The statistician of the Agricultural Department of the United States has shown in a recent report that the value of farm lands decreases in exact proportion as the ratio of agriculture to other industries increases. That is, where all the labour is devoted to agriculture, the land is worth less than where only half of the people are farm labourers; and where only a quarter of them are so engaged the farms and their product are still more valuable. It is, in fact, proved by statistics that diversified industries are of the greatest value to a State, and that the presence of a manufactory near a farm increases the value of the farm and its crops.*
>
> *It is further established that, dividing the United States into four sections or classes, with reference to the ratio of agricultural workers to the whole population, and putting those States having less than 30 per cent, of agriculture and of agricultural labourers in the first class, all having over 30 and less than 50 in the second, those between 50 and 70 in the third, and those having 70 or more in the fourth, the value of farms is in inverse ratio to the agricultural population, and that where as in the purely agricultural section, the fourth class, the value of farms per acre is only $ 5.28, in the next class it is $ 13.03, in the third $ 22.21, and in manufacturing districts $ 40.91. This shows an enormous advantage for a mixed district.*

> *Yet not only is the land more valuable the production per acre is greater, and the wages paid to farm hands larger. Manufactures and varied industries thus not only benefit the manufacturers, but are of equal benefit and advantage to the fanners as well."*

This will show that ours is a proven remedy. It can be laid down without fear of challenge that industrialization will foster the enlargement of holdings and that it will be the most effective barrier against sub-division and fragmentation. Agreeing in this, it may be observed that industrialization will not be a sufficient remedy for consolidation. That it will require direct remedies may be true. But it is also true that industrialization, though it may not bring about consolidation, will facilitate consolidation. It is an incontrovertible truth that so long as there is the premium on land consolidation will not be easy, no matter on how equitable principles it is proposed to be carried out. Is it a small service if industrialization lessens the premium as it inevitably must? Certainly not. Consideration of another aspect of consolidation as well points to the same conclusion:

> *That industrialization must precede consolidation. It should never be forgotten that unless we have constructed an effective barrier against the future sub-division and fragmentation of a consolidated holding it is idle to lay out plans for consolidation. Such a barrier can only be found in industrialization; for it alone can reduce the extreme pressure which, as we have shown, causes sub-division of land. Thus if small and scattered holdings are the ills from which our agriculture is suffering to cure it of them is undeniably to industrialize.*

Chapter 8

Entrepreneurship as an Economic Force in Rural Development

The Importance of Rural Enterpreneurship

The Entrepreneurship Concept

In order to understand the role played by entrepreneurs in developing an economy it is first important to understand the concept of entrepreneurship. (Petrin, 1992) While choosing a definition for entrepreneurship most appropriate to the rural area context, it is important to bear in mind the skills that will be needed to improve the quality of life for individuals, and to sustain a healthy economy and environment. Taking this into consideration, one can find that each of the traditional definitions has its own weakness. Hence, the most appropriate definition is a combination of three, wherein, entrepreneurship can be defined as

> *A force that mobilizes other resources to meet unmet market demand; the ability to create and build something from practically nothing. (Timmons, 1989) the process of creating value by pulling together a unique package of resources to exploit an opportunity.*

Determinants of Entrepreneurship

The need to understand the determinants of entrepreneurship is as important as understanding its concept. The origins and determinants of entrepreneurship span a wide spectrum of theories and explanations. However, it is generally accepted that policy measures can influence the level of entrepreneurship.

Research analyzing the determinants of the decision to start a new business has so far stressed the role of individual characteristics, access to capital and institutions. Social factors may also play a role in the decision to become an entrepreneur because, as shown by a growing literature, social interactions affect the payoffs from a variety of economic decisions. (Giannetti and Simonov, 2003).

A widely accepted view is the following: while personal characteristics as well as social aspects clearly play some role, entrepreneurship and entrepreneurs can also be developed through conscious action.(Petrin,1994)

Development of entrepreneurs and of entrepreneurship can be stimulated through a set of supporting institutions and through deliberate innovative action which stimulates changes and fully supports capable individuals or groups. Therefore, policies and programs designed specifically for entrepreneurship promotion can greatly affect the supply of entrepreneurs and thus indirectly represent an important source of entrepreneurship.

This view has important implications for entrepreneurship development in rural areas. If currently entrepreneurial activities in a given rural area are not thriving it does not mean that entrepreneurship is something inherently alien to rural areas. While this feeling could have some legacy due to the slower pace of changes occurring in rural areas compared to urban ones, proper action can make a lot of difference with respect to entrepreneurial behavior of people living in rural areas.

Role Played by Entrepreneurs in Rural Development

Entrepreneurial activity and new firm formation are unquestionably considered engines of economic growth and innovation. As such, they are among the ultimate determinants of the large regional differences in economic performance. The importance of new firm formation for growth has been recognized since Schumpeter (1934). According to the Global Entrepreneurship Monitor Report (2000), about 70 percent of an area's economic performance is dependent upon how entrepreneurial the area's economy is.

Entrepreneurial orientation in rural areas is based on stimulating local entrepreneurial talent and subsequent growth of indigenous companies. This in turn would create jobs and add economic value to a region, and at the same time it will keep scarce resources within the community.

According to Petrin (1992), to accelerate economic development in rural areas, it is necessary to build up the critical mass of first generation entrepreneurs.

Studies conducted by Economic Commission for Latin America and Caribbean (ECLAC) and Food and Agricultural Organization (FAO) in the Latin American and Caribbean region have indicated that rural enterprises can be an important modernizing agent for small agriculture. Governments have supported this process by creating incentives for agro-industry to invest in such regions.

This has not only been in developing countries, but it has also been a clear policy of the European Union (EU) which channels a large part of the total common budget to develop the backward and poor regions of Europe.

Lyson (1995) echoes the prospects of small-enterprise framework as a possible rural development strategy for economically disadvantaged communities and provides this description of the nature of small-scale flexibly specialized firms: "First, these businesses would provide products for local consumption that are not readily available in the mass market.. Second, small-scale technically sophisticated enterprises would be able to fill the niche markets in the national economy that are too small for mass producers. Third, small, craft-based, flexibly specialized enterprises can alter production quickly to exploit changing market conditions."

According to a study conducted in the United States it has been found that rural poverty has become as intense as that found in the inner cities, and has stubbornly resisted a variety of attempts at mitigation through economic development policies. The latest strategy for addressing this problem is the encouragement of emerging "home-grown" enterprises in rural communities.

The expectation is that these new ventures-

a) will provide jobs or at least self-employment;

b) will remain in the areas where they were spawned as they grow;

c) and will export their goods and services outside the community, attracting much-needed income. (Lyons, 2002)

Gavian, et al (2002), in a study on the importance of SME development in rural employment in Egypt, have suggested that SMEs are traditionally thought of as well poised to respond to increased demand by creating jobs.

It is important to stress here that rural entrepreneurship in its substance does not differ from entrepreneurship in urban areas. Entrepreneurship in rural areas is finding a unique blend of resources, either inside or outside of agriculture.

The economic goals of an entrepreneur and the social goals of rural development are more strongly interlinked than in urban areas. For this reason entrepreneurship in rural areas is usually community based, has strong extended family linkages and a relatively large impact on a rural community.

Policy Implications for Rural Entrepreneurship

Studies have shown that SMEs in rural areas in the UK (particularly remote rural areas) have outperformed their urban counterparts in terms of employment growth. Behind each of the success stories of rural entrepreneurship there is usually some sort of institutional support. Lu Rongsen(1998), in a study in Western Sichuan highlights the important factors responsible for the rapid development of enterprises in the area. These include-uniqueness of the products in so far as they are based on mountain-specific, local natural resources; development of infrastructure; strong and integrated policy support from government; and a well-planned marketing strategy and link-up with larger companies and organizations for marketing nation-wide and abroad.

According to Petrin (1994), the creation of such an environment starts at the national level with the foundation policies for macro-economic stability and for well-defined property rights as well as international orientation. The policies and programs targeted specifically to the development of entrepreneurship do not differ much with respect to location. In order to realize their entrepreneurial ideas or to grow and sustain in business, they all need access to capital, labor, markets and good management skills. What differs is the availability of markets for other inputs.

The inputs into an entrepreneurial process-capital, management, technology, buildings, communications and transportation infrastructure, distribution channels and skilled labor, tend to be easier to find in urban areas. Professional advice is also hard to come by. Consequently, entrepreneurial behavior, which is essentially the ability to spot unconventional market opportunities, is most lacking in those rural areas where it is most needed i.e., where the scarcity of 'these other inputs' is the highest.

Rural entrepreneurship is more likely to flourish in those rural areas where the two approaches to rural development, the 'bottom up' and the 'top down', complement each other. The 'top down' approach gains effectiveness when it is tailored to the local environment that it intends to support.

The second prerequisite for the success of rural entrepreneurship, the 'bottom up' approach, is that, ownership of the initiative remains in the hands of members of the local community. The regional development agencies that fit both criteria can contribute much to rural development through entrepreneurship.

The National Spatial Strategy (NSS), the national planning framework for Ireland for the next 20 years (2002-2020), recognizes the importance of making the most of cities, towns and rural places to bring a better spread of opportunities and a better quality of life. It advocates the following features as appropriate rural enterprise policy elements:

1) The nature of the enterprise encouraged to locate in rural areas must be appropriate to those areas in economic, social and environmental terms, e.g., location of overly large enterprises in rural areas should properly be avoided;
2) Enterprise policies must be flexible to facilitate local circumstances rather than being rigid national ones;
3) Policy towards enterprise must involve features which go beyond the bounds of traditional enterprise policy, eg, in relation to social infrastructure to attract and retain the necessary workforce;
4) Policies in relation to enterprise in rural areas and in smaller towns should be seen as an integrated package. There must also be flexibility in relation to how smaller towns' enterprise functions are perceived. These vary depending on the nature of the area;
5) Policy towards rural enterprise should encompass all rural enterprise and not just traditionally grant-aidable manufacturing, i.e., in a rural context any rural enterprise is in principle equally desirable;
6) There is a need to focus on new rural enterprises other than tourism. There is a danger that an overly heavy burden in terms of expectations is being placed on the shoulders of rural tourism as the only viable alternative to farming;
7) There will need to be consistency and co-ordination regarding the choice of rural enterprise locations among the various bodies involved rather than each having its own unilaterally chosen list.

A study conducted by Smallbone and North (1997), reveals that firms that demonstrated the highest level of innovative behavior were growing in terms of sales and also generating employment, although it is important to stress that the relationship between innovation and growth is an inter-dependent and mutually reinforcing one, rather than a simple cause and effect relationship.

Piore and Sabel(1984), in their book, "The Second Industrial Divide", outline a policy framework for small business development, which states that economic development is more likely to succeed if it takes place within a political context, where local communities actively nurture and support small-scale, industrially diverse, flexibly specialized enterprises. Within this context, small business development is one component of a comprehensive economic development strategy comprising both large-scale, mass-production enterprises and small-scale, flexibly specialized production units.

Organization for Economic Cooperation and Development's (OECD) (1999) work on government policy for enterprise development advocates best practices in four broad areas related to SMEs. These practices are appropriate for both agro industries and other rural enterprises. Specifically, OECD advocates facilitating:

- Efficient and unbiased financial markets for SMEs;
- A suitable business environment for SMEs;
- Education, training and the capability of SMEs to compete; and
- Access to information, networking and the global marketplace for SMEs.

To summarize, Petrin (1994) maintains that policy implications for rural entrepreneurship development can be:

1) Sound national economic policy with respect to agriculture, including recognition of the vital contribution of entrepreneurship to rural economic development;
2) Policies and special programs for the development and channeling of entrepreneurial talent;
3) Entrepreneurial thinking about rural development, not only by farmers but also by everyone and every rural development organization;

Problems Faced by Rural Entrepreneurs

According to a study by Tarling et al (1993), in rural UK, a number of potential weaknesses in the competitiveness of rural firms, in particular certain aspects of the operating environment and the firms' responses to them have become evident. In this respect, Vaessen and Keeble, (1995), also point out that the external environment in the more remote rural areas particularly, presents challenges for SMEs, which they need to adapt to if they are to survive and grow. These include the limited scale and scope of local market opportunities which make it necessary for firms to be particularly active in developing non-local markets if they are to grow.

Another aspect of the external environment in these remote rural areas is the labor market, in which relatively low wage levels in comparison with urban areas combined with qualitative characteristics of the rural labor force (e.g. loyalty to the firm) reduce the incentive for firms to invest in labor saving process innovations, particularly in the more craft-based sectors.

A further characteristic of the remote rural business environment is the lack of a local industrial and service milieu which means that there are fewer opportunities for firms to subcontract out locally than in an urban context. From the point of view of innovation specifically, the low density of the business population results in a small number of potential collaborating firms locally, as well as more sparsely distributed research and development, educational institutions and business support providers compared with some other types of location.

This raises questions about the extent to which the characteristics of remote rural environments constrain innovative activity in SMEs; another issue which concerns the implications of these features for the type of policy response that is likely to be effective. The National Spatial Strategy of Ireland (2002) also indicates the following issues as key constraints in the development of rural enterprise in Ireland:

a) The issue of transport and accessibility in general, and of remoteness.
b) The low skill base of many rural areas emerged as important.
c) The lack of sufficient funding continues to be perceived as a major constraint.
d) The low enterprise base in many rural areas is seen as a key issue, and there is a general feeling of being caught in a vicious circle where an existing lack of enterprise contributes to a low degree of enterprise potential.
e) The absence of facilities and services both for enterprises and for their workforces emerged as important.
f) Competition from larger centers was seen as crucial in a number of areas. In some cases it was suggested that the proximity to such areas can to some extent be a disadvantage from this perspective.

g) Issues of planning and zoning were seen in some areas as significant as was the fact that it may be more difficult to obtain planning permission for certain types of enterprises in rural areas.

Smallbone and North (1997) in a study in rural England have identified the specific areas of support needs that rural SMEs require: marketing, process innovation, improving access to specialized training and assistance in the use of internet. Gavian,et al (2002), in a study in Egypt point out that by continuing to provide supply-side solutions without expanding the market for their products and services is highly unlikely to generate employment through expansion.

Framework for Encouraging Rural Entrepreneurship

Jay Kayne with the Kauffman Foundation created the following figure during the Second Minnesota Academy working session in Rochester, Minnesota. This figure provides a general framework for encouraging rural entrepreneurship. In the final analysis, this framework provides the critical questions necessary to assessing the cntrepreneurial opportunity in any rural place or state.

Rural Enterprise Development in Swaziland

The smallest country in Southern Africa, Swaziland is classified as a middle-income economy, but the distribution of income is unequal and nearly half the population lives below the national poverty line. Its population is largely rural and the structure of the economy has shifted over the years from an agricultural base to manufacturing. According to the National Report to the World Summit on Sustainable development (2002), despite enjoying relative peace and prosperity and good economic performance over past decades in terms of growth and fiscal stability, Swaziland now faces a number of challenges. These include maintaining macro-economic stability while providing better education and health, governance issues and gender inequality, high unemployment rates, the need to attract new investment and adapt to a changing trade environment.

The African Development Bank (1999) states that one of the main constraints in Swaziland's economic development is a relatively low industrial resource base including the shortage of indigenous entrepreneurs. Over 70% of Swaziland's population lives in villages, it makes it all the more necessary to make an earnest attempt to create an environment and supporting policies which will aid in the development of rural entrepreneurs. An assessment of growth potentials of Swaziland show that the major potential sources of growth are in the agricultural sector, including agro-industrial activities, as well as in tourism and mining. The country's ecological conditions are ideal for growing a wide range of crops and diversifying commercial and traditional agriculture into high value horticultural crops, which have linkages with agro-industrial activities. Given Swaziland's pleasant and varied landscape, tourism prospects are extremely buoyant and as yet under-exploited. There are also several opportunities for growth in the mineral sector. Keeping in mind the various guidelines which have been discussed above, the dawn of Swaziland's rural economy lies in the hands of its entrepreneurs.

However there are a few factors which are acting as constraints to rural development. The National Report to the World Summit on Sustainable development (2002) asserts that these include inadequate access to development finance for investment; inadequate access to markets; and, there is currently no agricultural policy that would harmonize marketing, supply of inputs and extension services. A further constraint is the lack of knowledge and self-confidence of the people in rural communities due to limited experience and lack of education. People who have never been given a chance often have difficulties responding when all too rare opportunities arise. The country's government also has to accept that lack of knowledge and self-confidence is a very serious constraint to development and should come up with a national training plan and support infrastructure.

Another constraint faced by the country is to move away from the notion of poverty alleviation to wealth creation. Poverty alleviation focuses on the negative aspects of life and the process is often paternalistic – "we will alleviate your poverty". Wealth creation on the other hand leads to a focus on business and ownership, a proven combination in today's world.

To sum up in the words of Narayan J.P., (1962), "Rural industrialization would have to be based on two factors: (a) Local resources, both human and material, (b) and local needs. 'Local' does not mean a single village; it might mean a village, a group of villages, a block or a district-depending on the nature of the industry and the technology used. There are to be no pre-conceived limitations or inhibitions of a doctrinaire or sentimental type in regard to such matters as the use of power and technology.

The aim and total long-term effect of rural industrialization should be to convert the present lopsided purely agricultural communities into balanced agro-industrial communities."

Worldwide the last three decades have seen major shifts in rural economies. Rural enterprises are important generators of employment and economic growth internationally. It is important to stress that rural entrepreneurship in its substance does not differ from entrepreneurship in urban areas. Entrepreneurship in rural areas is finding a unique blend of resources, either inside or outside of agriculture.

This chapter has attempted to understand the role played by rural enterprises in economic development and how governing bodies can help to foster its growth. The promotion of entrepreneurship and the understanding where entrepreneurship comes from is as equally important as understanding the concept of entrepreneurship.

The environment which is considered most favorable for their growth forms the basis for the development of policies for entrepreneurship development. Policy implications for rural entrepreneurship development can be summarized as:

(a) Sound national economic policy with respect to agriculture, including recognition of the vital contribution of entrepreneurship to rural economic development;

(b) Policies and special programs for the development and channeling of entrepreneurial talent;

(c) Entrepreneurial thinking about rural development, not only by farmers but also by everyone and every rural development organization;

d) And institutions supporting the development of rural entrepreneurship as well as strategic development alliances.

However, despite their phenomenal growth rural enterprises have common systemic constraints to their development. Governments and donors can help to address these constraints by facilitating efficient and unbiased financial markets; a suitable business environment; education, training, and competitive capacity; and access to information, networks and the global market place. To conclude the paper has also pointed out the importance of rural enterprises in the development of the economy of Swaziland.

Integrated Wasteland Development Programme

India shares 16% of the world population, while its land is only 2% of the total geographical area of the world. Naturally, the pressure on the land is often beyond its carrying capacity. Therefore, the productive lands, especially the farmlands in the India are in the constant process of various degrees of degradation and are fast turning into wastelands. At present, approximately 68.35 million hectare area of the land is lying as wastelands in India. Out of these lands, approximately 50% lands are such non-forest lands, which can be made fertile again if treated properly. It was unprotected non-forestlands, which suffered the maximum degradation mainly due to the tremendous biotic pressure on it. In the last 50 years it is India's lush green village forests and woodlots have been deforested to the maximum. It is precisely to restore this ecological imbalance by developing the degraded non-forest wastelands, Govt. of India had created the Department of Wasteland Development during July,1992 under the Ministry of Rural Development, which has been subsequently reorganized and renamed Department of Land Resources, with a broader mandate.

A Degraded Wasteland

National Wasteland Development Board was established in 1985 under the Ministry of Forests and Environment mainly to tackle the problem of degradation of lands, restoration of ecology and to meet the growing demands of fuel wood and fodder at the national level. During the Seventh Five Year Plan, the strategy adopted by the National Wasteland Development Board emphasised more on tree planting activities rather than Community Participation for wasteland development, In the year 1992, the new Department under the Ministry Of Rural Development (now Ministry of Rural Areas and Employment) was created and the National Wasteland Development Board was placed under it. The Board was reconstituted in August 1992 and was made responsible for mainly development of wastelands in non forest areas in totality by involving local people at every stage of development. It aims at creating a scenario where the Government acts as a facilitator and the people at the grass root level become the real executioner of the programme.

Major programme implemented for improving the productivity of waste & degraded lands keeping in view the poverty, backwardness, gender & equity is Integrated Wasteland Development Programme.

Integrated Wasteland Development Programme (IWDP)

The Problem

The degradation of environment in the fragile Indian sub-topical eco-system is basically attributed to:-

- Increasing biotic pressure
- Absence of adequate investments and appropriate management practices.

- High rate of Population growth and high incidence poverty in rural areas.
- Over-exploitation of National Resources.
- The break-down of traditional institutions for managing common property resources and failure of new institutions to fill the vacuum.
- Faulty land use practices.

Consequences

- Soil Erosion & Land Degradation
- Depletion of natural resources
- Lower productivity
- Ground Water Depletion
- Shortage of Drinking Water
- Reduction in Species Diversity
- Increase in the extent of Wastelands.

The Strategy

Development of wastelands mainly in non-forest areas aimed at checking land degradation, putting such wastelands of the country to SUSTAINABLE use & increasing bio-mass availability especially that of fuelwood, fodder, fruits, fiber & small timber. Government of India is taking up this colossal task through its INTEGRATED WASTELAND DEVELOPMENT PROJECT SCHEME (IWDP) by revitalizing & reviving village level institutions & enlisting people's participation. It is people's own programme which aims at giving them actual decision making powers in terms of project implementation & fund disbursal.

It is one programme which is making sincere efforts towards the empowerment of the people so that a sense of collective responsibility can be evolved among them. The new guidelines for watershed development provides a paradigm shift in the traditional approach where the role of the Government is changed from that of governance to facilitation.

The institutional arrangements envisaged in the Guidelines can be seen as a true reflections of the Agenda 21 where the sustainability comes through the involvement of people & the local bodies. The approach of watershed development in a holistic manner automatically strikes a prudent balance between environmental concerns & developmental aspirations. The efforts being made under the guidelines can be termed as sincere & honest as here the survival of life itself is at stake with the watershed development rather than the quality of life itself as compared to similar situations in the developed countries. In fact, the effective community control has been an integral part of the Indian social fabric which was fragmented by the colonial rule.

This programme is an effort towards its restoration & a small step in the achievement of this goal which might turn into a big leap with the support from the people.

Villagers During a Meeting on Watershed

What is Watershed Development ?

Watershed development refers to the conservation regeneration and the judicious use of all the resources – natural (like land, water plants, animals) and human – within the watershed area. Watershed Management tries to bring about the best possible balance in the environment between natural resources on the one side and man and animals on the other. Since it is the man which is primarily responsible for degradation of environment, regeneration and conservation can only be possible by promoting awakening and participation among the people who inhabit the watersheds.

Why Watershed Development ?

Man and his environment are interdependent. The changes in the environment directly affect the lives of the people depending on it. A degraded environment means a degraded quality of life of the people. Environmental degradation can be tackled effectively through the holistic development of the watershed. A watershed provides a natural geo-hydrological unit for planning any developmental initiative.

What are Wastelands ?

Degraded land which can be brought under vegetative cover, with reasonable effort, and which is currently under utilised and land which is deteriorating for lack of appropriate water and soil management or on account of natural causes.

The programme does not focus solely on uncultivable wastelands because such lands are:

- Too degraded to recoupe in isolation
- Cost of treatment is very expensive and economical
- Such lands are too remote from the village through protection of vegetative measures and participation of local people is not possible.

Why People's Participation?

There is a close relationship between the environment and the community living within that area as the community derives sustenance from it. Increase in biotic pressure leads to over-exploitation and degradation of natural resources. Paucity of resources also leads to internal conflict giving opportunity to others to exploit the situation. It is thus necessary for people to realize the intrinsic relationship between population, poverty and degraded environment they live in. the poor, in the developing country like India are left with no option but to degrade their own environment for their very own survival. Still, it is only they who can restore the health to environment thus ruined, outside actors can only facilitate but never substitute for stake holders. Hence, there can be no sustainable natural resources management unless it involves all inhabitants of the affected areas in an active manner and development plans are formulated and executed by them.

Integration of indigenous technologies with development is vital. Rural people's knowledge and the technological advancements are complimentary in their strengths and weaknesses. Combined together, they may achieve what neither would achieve along. Low cost locally available technology with suitable intervention by latest advancements yields best solution. It is clear that the watershed development cannot be done in isolation. It is a natural entity and may contain different types of lands namely, forest lands, community lands, government lands or private lands. These lands can be treated on "ridge to valley" approach. A land lying in a valley cannot be improved if the land at upper reaches is not treated. Treatment of land in a scattered manner will not lead to wasteland development. Mere treatment of land is not enough. Land and people cannot and should not be viewed in isolation. So the best possible strategy would be treating the land by empowering the people who live in it. It is watershed plus approach which takes care of holistic development.

Therefore, the entire watershed community is to be involved for the integrated development of watershed and the assets created in such an effort are to also be maintained through the people of the watershed community in order to ensure sustainability. People's participation also ensure conservation and development of Common Property Resources. Besides when people decide what they have to do their stake in development become more pronounced leading to their intense involvement. This involvement in decision making is the key to success which brings sustainable development. Hence people's participation is the approach for the purpose.

Chapter 9

Gram Sabha and Village Level Governance

Gram Kosh Support Changed the Life of Vulnerable Women

Dharmi Paharni of Telo Tok, the widow belongs to vulnerable family. Her livelihood was depend on partial cultivation and casual labour and somehow managing their daily subsistence. DHARMI has three children. Being the head of the family she had to face various social and economic problems.

All their valuable assets including land alienated during the treatment her diseased husband died earlier. She become the member of SHG in the year 2007.But in the initial stage of SHG groups was not capable to meet the all requirements of the group members. Further in 2008she received a loan from Telo Gram Sabha Kosh and used this amount in cultivation.

After continuous cultivation since last three years this year she recovered her land from the Mahajans and also returned the loan to gram sabha with interest. The day has come when she got success and now this family is happy released from hunger and is doing well. The children are also admitted in mission school for formal education.

Restoration of Slienated Land and Liberation Families from Money Lenders Exploitation: In the area it was obvious that 68% land of primitive Paharia tribal community and 36 – 46% Santhal tribal community alienated due to the exploitative and exorbitant interest rate of local money lender specially at the time of disease treatment, agricultural season, hunger stressed conditions and other emergency situation.

Through the initiatives by the gram sabha with the support of Gram Kosh 199 families restored their land, which have been with the local exploiters group since 2 – 3 decades. Through the similar painstaking initiatives of the Gram Sabha, 324 families became free form the clutches of exploitators group.

Resolution of disputes and grievances: Strengthening of Gram Sabha and its prompt initiatives protected more than 422 families from falling into legal complications and wastage of money during legal procedures. Most of the civil disputes cropping up in the village have been resolving during the village Gram Sabha. Litigation related to land conflict on the social issues, distribution of shares families level disputes are the core disputes resulting during the meetings.

Revitalization of Bungalow Level Governance System

In the DAMIN-E-KOH area of Santhal Pargana there are 22 Damin bunglows, which have been acting as top decision makers and justicial system for tribals residing in the area. It is also mentioned in Santhal Pargana Tenancy Act (1949 Spl.) and supported by PESA 1996 under provision of Vth schedule of Indian constitution.

The top traditional leaders such as Sardar, Nayab were the chiefs among primitive Paharia tribes and Parganait and Chakladar had been the powerful top leaders among the Santhal tribes in the Damin-I-Koh area.

As indicated earlier, powers related to Revenue, Administration and Justice had been exercising by these traditional leaders since the execution of SPT Act (1949 Spl.) . Most of the bungalow level chiefs either died or somewhere alive, most of them are in isolation. Now through various capacity building programmes and meetings with community, the traditional governance system of 69 bungalows have been revitalized in the area.

These governance structures together with the gram sabha initiated their role as senior leadership to solve the larger disputes and issues cropping up in the area.

Besides its initiatives in different activities of the 11 bungalow level federation, 5 bungalow level federation i.e. Manjhi Baisi Samiti, Boarijore and Ato Baisi Swasasan Samiti Telo Dak Bunglow Lahanti Baisi Rajabhita, Manjhi Pargana Sardar Mahasabha, Dharmapur, Manjhi Lahanti Baisi, Maheshpur, Pakur and Even Manjhi Baisi, Devinagar, Maheshpur block Pakur and Manjhi Pargana Sardar Mahasabha, Kunjbona. Gram Sabha Sangh, Chandna, Sunderpahari,

Godda. initiated to control over NTFP to form the cooperatives. This year four cooperatives have been emerged as BACHAW DAHAR, Boarijore and CHANDO BABA SAHYOG SAMITI, Telo dak bunglow, Lahanti Baisi Cooperative, Rajabhita, Manjhi Pargana Sardar Cooperative Kunjbona.

Now more than 224 quintals of NTFP and grain is deposited to control over resources and negotiate the local market. More than 1142families got benefit from these cooperatives and secured the values of their products. As these families have been protected from the exploitative markets and prices

Village Democracy and Civil Society

India is a country of kaleidoscopic diversity. Its ancient and rich civilisation has been shaped by various combinations of geopolitical, economic, social and demographic forces, which have produced a rich variety of institutions, social movements, traditions, systems of belief and practices. This Sovereign Socialist Secular Democratic Republic of one billion people living in 25 States and 7 Union Territories (UTs) is governed by a Constitution which is federal in structure with unitary features.

The traditional social norms coexist with liberal democratic institutions in an uneasy, ambiguous, and contradictory relationship. One of the major limitations of Indian parliamentary democracy has been its centralised nature. Centralised democracy in India has failed and the pendulum has moved towards participatory and responsive government. Indians want a participatory and responsive democratic government. PRIA's study on Civil Society in the New Millennium discerns a shared dream among the citizens of India. Indians want peace, education and socio-economic security. They want to act and act responsibly, in the interest of shaping such a society and governance.

About 75 % of India's population live in more than half a million villages. Village communities and their organisations have been in existence in India for centuries. In olden days, Panchayats were functional institutions of grassroots governance in almost every village. The village Panchayat or elected council had large powers, both executive and judicial.

However, the autonomy of Panchayats gradually disappeared owing to many reasons. But the recent Constitution (73rd Amendment) Act, 1992, which came into force on 24th April 1993, was meant to provide constitutional sanction to Panchayats and establish democracy at grassroots level as it is at the State level or national level. Except for 3 north-eastern States (having tribal councils) and two urban UTs, all the States/UTs coming under the purview of this Act have amended their Panchayat Acts in conformity with the Central Act.

The Gram Sabha or village assembly has been envisaged as the foundation of the Panchayati Raj system. There are three tiers of Panchayats (PRIs) at village (Gram Panchayat – GP), intermediate (Panchayat Samiti – PS) and district (Zilla Parishad – ZP) levels. The States having a population not exceeding 2 million have not constituted the Panchayat at intermediate level. As a result, at present, there are about 3.4 million representatives of Panchayats at all levels comprising 3,198,554 at the village level, 151,412 at the intermediate level and 15,935 at the district level.

These members represent 227,698 Gram Panchayats, about 6,000 Panchayat Samitis and about 500 Zilla Parishads. All the seats in a Panchayat at every level are filled by elections from the respective territorial constituencies. Not less than one-third of the total seats and offices of chairperson at each tier have been reserved for women. Reserved seats for weaker castes and tribes (SCs, STs and Backward – *Dalits)* have been provided at all levels in proportion to their population in the Panchayats.

To supervise, direct and control the regular and smooth elections to Panchayats, a State Election Commission has been constituted in every State and UT. The Act has ensured constitution of a State Finance Commission in every State/UT, each term of office being five years, to suggest measures to strengthen the finances of PRIs.

To promote bottom-up-planning, the District Planning Committee (DPC) in every district has bÿen accorded constitutional status. An indicative list of 29 items has been given in the Eleventh Schedule of the Constitution. Panchayats are expected to play an effective role in planning and implementation of works related to these 29 items. The spirit of the Constitution visualises Panchayats as institutions of self-governance. However, given the federal structure of our polity, most of the financial powers and authorities to be bestowed on Panchayats have been left at the discretion of the State Legislature concerned. Consequently, the powers and functions vested in PRIs vary from State to State.

The constitutionally decentralised institutions have come into being. But they can't be a solution to all ills of governance. The reality is quite harsh. The distribution of rural assets and powers is heavily skewed in India – the bottom 39 % of rural households (belonging to lower castes) own only 5 % of all assets, while the top 5 % own 46 %. The literacy level among SC/ST and women is quite low. A rigid patriarchal structure inhibits women's participation in public affairs. Moreover, the majority of the elected representatives are first timers with little or no prior knowledge of the functioning of PRIs.

Most of the women PRI members are illiterate and have to comply with social taboos and patriarchal values. They are 'expected' to be shy and submissive, resulting in weak articulation skills. So it is not easy for the rural weaker population to actively participate in the development process.

Also at local levels, the powers held by individuals have traditionally always exceeded the limits imposed by social institutions. If the people and their institutions are not active, the state and its institutions, whether in centralised or decentralised form, are forced to assume leadership of the people. Under these conditions, people's ability to exercise¢options in civil society interactions and within social hierarchies often becomes the requisite condition for local government to be responsive and accountable.

PRIA, Panchayats and Civil Society

PRIA is an international centre for learning and promotion of participation and democratic governance. It promotes people-centred development initiatives within the perspective of participatory research. PRIA promotes deeper understanding of the mosaic of civil society actors and enhances their contributions to democratic governance in society. It also contributes towards making Panchayati Raj and municipal bodies effective institutions of local self governance.

For the last five years, PRIA, the Network of Collaborating Regional Support Organisations (NCRSOs) and other partners of PRIA have undertaken strategic interventions to strengthen PRIs in 12 States. These States are Andhra Pradesh, Bihar, Gujarat, Haryana, Himachal Pradesh, Kerala, Madhya Pradüsh, Maharashtra, Orissa, Rajasthan, Tamil Nadu and Uttar Pradesh – accounting for about two-thirds of the rural population of India.

The rationale for these interventions is to enhance the potential for community participation and responsibility in development, that is, the people-centred and people-controlled development that PRIA has always promoted. The constitutional provisions provide new opportunities and possibilities for building up leadership from among women and Dalits (SC/ST). The PRIs can»also become the basis for further elaboration and strengthening of civil society in the country. A broad framework for strategic intervention was developed on the following principles:

1. The PRIs are to be viewed as institutions of local self-governance, not as mere implementors of centrally determined development programmes. Bottom-up planning, based on micro-planning, is to be the basis of self-governance. The PRIs should not be allowed to become the third tier of development administration.
2. The emphasis must be placed on active participation in decision making by women (and other weaker sections) with a view to enhancing their role, status and leadership in local self-governance.
3. Interventions in strengthening PRIs should focus on building, promoting and empowering new leadership by women, SC/ST and Dalits.
4. The PRIs should assert their access to and control over natural and human resources as well as other development resources available with the State and the national government.
5. Strengthening PRIs will entail clarifying their roles, systems of governance, accountability, transparency and inter-linkages.

The said intervention is multi-sectoral. PRIA believes that only a strong, participatory, responsive and accountable government at local level can fulfil people's aspirations and their needs. The PRIs have to be supported by strong voluntary actions. The people's bodies like Gram Sabhas have to be strengthened.

There should be a healthy co-operation between community organisations and Panchayats. Finally, governmental policies should create an enabling environment for PRIs to act as vibrant and thriving institutions of local self-government.

Strengthening Voluntary Action and PRIs

One of the primary strategies of PRIA's work comprises capacity building. It entails direct strengthening of the capacities of citizens, citizens' organisations, voluntary development organisations, support organisations and networks and coalitions of such organisations. To promote democracy at local level, a variety of local civil society organisations have been involved in strengthening PRIs. In many areas, successful conscientisation, group building and promotion of local leadership among marginalized sections have already been achieved through the efforts of voluntary organisations and activists. As a result, these voluntary agencies (VAs) and activists have been enabled and mobilised to play a more direct role in the promotion and strengthening of PRIs. Therefore, building capacity and encouraging participation of such VAs and activists is an important strategic intervention.

PRIA began a programme of strengthening Panchayati Raj Institutions (PRIs) in collaboration with its partners in the Network of Collaborating Regional Support Organisations (NCRSOs) in mid-1995 in 9 States of the country. This Phase-I lasted two years, and built on the initial exploratory work undertaken by PRIA after the 73rd Constitutional Amendment mandated the Panchayati Raj Institutions as bodies of local self-governance. Phase-II of the programme was launched in September 1997 following a review of Phase-I. New strategies and broader partnership characterised this joint programme in Phase-II. It covered 12 States, nearly 1,500 Gram Panchayats, and more than 15,000 elected representatives, working with six Regional Support Organisations and other key partners.

PRIA's Strategic Review mandated a long term commitment towards strengthening local self-governance. A programmatic review was conducted during June-August 1999 to identify next steps in the elaboration of the programme for strengthening local self-governance. Discussions on the findings and recommendations of the review have since been carried out by PRIA and NCRSOs.

The review established the relevance of the mix of intervention strategies carried out in the programme during the past two years. The uneven development of Panchayati Raj Institutions in different states (arising largely out of the socio-political environment and civil society engagements) necessitates a more judicious and synergistic mix of these various interventions. The range of interventions available to strengthen Panchayati Raj Institutions as institutions of local self governance needs to be applied differently in different contexts and stages of development of Panchayati Raj Institutions.

Four broad categories of interventions are designed to respond to the programmatic priorities and strategies for strengthening PRIs. These categories are:

1. Promoting Public Ownership (Information Dissemination, Public Education, Linking Civil Society, and Accountability),
2. Building Capacity (Gram Sabha, Elected Representatives, New Leadership, Structural Functioning, Negotiating with Administration, and Networking),

3. Local Development (Micro-planning, Resource Use, Matching Funds, and Managing Services), and
4. Research and Advocacy (Monitoring Strategies, On-line Feedback, Policy Implementation, Policy Reform, Creating Enabling Environment and Knowledge Building).

In the following pages, we will discuss some of our experiences related to PRIs.

Strengthening People's Participation

In every village there is a people's body called Gram Sabha. The Gram Sabha is a body consisting of persons registered in the electoral roll at the village level. It is the only forum which provides opportunities to all the adult villagers to directly participate and suggest what can and needs to be done for their own village, and how. Only a strong Gram Sabha can ensure public regulation of authority. If not made accountable to the community, Gram Panchayats have a tendency to become *Sarpanch* (chairperson of GP) Panchayats. The Gram Sabha serves to keep Gram Panchayat accountable.

Gram Panchayats across the States have been constitutionally mandated to ensure that Gram Sabha meetings be held at least twice a year. But in reality, in most places, Gram Sabha meetings are held on paper only. Most of the GS members are unaware of their rights and responsibilities as GS members. Many of them can't distinguish between the GS and the GP of the village. It has been also found that villagers in general are not informed about GS meetings. Even if informed, women may not participate because of social customs. Lack of a common venue for meetings (and the distance to be travelled to attend GS meetings) where the GS is too large is also a barrier to people's participation in GS meetings.

VDCs, Local VA and Kehar Gram Panchayat

Kehar is a Gram Panchayat in Mandi district of the State of Hinachal Pradesh. PRIA initiated micro-planning in this Gram Panchayat with the help of RTDC, a local voluntary agency (VA). Being active in the area, RTDC has close linkages with community and ¨ommunity organisations of Kehar. This linkage facilitated the whole process smoothly. It also ensured that the process involved all the sections of Kehar Gram Sabha.

With the help of RTDC the Village Development Committees (VDCs) for each ward of the Gram Panchayat were constituted. These VDCs comprise 15-20 members from different groups of the Gram

Sabha. PRIA, RTDC, VDCs and Gram Panchayat have collaborated to influence the district government. The government has provided resources and the plan is being implemented. During the whole process, the GP and the civil society organisations acted in close affinity to strengthen each other.

Information dissemination to the people, and the process of bottom-up-planning or micro-planning are some of the most effective ways of strengthening participation by people in their own development. The local civil society organisations play a vital role in strengthening people's participation (in local governance) through these processes. They also help civil societies to strengthen their voice in people-centred people's development.

As per Article 243-G, Panchayats are constitutionally mandated to prepare plans for economic development and social justice. Thus every Panchayat has to prepare a plan taking into account local needs and local conditions. The whole process develops a framework of agreement within the Gram Sabha about development priorities. Villagers sit together to prioritise community problems, prepare a list of resources available and ask the Gram Panchayat to implement the plan. Since the plan is annual, it provides a rigorous framework for the Panchayat to be accountable to the Gram Sabha.

A plan facilitated by local organisations and local community groups like youth and women's groups, allows villagers to scrutinise and judge the performance of their GP. These organisations and the GS play a constructive role in augmenting Panchayat resources by enabling Panchayats to mobilise internal resources as well as to negotiate effectively with the government to provide resources to implement the village plans.

Collaboration with Community Groups

In every village there are a number of functional groups like Self Help Groups (SHG), Community Based Organisations (CBO) and Village Development Committees (VDC). Their interaction, co-operation and conflict with local bodies is an area of current debate in India. Besides statutory bodies like the GP and GS, there are a number of non-statutory participatory groups in almost every village. These groups may be of two types. One emerges from the community's own needs and initiative, that is, community-driven groups like Youth Groups, *Mahila Mandals* (Women's Groups) or even Caste Panchayat. Other types of groups are those which are created by external agencies/ projects/programmes, usually for a specified period. These groups possess specialised expertise and have a close linkage with their creators (external agencies). For example, the Government of India's project District Primary Education Programme (DPEP) has created Village Education Committees (VEC).

For effective collaboration between community organisations and PRIs, the GS should be made aware, active and strong. In every Gram Panchayat, there are sector-specific standing committees like a Health Committee, Education Committee, Social Justice Committee, etc. Each committee is headed by the Sarpanch or a member of the GP. An institutional mechanism may be developed so that these specialised organisations have close interaction with specialised standing committees of GPs. In this regard, project-based committees should be strengthened to be more effective, autonomous and participatory.

Linkages Between a GP and a Project-based VEC

Kaliram is a village in Kaithal block of Haryana. The Sarpanch of this GP, an educated man, is a member of the VEC. Both the Headmaster of the village primary school and the Sarpanch take the initiative in enhancing the enrolment of children in the school. The Sarpanch took the initiative to organise a competition for school-going children and also sponsored a Ma-Beti Mela (Mother-Daughter Fair), organised at the school. Both the events were successful in enhancing community participation in village education. The Sarpanch monitors the attendance of teachers and teachers are not resentful of this fact. They feel that this monitoring should be adopted in all schools.

However, in Khandalva village of the same block, there is no linkage between GP and VEC. The school is in very poor condition and the indifference of the GP also inhibits village participation in school affairs.

NGOs can play a very effective role in facilitating collaboration between community groups and the PRIs. However, our experiences in 9 States reveal that there is no structured institutional mechanism to build a relationship between these two types of bodies. Some policy changes are required in this regard.

Policy Advocacy

The public and policy environment for people's participation in governance is inadequate, if not downright hostile. Positive support from Union and State governments is required for genuine and functional devolution of financial resources and authorities to PRIs. It requires intense advocacy efforts to influence policy changes at Union and State levels. Policy advocacy entails influencing policies from the vantage point of enabling the participation and empowerment of the marginalised. It comprises systematic and ongoing monitoring of existing policies, their implementation and reform. PRIA promotes citizen advocacy, not just professional advocacy.

To advocate changes in government policy, in addition to public pressure, macro-level well-documented 'proofs of ground reality' become imperative. So, PRIA and NCRSOs are engaged in systematic documentation of different processes. The participatory research aiming at building the capacity of the people and CSOs are regularly undertaken. Simultaneously the findings of these studies are widely disseminated to create pressure (from different quarters) for required policy changes. The recent study on the Status of Functions and Finances of Panchayati Raj Institutions in India sensitised citizens, the media, NGOs, bureaucrats, ministers and political parties about the rather weak status of finances of PRIs.

A number of pro-Panchayat initiatives were taken by different governments. Even the Planning Commission of India, as admitted by its Deputy Chairman in a letter to PRIA, was influenced by this study to create a task force in the Commission to review rural development schemes of the government. PRIA in its role of contact point for a high-powered task force (sub-group) constituted by the Government of India, has made some concrete recommendations for strengthening of Gram Sabhas. These recommendations, when accepted by the government, will go a long way to strengthening local self-governance and consequently the civil society in India.

Lessons Learnt

India is the largest democracy in the world. It signifies, among other things, the aspirations of our people and the vision of our leaders. True democracy emphasises decentralisation of governance. The institutions of local self-governance should be strengthened to be participatory, responsive, transparent and accountable. For this citizens should be educated and people's bodies like Gram Sabhas must be strengthened to act as custodians of grassroots democracy. The capacities of PRI members should be enhanced through training and workshops. The government officials who are used to the top-down model need to be sensitised to the new realities of local self-governance.

The Panchayati Raj Institutions should be given control, responsibility and authority over all the resources lying in their geographical jurisdictions. They should be held accountable for local matters by their voters, the Gram Sabha. It must be ensured that women and *Dalits* participate actively and effectively in local self-governance. The State-led and other types of project committees should collaborate (not be played off as competitors) with PRIs, and PRIs should provide a space to these community organisations.

NGOs have played a very effective role in making people more and more conscious of their roles and rights. Through processes like micro-planning, special emphasis on weaker sections of the population, participatory research studies and advocacy, people's participation has been greatly enhanced in 'intervened' areas. However, sustained and more aggressive interventions are needed to deepen democratic local self-governance. Research and policy advocacy have to be promoted on an extensive and sustained basis to improve different aspects of local self-governance. And creative individual and collaborative efforts by civil society and the Government to strengthen local self-governance need to be scaled up.

Village Panchayats and the Governance in North-East India

Governance is defined as the manner in which power is exercised in the management of country's economic and social resources (The World Bank). UNDP viewed Governance as the exercise of political, economic and administrative authority in the management of a country's affairs at all levels. It comprises mechanisms, processes and institutions through which citizens and groups articulate their interests, exercise their legal rights, meet their obligations and mediate their differences.

Democracy derives its strength from the people and people need meaningful participation in local governance to make society vibrant and county prosperous and strong. Making Panchayat institutions of self-governance is the mandate of the constitution of India. The 73rd Constitution Amendment Act ushers in a new era of participation governance towards realizing Gandhiji's dream and his ideas of Gram Swaraj. Today, Panchayats are the bedrock of India's rural development and poverty alleviation efforts. It has the potential of building a progressive India in harmony with the felt needs and the aspirations of the people.

Historical Background

There were Panchayat republics in the Vedic age in ancient India. The Vedic *Sabha* and *Samiti* were not only elected bodies but also representative in character with full voting rights to women. These institutions could probe into the conduct of kings, the misdeeds of the ministers, the abuse of power by the powerful. An ancient Indian republic was a state where the strong were just and weak secure. The Vedic king was the protector of the people i.e., *Janaya* Along with that the self-governing institutions of ancient India ran parallel in the villages. They were the backbone of the true Indian democracy.

Between ancient, medieval and modern period, the growth of Panchayats had ups and downs. The famous Mayo's Resolution of 1870 gave impetus to the development of local institutions by enlarging their powers and responsibilities. In 1882 Lord Riponprovided democratic framework to these institutions. In 1907 the famous Royal Commission on Decentralization was established which gave a boost to the local – self government. There after, came a series of efforts in the form of committee, commission and Act. (The Govt. of India Act, 1911; the Govt. of India Act, 1935). However, the colonial rulers could not promote much to local self-government.

Post-Independence Period

Panchayats were included in Article 40 under the Directive Principles of the Constitution of India. Just after independence, Gandhiji urged that India's independence must begin at the bottom, so that the character of India's independence as conceived by the Congress was based on Village autonomy. The Post-independence phase of Panchayat Raj is marked with significant developments. In an attempt to usher in socio – economic and cultural transformation in the country side, in 1952, the Government of India launched a comprehensive Community Development Programme encompassing almost all activities of rural development.

However, the Programme could not make much headway in fulfilling the dreams of the rural masses. In order to examine the causes for its failure, the govt. of India constituted a high power study team in 1957, headed by Balwant Rai Mehta, a member of Parliament. The team observed that the failure of the Community Development Programme was due to the conspicuous absence of people's participation. In order to secure people's participation, the team suggested that "a set of institutional arrangements would have to be created. This resulted in the creation of a 'three tier' system of Panchayati Raj Institution to organize and manage the rural development programmes. Thus began a new experiment in the sphere of rural development through the participation of people. By 1959, all the states, had passed Panchayat Acts and by mid 1990s Panchayats had reached all the parts of the country. The framework of new institutional arrangement comprised "Village Panchayat" at the base,, "Panchayat Samities" at the middle and "Zilla Parishad" at the apex level.

But the interest and the support for Panchayat did not last long. The apathy towards Panchayat started growing. The central government headed by then Prime Minister of India, Morarji Desai appointed another committee under the Chairmanship of Sri Ashok Mehta in 1977, to report on the status of Panchayati Raj institutions and sugest measures for their revitalization.

The committee recommended constitutional status to the Panchayats, participation of political parties in Panchayat elections, adoption of a two– tier system at District and Mandal level and establishment of a finance body like Panchayati Raj Finance Corporation for providing credit to the Panchayats.

The Gram Sabha has been removed from Panchayati Raj Institutions (PRIs) in India. The removal of Gram Sabha has distanced the people at the grass–root level from the PRIs and within a short period the entire PRI became inactive and moribund in almost all states. In order to reinvigorate and revitalize Panchayats, the govt. of India had again appointed G.V.K. Rao committee (1985) and L.M Shingvi committee (1986).

Both the committees recommended, inter–alia, the following:

i). To grant constitutional status to the Panchayats;

ii). Devolution of financial resources to the PRIs;

iii). Conversion of PRIs from two – tier to three-tier by reintroducing Gram Sabha in the structure.

On the recommendation of the G.V.K. Rao (1985) and L.M Shingri (1986) committees, the Rajiv Gandhi Government in 1989 introduced a Bill for amending the constitution for giving constitutional status to Panchayats, But he failed to pass through the Bill. It was P.V Narashimha Rao Government who could amend the constitution in 1992 by introducing 73rd Amendment to the constitution alongwith the Nagarpalika 74th Amendment Act.

Thus, the Panchayati Raj institution became a constitutional machinery for rural administration in India. The tribal dominated states under 5th and 6th schedules of the constitution were, however, given option either to introduce Panchayati Raj institution or to continue with their traditional self-government institutions. All the states of India including 5th and 6th schedule states except Jammu & Kashmir, Nagaland, Meghalaya and Mizoram amended their Panchayati Raj Act to accommodate the provision of the 73rd Amendment Act.

The North –East India consists of seven states of Indian Union, viz. Assam. Arunachal Pradesh, Manipur, Meghalaya, Mizoram, Nagland and Tripura covering 8 Percent of the total geographical area and 3.78 percent of the total population of the country.

A large part of the North – East India is governed by the fifth and sixth schedules of the constitution of India. The Panchatyats (Extension to the schedule areas) Act, 1996 extends the 73rd Amendment: to the fifth schedule areas. Three states viz. Mizoram, Nagaland and Meghalaya, which are covered by the sixth schedule are exempted from the purview of the 73rd Amendment. The sixth schedule envisages establishment of Autonomous district councils.

These councils have been given legislative, administrative and Judicial powers under the sixth schedule. No law of the centre or the state in respect of the legislative powers conferred on the Autonomous District Councils could be extended to those areas without their prior approval. The district councils are also empowered to constitute Village councils and also Village courts. While the Autonomous District Councils have the advantage of legislative powers which the PRIs do not have, the Autonomous District Councils do not make provision for reservation for women, several important powers such as social forestry management which have been provided by the 73rd Amendment are attached in the PRIs.

Grass Root Governance in Assam

Historically Assam had a mosaic of tribal and non-tribal institutions. It was principally the system prevailing under the Ahoms which provided the background to the evolution of Panchayati Raj institutions in the state.

British Period

The promulgation of the Assam Local Self-Government Act, 1915 brought about a change of approach. The act provided for the establishment of the Village Panchayat, for the first time on a formal and legal basis. It also provided for an elective non-official majority in the Panchayat and for the election of non-Officials as Chairpersons and Vice-chairpersons. The act delegated powers and functions to the Village authorities relating to Village sanitation, village works, etc. In 1926 another act was passed as a Panchayat act because of the failure of the Panchayat scheme under the 1915 act. The functions of the Village authority under the act of 1926 were listed as water supply, medical relief and sanitation. The outcome of the act of 1926 was that some Village authorities were found to exist only on paper, and out of those that functioned, a sizeable number turned out to be ineffective for want of suitable machinery and necessary resources. Thus, despite formal establishment, Panchayat institutions under the British proved to be a dismal failure.

Post Independence Period

In the post independence period, Assam was one of the pioneering states to introduce Panchayati Raj by enacting Assam Panchayati Raj Act, 1948. It provided for the division of rural Assam into Panchayat areas, with each area consisting of a number of villages and each village having a primary Panchayat. All adult residents of a primary Panchayat area were made voters. The act provided that primary Panchayats would have executive bodies. This was a notable improvement on the earlier position. By 1959, however, of the total 742 rural Panchayats that were to be constituted under this act, only 422 (with 2,657 primary Panchayats) could be established.

On the recommendation of Balwant Rai Mehta committee Report, the Panchayati Rai system was introduced in the country and Assam was one of the states which framed a new Panchayati Raj Act, 1959, replacing the earlier Act, and a three-tier Panchayati system consisting of the Gram Panchayat at the Village level, Anchalic Panchayat at the intermediate level (co-terminus with the CD block) and Mahkuma Parishad at the Taluka or Sub-divisional level were constituted. The Assam Panchayati Raj Act covered the plain districts of the state and the Hill Autonomous Districts and villages located in the tea garden areas were excluded from the purview of the Act. With the introduction of the new act, the then existing local boards were abolished.

The act of 1959, amended in 1964, was repealed after the adoption of the Assam Panchayati Raj Act, 1972. Through this Act, the PR system in Assam was reverted back to the two–tier system, the Goan Panchayat (GP) at the village level with the population size ranging from 15,000-20,000 and Mahkum Parishad (MP) at the apex level. Due to the increase in the size of the Goan Panchayat, the number of GPs was reduced to 714 and the number of MPs was 32. The act also brought under its coverage the villages located in the Tea-garden areas. The state government once again made amendments to the earlier Panchayati Raj Act and introduced a new Act in 1986 replacing the

1972 Act. The new Act became operative with effect from 5th September 1990 only. With this new act the state again reverted to a three–tier set up – Goan Panchayat with 6000 – 10,000 Population size; Anchalik Panchayat (at the block level) and Mahkuma Parishad at the sub-divisional level. In February 1992, the first elections under the act of 1986 were held. For the earlier elections, the electoral rolls of the Assam Legislative assembly had served as the voters list for Goan Panchayat and Mahkuma Parsihads.

Due to various reasons, most importantly, the controversy over an acceptable electoral roll in the wake of the movement against the presence of foreign nationals in Assam, Panchayat elections had been stalled for more than a decade.

Present Position

As a sequel to the 73rd Amendment, the Assam Government enacted the Panchayat Act,1994 which covers almost all the features of the 73rd Amendment. The PR system continues to be the three-tier with a modification i,e, in place of Mahkuma Parishad there shall be Zilla Parishad at the District level. The reservation for women was increased from 30 % (as per the 1986 Act) to 33.3 percent in the 1994 Act. Reservation for the SCS/STs in non Autonomous district council (ADC) area shall be in proportion to their population. The Act provides all the 29 items as per the eleventh schedule to be transfereed to PRIs. At the Goan Panchayat and Anchalik Panchayat levels there shall be three standing committees.

The three standing committees at the GP level shall be – a). Development Committee; b). Social Justice Committee; and c). Social Welfare Committee. At AP level, the three committees shall be a). General Standing Committee; b). Finance, Audit and Planning Committee; and c). Social Justice Committee. The Zilla Parishad shall have four Committees a). General Standing Committees; b). Financial and Audit Committee; c). Social Justice Committee; and d). Planning and Development Committee.

The 1994 Act provides for the constitution of District Planning Committee. The Zilla Parishad Chairman shall be the Ex-Officio Chairman and CEO of Zilla Parishad shall be the ex-officio Secretary of the DPC. MPs, MLAs, Mayor/Chairman of the Zilla Parishad standing committee shall be the members. The Deputy Commissioner shall be the permanent invitee in the DPC.

In conformity with the 73rd constitutional Amendment, the Act of 1994, has provided for the constitution of a State Finance Commission covering Panchayat institutions and Municipalities. The Finance Commission has been constituted and it had submitted its report to the state govt. A state Election Commission was also constituted for holding elections to the Panchayats and Municipal Bodies. After a long pending Panchayat election was held in 2002 and Panchayat has been constituted all over the state except in the Hill Autonomous District Council Areas.

Panchayat Raj in Arunachal Pradesh

Arunachal Pradesh was created out of the frontier tribal areas of Assam. It was formerly known as North–East Frontier Agency (NEFA). It was made an union territory in 1972 and given its present name – Arunachal Pradesh (Land of the Dawn-lit Mountains). In 1987, it became a state. The state is surrounded on three sides by the international border with Bhutan to the west, China to the north and Burma to the east and Assam to the South. It is the only hill state in North-Eastern Region which introduced a Panchayat system as early as in 1969, under the NEFA Panchayati Raj Regulation 1967. The state has a large number of tribes, like Adi, Nishi, Apatani, Tagin, Mishimi, Khampti, Nocte, Wancho, Tangsha, Singpho, Monpa, Sherdukpen and Aka. Traditionally, the tribal people had been managing their affairs through Village Councils, certain tribes even developed into some sort of Anchal councils (for example in Bango Kebang and the Bogum Bokang Kebang of the Adis) operating above the Village level. However, these councils lacked uniformity at different stages of development.

Under the NEFA Panchayati Raj Regulation 1967, a three-tier structure was consitued on 2nd October 1968. It comprised Gram Panchayat at the Village level, Anchal Samities at the anchal level and Zilla Parishad at district level.

Gram Panchayat

The Gram Panchayat consisted of one to ten members directly elected by the villagers. Each hundred villagers has one member. Each Gram Panchayat was to have a minimum of three hundred electors. There was no provision for a Chairman of a Gram Panchayat.

Anchal Samiti

Each Gram Panchayat in the anchal elected one of its members to the Anchal Samiti, which had a maximum of twenty-five members. These members elect their vice– president from amongst themselves. Besides the elected members, the Anchal Samiti could have a maximum of five members nominated by the Deputy Commissioner from among the tribes not represented by the elected members. The Deputy Commissioner of the district could appoint the Sub-divisional Officer or any other Officer of the same rank as the President of the Anchal Samiti, and another Junior Officer, not below the rank of a circle Officer, as its executive Officer.

The Anchal Samiti had wide-ranging financial powers and in fact regulated the flow of resources for various development schemes. It also co-ordinated the activities of the Gram Panchayats. That it had an Official as its President and acted generally under the influence of its Official members, however, meant that it would not always exercise this supreme authority in the best interest of its constituents.

Zilla Parshad

The Zilla Parshads consisted of all the Vice –Presidents of the Anchal samities, one elected representative each from the Anchal Samities and not more than six members nominated by the Deputy Commissioner of the district form among the tribes who have not secured representation in the Zilla Parishad. The Deputy Commissioner of the District is the ex-officio Chairman of the Zilla Parishad. The term of Office of the panchayat were three years. The Zilla Parishad was mainly an advisory body and had no executive function. In view of the dominant position that officials continued to occupy in the Panchayati Raj bodies at all the three levels and the influence they exercised in these councils, it would be unrealistic to call them self-governing institutions in the real sense of the term. Arunachal Pradesh has a population below twenty lakh. Therefore, it had the option of constituting only two tiers under the constitution 73rd amendment Act, 1992, but an ordinance framed on 18th April 1994, that is, the Arunachal Pradesh Panchayat Raj ordinance, included the constitution of three tiers in the state.

Present Status

The passage of the 73rd constitutional Amendment Act 1992 created a unique situation in Arunachal Pradesh. To meet the requirement of the 73rd Amendment Act, the Arunachal Pradesh Government issued the Arunachal Pradesh Panchayati Raj ordinance 1994 replacing the NEFA Panchayati Raj Regulation 1967 to meet the requirements of an Amendment Act.

The ordinance was sought to be replaced by the Arunachal Pradesh Panchayati Raj Bill 1994 passed by the Arunachal Pradesh Legislative Assembly in September 1994. It contained the same provisions as in the Panchayati Raj Ordinance. However, the Bill could not become an

Act as the Governor of Arunachal Pradesh reserved it for the assent of the President of India. The President of India did not give assent to the Bill remitted it to the Legislative Assembly with the observation that. It does not provide for Gram Sabha, and that. It does not provide for reservation for scheduled castes.

The State Legislative assembly reconsidered the Bill in March 1997 and modified it to provide for a Gram Sabha at the lowest level of Panchayats but it did not agree to make a provision for reservation for scheduled castes on the plea that Arunachal Pradesh does not have any scheduled caste population. The negligible scheduled caste population (0.47% as per the 1991 census) in the state is only floating population and is mainly concentrated in urban areas. The bill was sent again to the President of India in April 1997. It is now awaiting the President's assent.

Meanwhile the Arunachal Pradesh Governor trice extended the life of the Panchayat bodies elected in 1992 under the NEFA Panchayat Raj Regulation 1967, first time in August 1995 for one year and then in September 1996 and in March 1997 extending it for six months each time. The original term of Panchayats were three years. It was extended upto five years with the plea that the 73rd Amendment Act, 1992 makes an uniform 5 years term for the Panchayats, throughout the country, overlooking the fact that it does not allow any extension of terms of the Panchayats elected under the existing Acts. It only allows them to complete the term if it extends beyond 1994.

Hence, on 14th September 1997 on completion of the two-year term of the Panchayats, the state government ordered their dissolution. Thus, the 73rd Amendment Act has created an entirely reverse position of its intended objectives of strengthening and ensuring introduction of Panchayats in every state. In Arunachal Pradesh, it had led to a situation where existing Panchayats are also eliminated. This probably is a violation of the 73rd Amendment Act and thus constitution of India. There are however, frequent and ever increasing demand from the people to restore the Panchayats in the state as soon as possible.

Panchayats in Manipur

Manipur came under British rule as a princely state in 1891. The Manipur Constitution Act, 1947, established a democratic form of government with the Maharajah as the executive head and a legislature constituted by election based on adult franchise. The Legislative Assembly so constituted was dissolved on the integration of the state with the Dominion of India in October 1949.

It became as a part 'C' state under the Indian constitution with effect from 26-1-1950. Manipur achieved full statehood on January 21, 1972. Manipur is geographically divided into the hills and the centrally situated valley. The Hill areas are inhabited predominantly by the Naga and Kuki tribes with a sprinkling of the Nepalese in the immediate neighborhood of the valley. In the valley live Meiteis, (Manipuri Hindus), Pangals (Manipuri Muslims), the Nepalese, and the Business communities like Marwaris, Punjabis, Biharis and so on. The Barak basin is inhabited by the Meiteis and the Bengalis.

The Panchayati Raj institutions were functioning only in the valley districts and Jiribam sub-division. In the hill districts, there were village authorities, almost similar to village Panchayats, functioning under the provisions of the 1956 Manipur (Village Authorities in Hill Areas) Act.

Evolution of Panchayats

Traditional form of Panchayats had been existing both in the valley and hill areas of Manipur from time immemorial. In the villages of valley there were institution viz, Singlup or wood clubs, resembling the Panchayats of Bengal, under the Sirdar or head of village. Besides generally controlling village affairs, these singlups used to adjudicate petty disputes in the villages.

In December 1896, the singlups were replaced by Panchayats. These Panchayats were constituted with five members. These members were remunerated through free grant of land up to a maximum of 25 pari/hectare. In 1906 a cash payment of 15 rupees per month for each Panchayat member was sanctioned in addition to the free grant of land. These Panchayats had the power to impose fines up to fifty rupees, and of deciding civil suits involving a value of fifty rupees or less.

The apex Panchayat at Imphal, known as Sadar Panchayat, adjudicated in civil cases of appeals from the village Panchayats besides looking after the civil cases of the Imphal area.

Under the Manipur State Courts Act, 1947, Village Panchayats were conferred with the powers of the lowest court for the administration of Justice in criminal and civil cases.

Modern Panchayat System

The Panchayat system in Manipur was introduced in 1960 under the provisions of the United Provinces Panchayat Raj Act 1947, which was extended to the state. Under the Act, a two-tier system was introduced in the state.

The state govt. enacted the Manipur Panchayati Raj Act in 1975 which provided a three tier system of Panchayat in the state comprising Gram Panchayats at the Gram Sabha level, Panchayat Samities at the block level and Zilla Parishads at the district levels, besides Nyaya Panchayats for judicial purposes.

After the election in 1978, 167 Gram Panchayats, 37 Nyaya Panchayats and 6 Panchayat Samities were constituted. Though the act provided for the establishment of three-tier system of Panchayats, only Gram Panchayats and Panchayat Samities were constituted.

The Act provides for the establishment of a Gram Fund and Panchayat Samiti fund raised through taxation, donations and contributions from the state and central governments. The state govt. allocated funds for the development of Panchayati Raj institutions under the five year plans. Gram Panchayats received funds directly from the central govt. and from state government for executing various rural and community development schemes.

Post 73rd Amendment Developments

In conformity with the 73rd constitution Amendment Act of 1992, the Manipur Panchayati Raj Act 1994 was passed on 23rd April 1994 by repealing the Act of 1975. The new Act has provided for the constitution of a two-tier Panchayati Raj in the valley areas, the Gram Sabha at the village level and Zilla Parishad at the district level. The Act of 1994 was amended substantially in 1996 to accommodate gram sabha at the village level having population of not less than 3000 and not more than 6000.

District Councils in the Hill Areas

In the hill area of Manipur, district councils under the sixth schedule are in existence. As such, these areas are outside the purview of part IX of the constitution.

Local Self – Governance in Tripura

Tripura is the second smallest state in India. It was formally declared a Union Territory on November 1, 1957 and elevated to the status of a full-fledged state on January 21, 1972.

The PR system in Tripura was initially guided by the United Province Panchayat Raj Act, 1947, and Goan Sabhas in development blocks were constituted in a phased manner. As the ambit of the Gram Panchayats activatees and their effectiveness increased and participation of the villagers became more intensive, the state govt. felt it necessary to enact a new Legislation. The Tripura Panchayats

Act, 1983, was brought into force in January 1984, replacing the United Provinces Panchayat Raj Act, 1947.

Tripuraa has a long history of good local self governance. Where a single tier system of Panchayati Raj was started at the village level. The Gram Panchayat is the executive body of the Goan Sabhas constituted through open election by raising hands. Naya Panchayat was also formed at circle level by comprising several Goan Sabhas.

The Tripura Panchayat Act, 1993 established a three-tier structure in the state with the Gram Panchayat as the lowest tier, the Panchayat Samitis at the block level and Zilla Parshad at the district level. The Act also provides for a Gram Sabha which shall meet annually to consider matters relating to accounts, budget, and report of development works in the Gram Panchayat.

The State also set up the Tribal Areas Autonomous District Council (TAADC) in 1982 under the sixth schedule of the constitution and it provides for separate elections to village councils.

Gram Sabhas are there irrespective of schedule or non-schedule area. Hence, Tripura's local self governance is quiet unique. The members of Gram Sabha in Tripura have never been silent observer. They actively participate in almost all the village affairs like crime and punishment, guarding the villages and forests, resolving community conflicts, land alienation and management matters, general cleanliness of the village and other service areas like cleaning the local health centre. Gram Sabhas are capable of determining and analyzing the resources they have including opportunities as well as problems and obstacles to development.

Traditional Institutions and District Councils of Meghalaya

Meghalaya, literally 'the abode of the clouds' was inaugurated as an autonomous state on April 2, 1970. It was declared as state on January 21, 1972. Khasi, Jaintia and Garo are the three major tribes and other smaller tribes are Hajong, Rabha, Delu, Babai and Mann.

There are three District councils under the sixth schedule of the constitution covering 7 districts of the state.

Garo Hills

Garo Hills, below the level of District Council there is an institution called Lasker which is recognized by the District Council as a traditional body. During the colonial rule they were under the control of the Deputy Commissioner. They have Executive function both and Judiciary function within their area. In Garo Hills there is another institution at the village level called Nokma. Nokma who holds control over clan land is called A'king Nokma and there are village level Sardars to assist the Nokmas in day to day village administration. The Nokmas and Sardars to are under the administrative control of the District council. Nokmanship is inherited by the clan members under the District council administration, the A'king Nokmas have been reduced to mere custodians and supervisors of their A'kings on behalf of their wives and their clans. However, the Garo Hills District (Jhum) Regulation Act, 1954, conferred on the A'king Nokmas the right to allot land for jhumming to each family within his A'king in consultation with the residents thereof. But in the event of any dispute with regard to the land so allotted by the A'king Nokma to any particular person or a family, the matter has to be referred to the village council, a power which was earlier exercised by the A'king Nokma.

The Garo Hills Autonomous District Council passed the Constitution of Village Council Act in 1958 in order to establish and develop local self government in the rural areas and to make better provisions for rural administration and to develop them as self-sufficient units. A village council was constituted for each village and group of villages. There was a President and a Secretary for each village council. The duties and functioned allocated to the Village Council included: cleaning and lighting of village roads and paths; sanitation, construction, maintenance and improvement of public wells and tanks; preventive measures in case of epidemic, opening and regulation of burial and creruation ground and places for disposal of dead animals, construction and maintenance of places for the storage of cowdung and other manures, maintenance of record of population census, census of unemployed persons and landless persons and persons having no economic holdings and other statistics; construction; maintenance and improvement of village communication, drains and water-ways; control of village grazing grounds; village common and other communal property; the relief of the poor victims of famine, flood and other calamities; regulating slaugter houses; controlling and maintenance of owned or transferred buildings, institutions or property; regulating the construction of new building or houses or extension or alteration of existing one; Primary School education. Registration of births and deaths.

Khasi and Jaintias

In the Khasi Hills the syiem is recognized as traditional institution who holds office usually for life but in some cases for short period of five years. The syiem is elected in accordance with the customary law and practice by traditional executive called myntris. The institution is under the administrative control of the District Councils.

In the Jaintia Hills District also there is a traditional authority called *Doloi* who functions more or less on the same pattern of syiems among the Khasis. A district council for the then Khasi and Jaintia Hills District was inaugurated in 1952.

The United Khasi Jaintia Hills Autonomous District (Appointment and Succession of Chiefs and Headman) Act, 1959 (hereafter referred to as the Principal Act), made provision not only for its authority to appoint the chiefs and headmen, but also that of the removal and suspension of the same by the executive committee of the district council, if in its opinion, these incumbents violated, the terms and conditions of their appointment. This act not only brought radical changes in the pattern and procedure of the election and appointment of chiefs, but also reduced their position and status.

According to Article 243 M of the constitution, the provisions relating to Panchayati Raj institution are not applicable to Meghalaya. Hence constitution 73rd Amendment does not apply to Meghalaya.

Local self-governance in Mizoram

Mizoram, in the local language, means the land of Mizos. 'Mizo' itself means highlander. Under the British administration, Mizoram was know as Lushai Hills District. In 1954 by an Act of Parliament the name was changed to Mizo Hills District. In 1972, when it was made a Union Territory, it was named Mizoram. Mizoram became 23rd state of Indian Union on 20.2.1987.

The Mizos have various tribes viz, the Lushais, Pawis, Paites, Raltes, Hmars, Kukis, Maras, Lakhers etc. Mizoram has democratically elected Village Councils since 1954 which have been set up by the enactments of the District Council as per sub-clause (e) of the clause of the sixth schedule to the Constitution of India with a very limited functions and powers mostly administrative and judicial of petty nature. The Lushai Hills District (Village Councils) Act 1953 and the Pawi-Lakher Autonomous Region (Village Council) Act 1994 have been adopted by the Govt. of Mizoram and the District Councils (Mara District Council, Lai District Council and Chakma District Council) since 1972. The provisions of the Acts are amended by an executive/ administrative orders of the government and District Councils.

The 73rd Constitutional Amendments Act does not apply to Mizoram.

Village Councils of Nagaland

The Nagaland state comprises of the former Naga Hills district of Assam and the former Tuensang Frontier division of the North East Frontier Agency. These were made a Centrally Administered Area in 1957. In January 1961, it became the state of Nagaland. The state of Nagaland was officially inaugurated on 1st December 1963. The population of Nagaland is entirely tribal. There are as many as 16 tribes and among the Nagas with their own distinctive languages and cultural features. The major tribes are Angami, Rengma, Sema, Lotha, Zaliang, Ao, Chang, Sangtam, Khemnungan, Yimchunger, Phom, Konyak, Dimasa Kachari and Kuki.

Village level institutions have been strong in Nagaland. Since time immemorial Naga villages were independent in nature. There had been two major forms of village governments in Naga society, viz. democratic and autocratic. For instance, the Angamis, the Aos, the Chakhesang, the Kacharis etc, have democratic form of government where as the Kukis, the Semas, and the Konyaks practiced autocratic type of village government. The governments were run without written laws. However, the customary laws and usages were strictly adhered to. Even today customary laws are considered as the guiding principles of life in society.

Traditionally, life in every village in Nagland is managed by a council of elders – village council. Village organization in Nagaland is primarily based on institution of clan. A clan is a group of families amongst whom inter-marriage is strictly prohibited. It is the basic unit of the society Two or more such clan form a Naga village. Geographically a Naga village is divided into Khels (wards or sectors) which indicates a cluster of families.

Village Council

The history records that Naga villages were organized as small states or republics. However, there was no uniform legal system of village government in Naga society till 1970. After realizing the importance of village government, the state government of Nagaland passed an Act known as Nagaland Village, Area and Regional Council Act, 1970. Thereafter, it was further amended in 1973 and 1978 as Nagaland Village and Area Council Act with a view to bringing uniformity in Village Council structure all over Nagaland. A Village Council consists of members chosen by villagers in accordance with the prevailing customary practices and usages, the same being approved by the state government, provided that hereditary village chiefs, Goan

Booras (GBs) and Angs shall be e-officio members of such councils and shall have voting rights. The village council will choose a member as Chairman of the council. The Village council may select and appoint a Secretary who may or may not be a member of the council. If the Secretary is not a member of the council, he shall have no voting power.

Powers and Duties

The Village Council has the following powers and duties.

1. to formulate village development schemes, to supervise proper maintenance of water supply, roads, forest, education and other welfare activities,
2. to help various govt. agencies in carrying out development works in the village,
3. to take development works on its own initiative or on request by the government.
4. to borrow money from the government, Banks or financial institution for application in the development and welfare work of the village and to repay the same with or without interest,
5. to apply for and receive grant–in–aid, donations, subsidies from the government or any agencies,
6. to provide security for due repayment of loan received by any permanent resident of the village from the government, Banks or financial institutions.
7. to lend money from its funds to deserving permanent residents of the village and to obtain repayment thereof with or without interest.
8. to forfeit the security of the individual borrower on his default in repayment of loan advanced to him or on his commission of a breach of any of the terms of loan agreement entered into by him with the council and to dispose of such security by public auction or by private sale.
9. to enter into any loan agreement with the government, Bank and financial institutions or a permanent resident of the village.
10. to realize registration fee for each litigation within its jurisdiction;
11. to raise fund for utility service within the village by passing a resolution subject to the approval of the state government; provided that all monetary transactions shall be conducted through a scheduled Bank or the Nagaland state Co-operative Bank;

12. to constitute village Development Board;
13. power to do certain acts on the event of epidemic. On the outbreak of an epidemic or infectious disease village council shall initiate all preventive measure.

Administration of Justice

The Village council can administer justice within the jurisdiction of the village, in accordance with the customary law and usages as accepted by the canons of justice established in Nagaland, and the law in this respect as enforced from time to time.

In case of disputes between villages falling in different areas or districts, two or more village council may settle dispute in a joint session or refer it to the appropriate authority.

Village Administration

The village council is authorized to act as the supporting agent to the government in the village administration which includes the following:

a). Maintenance of law and order;

b). In serious case offender may be arrested but such person should be handed over to the nearest Administrative Officer or Police Station without undue delay;

c). to report to the nearest Administrative Officer of occurrence of any un-natural death or serious accident;

d). to inform the presence of strangers, vagabonds or suspects to the nearest Administrative Officer or Police Station;

e). to enforce order passed by the competent authority on the village as a whole;

f). to report outbreak of epidemics to the nearest Administrative Officer or Medical Officer;

g). no transfer of immovable property shall be effected without the concept of the village council. Written record of this shall be maintained by the village council.

Area Council

At the circle level there was Area council. Area council was a council constituted by the representative sent by each village council within the circle.

Area council is an intermediary body in between district and village. However, Area council has been eliminated since 1990.

Village Development Boards (VDBs)

In accordance with the Nagaland Village Area and Regional Council Act 1970(Amended in 1973 and 1978) VDB came into existence in 1980,as a subsidiary to Village Council. At present Nagaland has 1045 recognized villages and each village has a Village Council to look after law and order situation of the village and a VDB to undertake developmental activities of the village. VDB deliver developmental works to the village through centrally sponsored Schemes as well as State govt. Schemes.

The constitution 73rd Amendment Act does not apply to the state of Nagaland.

Comparison between Panchayats, Districts Council and traditional Institutions

Making Phanchayat institution of self governance is the mandate of the constitution. The 73rd constitution Amendment Act ushers in a new era of participatory governance towards realizing Gandhiji's dream and his ideas of Gram Swaraj.

The objective of the 73rd Amendment Act to the Constitution is the devolution of power, where as Village Council Acts do not stipulate the same. The village Councils thus have no comparison with constitutional provisions relating to Panchayats. When all the provisions of the 73rd Amendment about the powers, scope of function and financial support for the exercises of the powers and discharge of the responsibilities by the Panchayat bodies are compared with those attached to the District Councils attached to the sixth schedule area, it is found that while the District Councils have several regulatory powers subject to state government control, the PRIs are in more advantageous position in respect of developmental functions. The sources of income of district councils are a less stable. Infact, they are solely at the mercy of the state government, whereas the Panchayat bodies are entitled to get funds from the state and central government under several schemes, in addition, to their own regular sources of income by taxation, mobilization of locally available resources, and the like. To prevent the Panchayat bodies from falling into financial Starvation Financial Commission has been established.

In case the Panchayat bodies are dissolved, the 73rd Amendment to the constitution stipulates that they must be reconstituted within a period of six months from the date of their dissolution. In the case of district councils, fresh elections can be held subject to the approval of the state legislature within a period not exceeding twelve months. Moreover, where as there is a provision of reservation of seats for women in Panchayat bodies, their representation is neglected in the traditional institutions and in the District Council.

Corruption: A Major Threat to Development

The overriding issue of corruption has emerged as problem number one in the country. It is now being accepted all over that one of the major drawbacks of the process of development planning has been corruption in rural development works, even at the high levels of bureaucracy and political leadership.

In the north-eastern region the pace of development is comparatively slower in case of District Councils in comparison to the Panchayat areas, which is mainly due to rampant corruption.

In tribal areas the elite class of the people or the local leaders are emerging as an opportunist class and they take the largest share of benefits depriving the poorest section of the society.

Panchayats are party based and it is the ruling party that dominates. However, since the members are from different political parties there is scope to take meticulous measures to prevent or reduce corruption. In Tripura, common people's feeling is that the distribution of social goods and benefits are always partial, i.e. the party supporters get the priority in the matter of such benefits; then it is given to the party sympathizers and the rest are deprived of such benefits.

This is the general remark made by the opposition party members and a section of the people. Same is true in the case of Assam. In Assam, there are allegations of misuse of rural development fund at the top level. It is alleged that bureaucrats, Panchayat Sabhapatis are engaged in corruption and earning disproportionate property with the help of local MLAs/politicians and bureaucrats. In Nagaland, common people feel that hardly 10 percent of development fund goes for developmental works. When the VDB workers blame the rural development officials of misusing and sharing of their development fund, the officials counteract by accusing them of mis-utilization of development funds. There are reports and allegations from Manipur and Arunachal Pradesh also of channelizing development fund to the pockets of politicians and bureaucrats.

Rural reconstruction can be achieved through changing the mindset of the rural people, particularly that of the marginalized sections. They should not consider themselves merely as a cog in the wheel, but as the cornerstone of the governing system. This could only happen when they become participators in decentralized governance, planning and development. Governance from grass root level gives much scopes for development, but lack of awareness among the poor, manipulation and exploitation of the masses by the local elite are blocking the benefits of development from reaching to the most needy rural people. It is one of the saddest part of our development endeavor. However, people are the real witness, guard and also the beneficiaries of their development projects. So, they have to be cautious. As Rabindra Nath Tagore said: "There is no power which can awaken you from outside. The awakening can come only from within you through your own united strength".

Local Self Governance

Local Self Governance has been a priority working issues for the organization with special emphasis on governance at Panchayat Level. GENVP consolidated its work on Promotion of pro–poor governance through the project titled 'Strengthening of Panchayat Raj Institution with special emphasis to Gram Sabha', supported by DFID PACS Program in the Blocks of Chandi and Nagarnausa in Nalanda district of Bihar.

Pre-Election Voter Awareness Camps (PEVAC): The year witnessed consolidation of the activities of the Dalit Sangarsh Morcha (DSM). The DSM played an active role in the panchayat election by organizing pre-election voter awareness camps to sensitize dalit voters, especially women to vote for the right candidate of their choice. The DSM was successful in identifying dalit candidates through consensus in many constituencies. In several Panchayats the DSM emerged as a strong pressure group to be recognized. 70 DSM supported candidates won the Panchayat election in the block of Chandi and Nagarnausa. Awareness camps were organized to sensitize the candidates on the provisions of the election. The PEVAC was successful in promoting awareness among the dalit communities as their rights as voters and motivating them to cast their votes in large numbers.

Promoting DSM (Dalit Sangarsh Morcha) as Organized Group: The year witnessed further expansion of DSM to neighboring panchayats and larger population. The DSM was successful in mobilizing the dalit community for active participation at the Gram Sabha and to raise their voice for their rights and entitlements. Regular meetings of DSM was organized for regular up gradation of the Dalit leaders on the initiatives undertaken and to share the outcomes of initiatives on issues such as social inclusion, Livelihood, access to entitlements and dalit dignity.

Community based initiatives at block level meetings and dharna (demonstration) were organized by the Dalit Sangarsh Morcha to sensitize block level officials and other stakeholders on the issues, i.e., irregular distribution of PDS, IAY and other schemes of the Panchayat.

Dalit Sammelan was organized to sensitize larger dalit community on the collective efforts of the DSM in the two blocks of Nalanda district and achievements of the organization. It was unanimously accepted that there is urgent need for building up such organizations.

Block level meeting of DSM

Significant Learning: Organized Community can effectively advocate for its rights. Livelihood issues and rights cannot be addressed as isolated issues, rather a combination of both ensures active participation from the community.

Cadre based organization has larger influence on the community than headed by a single leader.

The DSM was successful in mobilizing the dalit community specially women in large numbers to actively participate at Gram Sabha and raise their voice for access to developmental schemes being implemented by the panchayats and Developmental Blocks

Dalit Dignity

National Rural Employment Guarantee Act (NREGA): Two panchayats (Madhopur & Tulsigarh) of Chandi block in Nalanda District were covered under awareness generation programme on NREGA with a support from Development Alternative. Following activities organized under this campaign:

Study on NREGS: Baseline information on NREGS was collected at village level to asses the implemented schems and programs by the govt. and Impact evaluation was also conducted with the PRI functionaries.

Village Meeting: Awareness building meetings were organized in 8 villages with the beneficiaries and sensitizing them on the implementation of NREGS.

Observations from Village Meeting: It has been noticed that the NREGS is not reaching to the needed people because of the reluctant attitude of the govt. on one hand and lack of awareness among the common mass on the other.

Therefore, we deem it necessary to conduct such meetings on much larger level/scale.

Immediate Impact of the Village Meeting: People were sensitized of the issue.

Sense of demand making process developed to an extent among villagers.

People shown more interest after knowing the simple procedure to obtain the same.

The pressure group formed at the end of the meet is now actively promoting the issue among the villagers.

Panchayat level meeting : Panchayat level meeting were organized to create sensitivity of the local governance PRI functionaries and Gram Sabha. The PRI representatives and gram Sabha members were sensitized on NREGA and various schemes. The members were inducted the concept of the NREGS and role of members in planning, monitoring, facilitating identification of BPL families, their registration and job card preparation. The PRI members understood the concept and actively participating in the programme.

District level Workshop : District level workshop was organized At Zila Parishad hall at Bihar Sharif, Nalanda where the dignitaries from al concern with NREGS participated in the workshop. The proceedings and outcome of the study documents were presented before the officers present at the workshop. The gaps were identified at the village, panchayats & district level and reactions from different corners were also registered for reparation. The 5000 applications for job cards were submitted to the District Collector.

Decentralized Planning

Samarthan has undertaken several initiative to demonstrate decentralised planning. While some of these assignments were carried out on pilot basis with support from bilateral/multi-lateral donors and other donor organisations, Samarthan has recently focused in engaging with the state government in promoting decentralised planning. This has helped in converging the initiatives from different actors and has also helped in spreading the coverage to a larger cross-section of community. Here are some of the key projects related to decentralised planning that Samarthan has undertaken recently:

Promoting Livelihood through Micro Planning in MPRLP Villages

Samarthan is engaged with the Madhya Pradesh Rural Livelihood Project (MPRLP) as the nodal agency for providing handholding support to the staff of the project on decentralised governance and decentralised planning. The MPRLP is a GoMP project supported by DFID. The assignment involves large scale capacity building of government staff, elected representatives and the community members on the process decentralised governance of micro planning.

In the last one year, Samarthan provided capacity building support by developing 80 Master Trainers from MPRLP team on governance and micro planning. Samarthan also supported these master trainers through mentoring and handholding support to further build capacities of 856 Project Facilitation Team (PFT) members and nearly 21500 community members.

Samarthan supports the district teams and PFTs of MPRLP in planning for livelihood based activities in the intervened villages. Over the past one year, Samarthan has been able to provide handholding support to the MPRLP in developing plans in 1872 villages. A lot of emphasis is given on making the plans convergent with the other departments that are working in the village.

District Perspective Planning under BRGF

With support from the Government of Chhattisgarh, Samarthan prepared the District Perspective Plans under the Backward Region Grants Fund (BRGF) with Bastar, Dantewara and Koriya districts of Chhattisgarh. Samarthan worked as the technical support unit for planning in these Districts. Under the assignment a District level Situation Analysis was undertaken which led to the development of the District Vision Document. This was prepared in close consultation with all the departmental heads of the district. The vision document was prepared keeping in mind the 7 priority sectors identified by the Chhattisgarh government in line with the planning commission guidelines. These sectors include Livelihood, Education, Health, Power, Infrastructure, Urban Development and Social Security.

Based on the Vision 2020 document for the district, 5 year plans were prepared at the Panchayat and Urban Local Bodies level which was integrated into block and district level plans. Samarthan provided technical support in capacity building of the field investigators (from the line department), data collection and analysing the data. A software was also developed for integrating the plans at the block and district level. Special focus was given on developing the plans so as to converge the activities of different departments together.

Rural Decentralisation and Participatory Planning for Poverty Reduction

Samarthan implemented the "Rural Decentralization and Participatory Planning for Poverty Reduction" project in two districts in Chhattisgarh. This was a joint initiative of UNDP, Government of Chhattisgarh and Samarthan. The overall objective of the project is to provide catalytic support and create an enabling environment for decentralization by demonstrating how Panchayats can plan effectively and how the plans can be integrated into a block level plan.

Samarthan implemented this project in 48 villages in Dongargaon block of Rajnandgaon district and Bastar block of Bastar district of Chhattisgarh. This is an initiative to demonstrate an effective model of bottom-up planning where citizens' aspirations and relevant demand find centrality in the planning, execution and monitoring. The bottom up planning resulted in 17 Panchayats getting national Nirmal Gram award. Various participatory tools and methods were used to make the process participatory. Villagers and Panchayati Raj representatives actively participated in formulating plans for 5 years on livelihood issues.

Micro Planning for CGDPRP in Bastar and Churia Blocks

Samarthan carried out the intensive micro planning exercises block in 53 Panchayats in Churia block of Rajnandgaon district and 55 Panchayats of Bastar Block of Bastar district with support from the Chhattisgarh District Poverty Reduction Project (CGDPRP). The Government of Chhattisgarh is implementing the CGDPRP project with assistance from The World Bank. The broad objective of the project is to support the rural poor and particularly the poorest of the poor, strengthen and secure their asset base, to improve income generating opportunities and quality of life. The micro planning assignment required preparation of Gram Panchayats wise micro plan for a Churia and Bastar block. Using various tools and methods it was taken care that the villagers and Panchayati Raj representatives actively participate in the plan formulation. The problems of the area and peoples' priority in solving these problems were addressed in the Panchayat developmental plan. Based on the findings from the structured set of questionnaires and the tools of Participatory Rural Appraisal (PRA) the team developed a detailed micro plan for a period of 5 years, in consultation with villagers and functionaries of Gram Panchayat. The micro plans were presented and approved in a special meeting of the Gram Sabha.

Supporting SPB Guidelines by Strengthening Village Level Planning Process

In association with UNICEF and the State Planning Board (SPB), Samarthan is working on demonstrating bottom up planning process in two districts of Madhya Pradesh. The assignment includes building capacities of the line department staff in a ToT model. Further the trainers are supported in building capacities of the district and village level functionaries on participatory planning.

Under the assignment, Samarthan is developing an operational manual for the field level functionaries for conducting development planning at Panchayat/town level. It is also developing a software which would help in aggregating the village and Panchayat level plan at the block and district level.

The assignment would help in demonstrating how plans can be developed at the village and ward level and then aggregated at the block and district level to develop the district level plans. It focuses on strengthening the village planning process in order to develop meaningful plans for the districts.

Village Level Planning – UNICEF

The village planning process was initiated in the Dongargaon blocks of Rajanandgaon district with the support of Unicef. The program was implemented with an objective of creating awareness leading to empowered communities for action, inclusive planning, implementing and monitoring activities related to children with participation from the most vulnerable sections. It also focused to ensure that the planning is followed by regular community based monitoring in order to ensure that the system responds to the needs of the community by providing timely and quality services.

To develop ownership among the community members, facilitators were identified from within the community and their capacities were built on village planning. The trained facilitators worked in 107 villages to assess the situation related to health, nutrition, education, water and sanitation etc. Data was collected using participatory approaches and it was analysed with the community to develop a village level plan.

These exercises provided opportunities to discuss in-depth issues related to adverse sex ratio, teenage marriages and other behaviours that influence the health related issues of women and children. The participation of village functionaries from different sectors was an integral part in these discussions and that lead to a better understanding and appreciation of the roles and responsibilities of these functionaries and the building of a strong bond between the community and the functionaries. The 5 to 10 day exercises lead to the development of village action plans and the formation of village committees for overseeing and monitoring implementation. Prior to the village planning exercises a day orientation of the local representatives in the blocks was conducted. The orientation imparted knowledge about the roles and responsibility of the Sarpanch during the plan preparation and how social issues could be converged in the Gram Sabha plans.

India-Participation of Tribal Women in Village Organizations

THEME: Tribal women are gradually becoming integrated into village organizations.

A 1997 IFAD report focuses on a number of social issues in the poor tribal areas of Madhya Pradesh in India. The study area comprises villages and hamlets. The panchayat, or village governing body, is located in the main village, or gaon, which is an independent unit of social organization. Normally villages comprise 70-90% tribal and 10-30% non-tribal households. The institutional framework of these villages is often complex. In the past, the villages were entirely male dominated. But, increasingly women are becoming involved in the important village-level organizations of the gram sabha and the panchayat, as well as in less important mixed-gender and women-only organizations.

There are degrees of organization among villages. Villages closer to a highway or town and that have a higher level of ongoing economic development are likely to have a greater number of organizations than villages that are more remote. Such villages are also likely to have a higher proportion of non-tribes, and a greater mixture of different kinds of tribes. The dominant tribe will also influence the extent of organization in a village.

Gram Sabha (Village Council)

Traditionally, even among more egalitarian tribal communities, women have not taken part in the gram sabha, but this is slowly changing. The gram sabha is the traditional community organization and the supreme decision-making body, presided over by the elders. Every caste group is represented on it. Normally it is unregistered. Villagers see it as their organization. The more isolated the village from government programmes, the more important the gram sabha is in organizing community development action. The study notes that the gram sabha should always be consulted and involved in any village-level decision-making.

The Panchayat

Women are coming to have a more visible role in the panchayat. Villagers regard the panchayat as the official 'agency of the government' that mediates government instructions and works. The study notes that the panchayat is an ideal organization for undertaking infrastructure development on behalf of the Government, but should not be viewed as representing village wishes and ideas. Thirty-three per cent of the panchayati raj is reserved for women, resulting in five to seven women members.

The president, or panch, of the panchayat is elected from among the tribals, with the vice-president occasionally elected from non-tribals. On occasion, women compete with men for the panch, and do get elected. There are panchayat presidency posts expressly reserved for women, but the study found that even in those panchayats, the women seemed to be acting only as figureheads or official contact persons. In fact, it is the traditional male leaders or husbands who conduct the affairs of the panchayat. The women presidents whom the researchers met were completely marginalized and did not even know the number of existing members in their panchayats.

In one case, the female president was conveniently deaf and dumb. Generally, the study found that women consider the panchayat and the gram sabha to be male dominated, and to not adequately consider their point of view.

Mahilla Sangatan (Women's Organizations)

The traditional Mahilla Sangatan are self-formed women's associations. They can be registered or unregistered. Their original role is singing gaura, or marriage songs, and they may meet once a fortnight or so to practise. However, these days some Mahilla Sangatan are beginning to represent women's concerns at the village level, such as men's drinking. The study notes that the dynamism and power of women's organizations are highly dependent on strong women leaders. In at least a few cases, such traditional women's associations are taking on income-generating programmes. In one instance, they applied for and received funds from the block office and started manufacturing various goods from forest products. In that case, a literacy volunteer had been a key facilitator.

Locally Originating Women's Action Groups

In addition to the preceding, some villages also have other, often temporary, women's groups, which are never registered. These are usually set up by the women themselves in response to their common concerns over a given social or economic problem. Examples of such groups are those motivated by local schoolteachers or forest guards to fight for causes such as the scarcity of drinking water or roads.

Women's Development Groups

Because women's development groups are established by outsiders, they may not have the same level of motivation as locally originating ones. Government agencies and NGOs have established various women's groups in many villages around development initiatives. The most common are women's groups for savings and credit and income-generating schemes. Occasionally, groups are also formed around social issues. Usually, but not always, these are informal and unregistered associations, though they may become formal legal entities over time. The women's groups that have grown out of the Watershed Development Committees of the Rajiv Gandhi Watershed Mission are an example. In this case, women are encouraged to undertake income-generating activities, open separate bank accounts and register their organizations.

Chapter 10

Self-governance and Forest Resources

Executive Summary

Forest resources share attributes with many other resource systems that make difficult their governance and man-agement in a sustainable, efficient and equitable manner. Destruction or degradation of forest resources is most likely to occur in open-access forests where those involved, or external authorities, have not established effective governance. Conventional theories applied to forest resources presumed that forest users themselves were incapable of organising to overcome the temptations to over harvest. Extensive empirical research, however, has challenged this theory and illustrated the many ways that forest users themselves have devised rules that regulate harvesting patterns so as to ensure the sustainability of forest resources over time.

There is now a large body of literature analysing common-pool resources such as many fisheries, irrigation systems and rangelands. A growing consensus exists in this literature concerning the attributes of common-pool resources and of resource users that enhance the probability that self-organisation will occur. Many of these attributes seem also to help predict when forest users will self-organise. Forest users are more likely to devise their own rules when they use a forest that is starting to deteriorate but has not substantially disappeared, when some forest products provide early warning concerning forest conditions, when forest products are predictably available, and when the forest is sufficiently small that users can develop accurate knowledge of conditions. Self-organisation is more likely to occur when forest resources are highly salient to users, when users have a common understanding of the problems they face, when users have a low discount rate, when users trust one another, when users have autonomy to make some of their own rules, and when users have prior organisational experience. These attributes of forests and of the user community affect the benefits and costs of organising to protect and enhance forest resources. When users create organisations consistent with a set of design principles, they are likely to be able to sustain their own institutional arrangements over a long period of time.

This growing consensus about the attributes of users and resources has been applied in the design of policies intended to enhance the participation of local users in the governance and management of common-pool resources, including many forests. Supporting further research especially studies of forests and their users over time is an important foundation for even more effective public policies in the future.

Forest resources share attributes with many other resource systems that make difficult their governance and management in a sustainable, efficient and equitable manner. While some forests are small enough that fencing them or protecting their borders from intrusion is relatively easy, excluding beneficiaries from access and use of most forests is costly. The difficulty of exclusion creates the possibility that individuals who benefit from the use of a forest will not contribute to its long-term sustainability.

For many uses of a forest, one persons harvesting subtracts products that are not available to others. Thus, many aspects of forests can be considered as common-pool resources. Common-pool resources are characterised by difficulty of exclusion and generate finite quantities of resource units so that one persons use subtracts from the quantity of the resource available to others (E. Ostrom *et al.* 1994). The ecosystem services generated by forest resources watershed protection, carbon sequestration, biodiversity enhancement, etc. may be considered as externalities or as public goods.

Ecosystem services are, however, closely tied to the sustainability of the forest stock, and are thus threatened by the same set of incentives that tempt users of an unregulated forest resource into a race to use up the timber and destroy the forest itself. Destruction or degradation of forest resources is most likely to occur in open-access forests where those involved and/or external authorities have not established an effective governance regime to regulate the following: who is allowed to appropriate forest products; the timing, quantity, location and technology of appropriation;

- who is obligated to contribute labour or funds to provide or maintain the forest;
- how conflicts over appropriation and obligation activities are to be resolved; and
- how the rules affecting the above will be changed over time with changes in the extent and composition of the forest and the strategies of participants.

A self-governed forest resource is one where actors, who are major users of the forest, are involved over time in making and adapting rules within collective-choice arenas regarding the inclusion or exclusion of participants, appropriation strategies, obligations of participants, monitoring and sanctioning, and conflict resolution. Some extremely remote forests are governed entirely by users and not at all by external authorities. In most modern political economies, however, it is rare to find any resource system including the treasuries of private for-profit corporations that are governed *entirely* by participants without rules made by local, regional, national, and international authorities also affecting key decisions (V. Ostrom 1991, 1997). Thus, in a self-governed system, participants make many, but not all, rules that affect the sustainability of the resource system and its use.

The Conventional Theory of Common-pool Resources

Much of the literature on common-pool resources is derived from work on irrigation systems, fisheries and rangelands, but forests are also frequently studied as common-pool resources. Most theoretical studies by political economists have analysed simple common-pool resource systems using relatively similar assumptions (Feeny *et al.* 1996). In such systems, it is assumed that the resource generates a highly predictable, finite supply of one type of resource unit (hardwood timber, for example) in each relevant time period. Users are assumed to be homogeneous in terms of their assets, skills, discount rates and cultural views. They are also assumed to be short-term, profit-maximising actors who possess complete information. In this theory, *anyone* can enter the resource and appropriate resource units. Users gain property rights only to what they harvest, which they then sell in an open competitive market. The open-access condition is a given. The users make no effort to change it. Users act independently and do not communicate or coordinate their activities in any way. The prediction from this theory is that over harvesting will result.

Until recently, textbooks in resource economics presented this conventional theory as the *only* theory needed for understanding common-pool resources. With the growing use of game theory, use of a common-pool resources is frequently represented as a one-shot or finitely repeated, Prisoners Dilemma game (Dawes 1973; Dasgupta and Heal 1979).

These models formalise the problem differently, but do not change any of the basic theoretical assumptions about the finite and predictable supply of resource units, complete information, homogeneity of users, their maximisation of expected profits, and their lack of interaction with one another or capacity to change their institutions. Nor is the prediction changed.

The empirical validity of the theory was not effectively challenged until the mid-1980s since there were many dramatic examples of resources destroyed by users acting independently. The massive deforestation in tropical countries and the desertification of the Sahel confirmed the worst predictions to be derived from this theory for many scholars. Garrett Hardens (1968) dramatic article in *Science* convinced many non-economists that this theory captured the essence of the problem facing users of most forests in the world. Since users are viewed as being trapped in these dilemmas, recommendations were repeatedly made that external authorities must impose a different set of institutions on such settings. Some recommend private property as the most efficient form of ownership. Others recommend government ownership and control (Ophuls 1973).

Implicitly, theorists assume that regulators will act in the public interest and understand how ecological systems work and how to change institutions so as to induce socially optimal behaviour (Feeny *et al.* 1996: 195). The possibility that the users themselves would find ways to organise had not seriously been considered in much of the policy literature until the last decade. Organising so as to create rules that specify rights and duties of participants creates a public good for those involved. Anyone who is included in the community of users benefits from this public good, whether they contribute or not. Thus, getting out of the trap is itself a second-level dilemma.

Further, investing in monitoring and sanctioning activities in order to increase the likelihood that participants follow the agreements they have made also generates a public good. These investments, therefore, represent a third-level dilemma. Since much of the initial problem exists because the individuals are stuck in a setting where they generate negative externalities for each other, it is not consistent with the conventional theory that they solve a second-and third-level dilemma in order to address the first-level dilemma under analysis.

Until the work of the National Academy of Sciences

Panel on Common Property (National Research Council 1986), the conclusions derived from this basic theory were applied to all common-pool resources regardless of what kind of institutions local users developed. The growing evidence from many field studies of common-pool resources, however, called for a serious rethinking of the generalisability of the conventional theory. Empirical studies have challenged the applicability of the conventional theory to forests by showing how forest users in many locations have organised themselves to vigorously protect and, in some cases, enhance local forests (Fortmann and Bruce 1988; Fox 1993; Fairhead and Leach 1996). Often, problems in forest management have emerged when local self-organisation has not been recognised by policy makers, and the autonomy of forest users to continue their own forest use practices has been threatened. Loss of ownership combined with substantial increases in population, greater commercialisation of forest products and technological changes that made rapid deforestation possible, have increasingly threatened forests in all parts of the world. Evidence has been mounting from a wide variety of sources, however, that local forest users are still capable of managing forest resources in many diverse locations. Considerable interest has been rekindled in promoting various forms of community forestry institutions.

The International Forestry Resources and Institutions (IFRI) research programme is also conducting a series of studies on forests owned by governments, communally and privately. These studies are designed and implemented by a network of Collaborating Research Centres (CRCs) located in Bolivia, India, Kenya, Madagascar, Mali, Nepal, Tanzania, Uganda and the United States. As each of the CRCs is able to expand the number of research sites and to return to these sites on a regular basis, we hope to provide the kind of systematic evidence needed to ground theory developed from a broad range of common-pool resources in a strong empirical foundation specific to forests. Colleagues associated with the Centre for the Study of Institutions, Population, and Environmental Change (CIPEC) at Indiana University are also intensively studying diverse forests in Brazil, Guatemala, Honduras and Mexico. Initial findings are highly congruent with the emerging theory described below (Agrawal 1998; Banana and Gombya-Ssembajjwe 1998; Becker and Gibson 1998; McKean 1998; Schweik 1998; Varughese 1998).

A Growing Consensus on Variables Enhancing Self-organisation

Evidence from field research on common-pool resources challenges the generalisability of the conventional theory. While the conventional theory is successful in predicting outcomes in settings where users are alienated from each other or cannot communicate effectively, it does not provide an explanation for settings where users are able to create and sustain agreements to avoid serious problems of over appropriation. Nor does it predict well when government ownership will perform appropriately or how privatisation will improve outcomes.

A fully articulated, reformulated theory encompassing the conventional theory as a special case does not yet exist.

On the other hand, scholars familiar with the results of field research substantially agree on a set of variables that enhance the likelihood of users organising themselves to avoid the social losses associated with open-access, common-pool resources.

Drawing heavily on Ostrom (1992b: 298-9) and Baland and Platteau (1996: 286-9), considerable consensus exists that the following attributes of common-pool resources and of users are conducive to an increased likelihood that self-governing associations will form.

Though further empirical work is needed to test their relevance and explanatory power for self-organised forest management, these attributes do appear to have broad applicability.

Attributes of the Resource:

R1. Feasible improvement: The resource is not at a point of deterioration such that it is useless to organise or so underutilised that little advantage results from organising.

R2. Indicators: Reliable and valid information about the general condition of the resource is available at reasonable costs.

R3. Predictability: The availability of resource units is relatively predictable.

R4. Spatial extent: The resource is sufficiently small, given the transportation and communication technology in use, that users can develop accurate knowledge of external boundaries and internal microenvironments.

Attributes of the Users:

A1. Salience: Users are dependent on the resource for a major portion of their livelihood or other variables of importance to them.

A2. Common understanding: Users have a shared image of the resource (attributes R1, 2, 3 and 4 above) and how their actions affect each other and the resource.

A3. Discount rate: Users have a sufficiently low discount rate in relation to future benefits to be achieved from the resource.

A4. Distribution of interests: Users with higher economic and political assets are similarly affected by a current pattern of use.

A5. Trust: Users trust each other to keep promises and relate to one another with reciprocity.

A6. Autonomy: Users are able to determine access and harvesting rules without external authorities countermanding them.

A7. Prior organisational experience: Users have learned at least minimal skills of organisation through participation in other local associations or learning about ways that neighbouring groups have organised.

Many of these variables are in turn affected by the type of larger regime in which users are embedded. Larger regimes can facilitate local self-organisation by providing accurate information about natural resource systems, providing arenas in which participants can engage in discovery and conflict-resolution processes, and providing mechanisms to back up local monitoring and sanctioning efforts.

The probability of participants adapting more effective rules in macroregimes that facilitate their efforts over time is higher than in regimes that ignore resource problems entirely or, at the other extreme, presume that all decisions about the governance and management of resources need to be made by central authorities.

The key to further theoretical integration is to understand how these attributes interact in complex ways to affect the basic benefit-cost calculations of a set of users utilising a resource (E. Ostrom 1990).

Each useri has to compare the expected net benefits of harvesting from a resource continuing to use the old rules (BO) to the benefits he or she expects to achieve with a new set of rules (BN) Each user i must ask whether his or her incentive to change (Di) is positive or negative.

$$Di = BNi\text{-}BOi.$$

If Di is negative for all users, no one has an incentive to change. If Di is positive for some users, they then need to estimate three types of costs: C1. the up-front costs of time and effort spent devising and agreeing upon new rules; C2. the short-term costs of adopting new harvesting strategies; and C3. the long-term costs of monitoring and maintaining a self-governed system over time (given the norms of the community in which they live). If the sum of these expected costs for each user exceeds the incentive to change, no user will invest the time and resources needed to create new institutions. Thus, if

$$Di < (C1i + C2i + C3i)$$

for all I A (where A is the entire set of users), no change occurs.

In field settings, not everyone is likely to expect the same costs and benefits from a proposed change. Some may perceive positive benefits after all costs have been taken into account, while others perceive net losses. Consequently, the collective-choice rules used to change the day-to-day operational rules related to harvesting, planting, monitoring and other management activities affect whether an institutional change favoured by some and opposed by others will occur. For any collective-choice rule, such as unanimity, majority, ruling elite or one-person rule, there is at least one minimal coalition of users that must agree prior to the adoption of new rules. If there is an individual k in all minimal coalitions for whom

$$Dk £ (C1k + C2k + C3k),$$

no new rules will be adopted. And if for at least one minimal coalition

$$Dk > (C1k + C2k + C3k),$$

for all members, it is feasible for a new set of rules to be adopted. If there are several such coalitions, the question of which coalition will form, and so which rules will result, is a theoretical issue beyond the scope of this discussion. This analysis is applicable to a situation where a group starts with an open-access set of rules and contemplates adopting its first set of rules limiting access. It is also relevant to the continuing consideration of changing rules over time.

Thus, the existing collective-choice arrangements in a location for making operational rules related to the entry and use of forests affects whether self-organisation will occur. Existing institutional arrangements also have a major effect on the distributional impacts of any rule changes that may occur.

The rule used to modify institutional arrangements in field settings varies from reliance on the decisions made by one or a few leaders, to a formal reliance on majority or super-majority vote, to reliance on consensus or close to unanimity. If there are substantial differences in the perceived benefits and costs of users, it is possible that a minimal coalition will impose a new set of rules that strongly favours those in the winning coalition and imposes losses or lower benefits on those in the losing coalition (Thompson *et al.* 1988). If expected benefits from a change in institutional arrangements are not greater than expected costs for many users, however, the costs of enforcing a change in institutions will be much higher than when most participants expect to benefit from a change in rules over time.

Where the enforcement costs are fully borne by the members of a minimal coalition, operational rules that benefit the other users lower the long-term costs of monitoring and sanctioning for a governing coalition. Where external authorities enforce the rules agreed upon by a coalition of users, the distribution of costs and benefits is more likely to benefit that coalition and may impose costs on the other users. The attributes of a resource (listed above) affect both the benefits and costs of institutional change. If resource units are relatively abundant (R1), there are few reasons for users to invest costly time and effort in organising. If the resource is already substantially destroyed, the high costs of organising may not generate substantial benefits. Thus, self-organisation is likely to occur only after users observe substantial scarcity. The danger here, however, is that exogenous shocks leading to a change in relative abundance of the resource units occur rapidly and users may not adapt quickly enough to the new circumstances (Libecap and Wiggins 1985).

The presence of frequently available, reliable indicators about the conditions of a resource (R2) improves the capacity of users to adapt relatively quickly to changes that could adversely affect their long-term benefit stream (Moxnes 1996). A resource flow that is highly predictable (R3) is much easier to understand and manage than one that is erratic. In the latter case, it is always difficult for users (or, for that matter, for scientists and government officials) to judge whether changes in the resource stock or flow are due to over harvesting or to random exogenous variables. Unpredictability of resource units in microsettings, such as private pastures, may lead users to create a larger common-property unit to increase the predictability of resource availability somewhere in the larger unit (Netting 1972; Wilson and Thompson 1993). The spatial extent of a resource (R4) affects the costs of defining reasonable boundaries and then of monitoring them over time.

The attributes of the users themselves (listed above) also affect their expected benefits and costs. If users do not obtain a major part of their income from a resource (A1), the high costs of organising and maintaining a self-governing system may not be worth their effort. If users do not share a common understanding of how complex resource systems operate (A2), they will find it extremely difficult to agree on future joint strategies.

Given the complexity of many forest resources especially multispecies or multiproduct resources understanding how these systems work may be counterintuitive even for those who make daily contact with the forest. In forests that are highly variable (R3), it may be particularly difficult to understand and to separate those outcomes stemming from exogenous factors and those resulting from the actions of users. Of course, this is also a problem facing officials as well as users. Users with many other options, who thus discount the importance of future income from a particular resource (A3), may prefer to mine one forest without spending resources to regulate it. They simply move on to other forests once this one is destroyed, assuming there will always be still more forests available to them.

Users who possess more substantial economic and political assets may have similar interests to those with fewer assets (A4) or they may differ substantially on multiple attributes. When the more powerful have similar interests, they may greatly enhance the probability of successful organisation if they invest their resources in organising a group and devising rules to govern that group. Those with substantial economic and political assets are more likely to be a member of a winning coalition and thus have a greater impact on decisions about institutional changes.

Mancur Olson (1965) long ago recognised the possibility of a privileged group whereby some were sufficiently affected to bear a disproportionate share of the costs of organising to provide public goods (such as the organisation of a collectivity). On the other hand, if those with more assets also have low discount rates (A3) related to a particular resource and lower salience (A1), they may simply be unwilling to expend inputs or may actually impede organisational efforts that might lead to them having to cut back on their productive activities.

Users who trust one another (A6) to keep agreements and use reciprocity in their relationships face lower expected costs for monitoring and sanctioning over time. Users who lack trust at the beginning of a process of organising may be able to build this form of social capital (Coleman 1988; E. Ostrom 1992a) if they initially adopt small changes that most users follow before trying to make major institutional changes. Autonomy (A7) tends to lower the costs of organising. A group that has little autonomy may find that those who disagree with locally developed rules seek contacts with higher-level officials to undo the efforts of users to achieve regulation.

With the legal autonomy to make their own rules, users face substantially lower costs in defending these rules against other authorities. Prior experience with other forms of local organisation (A7) greatly enhances the repertoire of rules and strategies known by local participants as potentially useful to achieve various forms of regulation.

Further, users are more likely to agree upon rules whose operation they understand from prior experience, than upon rules that are introduced by external actors and are new to their experience. Given the complexity of many field settings, users face a difficult task in evaluating how diverse variables affect expected benefits and costs over a long time horizon.

In many cases, it is just as difficult, if not more so, for scientists to make a valid and reliable estimate of total benefits and costs and their distribution. The growing theoretical consensus does *not* lead to a conclusion that most users utilising common-pool resources will undertake self-governed regulation. Many settings exist where the theoretical expectation should be the opposite. Users will overuse the forest unless efforts are made to change one or more of the variables affecting perceived costs or benefits. Given the number of variables that affect these costs and benefits, many points of external intervention can enhance or reduce the probability of users agreeing upon and following rules that generate higher social returns.

But both social scientists and policy makers have a lot to learn about how these variables interact in field settings and even how to measure them so as to increase the empirical legitimacy of the growing theoretical consensus. Many aspects of the macro institutional structure surrounding a particular setting affect the perceived costs and benefits. Thus, external authorities can be effective in enhancing the likelihood and performance of self-governing institutions. Their actions can also seriously impede these developments as well. Further, when the activities of one set of users, A, have spill over effects on others beyond A, external authorities can either facilitate processes that allow multiple groups to solve conflicts arising from negative spill overs or take a more active role in governing particular forests themselves.

Researchers and public officials need to recognise the multiple manifestations of these attributes in the field. Users may be highly dependent on a forest (A1), for example, because they are in a remote location and few roads exist to enable them to leave. Alternatively, they may be located in a central location, but other opportunities are not open to them due to lack of training or a discriminatory labour market. Users discount rates (A3) in relation to a particular forest may be low because they have lived for a long time in a particular location and expect that they and their grandchildren will remain in that location, or because they possess a secure and well-defined bundle of property rights to this forest.

Reliable indicators of the condition of a forest (R2) may result from activities of users themselves such as regularly harvesting of medicinal plants or because of efforts to gather reliable information by users or by external authorities (Blomquist 1992). Predictability of forest resources (R3) may result from relatively constant weather conditions or because of actions taken by users to even out the availability of forest products over time.

They may have autonomy to make their own rules (A6) because a national government is weak and unable to exert authority over forests that it formally owns, or because national law formally legitimates self-governance of forests as in Uttar Pradesh in India. When the benefits of organising are commonly understood by participants to be very high, users lacking many of the attributes conducive to the development of self-governing institutions may be able to overcome their liabilities and still develop effective agreements. The crucial factor is not whether all attributes are favourable but the relative size of the expected benefits and costs they generate as perceived by participants. While all of these variables affect the expected benefits and costs of users, it is difficult particularly for outsiders to estimate their impacts given the difficulty of making precise measures of these variables and weighing them on a cumulative scale. Further empirical analysis of these theoretical propositions is, thus, dependent on the conduct over time of careful comparative studies of a sufficiently large number of field settings using a common set of measurement protocols.

On the Design Principles of Robust, Self-governed Common-pool Resource Institutions

Of course, the performance of self-governed common-pool resource institutions varies across systems and time. Some self-governed resources have survived and flourished for centuries, while others have faltered and failed. As discussed above, some never get organised in the first place. In addition to the consensus concerning the theoretical variables conducive to self-organisation, considerable agreement also exists about the characteristics of those self-governing systems that are robust in the sense that they survive for very long periods of time utilising the same basic rules for adapting to new situations over time (Shepsle 1989).

The particular rules used in the long-surviving, self-governing systems vary substantially. Consequently, it is not possible to arrive at empirical generalisations about the particular types of rules used to define who is a member of a self-governing community, what rights they have to access a resource, and what particular obligations they face. It is possible, however, to derive a series of design principles that characterise the configuration of rules that are used. By design principles, I mean a condition that helps to account for the success of these institutions in sustaining a forest or other common-pool resource and gaining the compliance of generation after generation of users to the rules applied in a location. Based on considerable research on common-pool resources, robust, long-term institutions are characterised by most of the design principles listed in Table 1. Fragile institutions tend to be characterised by only some of these design principles. Failed institutions are characterised by very few of these principles.

These principles work to enhance the shared understanding of participants of the structure of a resource and its users and of the benefits and costs involved in following a set of agreed-upon rules. Design Principle 1. having rules that clearly define who has rights to use a resource and the boundaries of that resource. ensures that users can clearly identify anyone who does not have rights and take action against them. Design Principle 2 involves two parts. The first is congruence between the rules that assign benefits and the rules that assign costs. The crucial issue here is that these rules be considered fair and legitimate by the participants themselves. In many settings, fair rules are those that keep a relatively proportionate relationship between the assignment of benefits and of costs. Otherwise, those who contribute time, funds and effort to sustaining a forest or other common-pool resource system resent the unfair allocation of benefits to those carrying a lesser load.

The whole distribution system can disintegrate if it is not perceived as fair. The second part of this design principle is that both types of rules need to be well matched to local conditions, such as soils, slope, number of diversions, crops being grown. Design Principle 3 is concerned with the collective-choice arrangements used to modify operational rules those that directly affect where, when and who can harvest from a resource. If most users are not involved in modifying these rules over time, the information about the benefits and costs as perceived by different participants is not fully taken into account in any efforts to adapt to new conditions and information over time. Users who begin to perceive the costs of their system being higher than their benefits, and who are prevented from making serious proposals for change, may simply begin to cheat whenever they have the opportunity. Once cheating on rules becomes more frequent for some users, others will follow suit.

In this case, enforcement costs become very high or the system fails. No matter how high the level of acceptance of an initial agreement, there are always conditions that tempt some individuals to cheat (even when they perceive the overall benefits of the system to be higher than the costs). If one person is able to cheat while others conform to the rules, the cheater is usually able to gain substantially to the disadvantage of others. Thus, without monitoring of rule conformance. Design Principle 4 few systems are able to survive very long.

The sanctions that are used, however, do not need to be extremely high in the first instance. The important thing about a sanction for a user who has succumbed to temptation is that their action is noticed and that a punishment is meted out. This tells all users that cheating on rules is noticed and punished without making all rule infractions into major criminal events. If the sanctions are graduated (Design Principle 5), a user who breaks rules repeatedly and who is noticed doing so, eventually faces a penalty that makes rule breaking an unattractive option. While rules are always assumed to be clear and unambiguous in theoretical work, this is rarely the case in field settings.

It is easy to have a disagreement about how to interpret a rule that limits harvesting or requires inputs. If these disagreements are not resolved in a low-cost and orderly manner, then users may lose their willingness to conform to rules because of the ways that others interpret them in their own favour (Design Principle 6).

Design Principles 7 and 8 are related to autonomy. When the rights of a group to devise their own institutions are recognised by national, regional and local governments, the legitimacy of the rules crafted by users will be less frequently challenged in courts, administrative and legislative settings. Further, in larger resources with many participants, such as many forests, nested enterprises that range in size from small to large enable participants to solve diverse problems involving different scale economies. By utilising base institutions that are quite small, face-to-face communication can be used for solving many of the day-to-day problems in smaller groups. By nesting each level of organisation in a larger level, externalities between groups can be addressed in larger organisational settings that have a legitimate role to play in relationship to the smaller entities.

Theoretical Puzzles

In addition to the consensus concerning the variables most likely to enhance self-organisation and the design principles characterising successful, long-term governance arrangements, many unresolved theoretical issues still exist about the self-governance of common-pool resources. Two major theoretical questions relate to the effect of size and heterogeneity.

Size

The effect of the number of participants facing problems of creating and sustaining a self-governing enterprise is unclear. Drawing on the early work of Mancur Olson (1965), many theorists argue that size of a group is negatively related to solving collective-action problems in general. Many results from game theoretical analysis of repeated games conclude that cooperative strategies are more likely to emerge and be sustained in smaller rather than larger groups. Scholars who have studied many user-governed forestry institutions in the field have concluded that success will more likely happen in smaller groups. In a systematic study of forest institutions, Agrawal (1998) has found that smaller forest user groups are less able to undertake the level of monitoring needed to protect forest resources than moderately sized groups. In a study of over 100 irrigation systems, Lam (1998) did not find any significant relationship between either the number of users or the amount of land included in the service area and any of the three performance variables he studied.

One of the problems of focussing on size of group as a key determining factor is that many other variables change as group size increases (Chamberlin 1974; R. Hardin 1982). If the costs of providing a public good related to the use of a forest, say a sanctioning system, remain relatively constant as group size increases, then increasing the number of participants brings additional resources that could be drawn upon to provide the benefit enjoyed by all. Marwell and Oliver (1993: 45) conclude that when a good has pure jointness of supply, group size has a *positive* effect on the probability that it will be provided.. On the other hand, if one is analysing the conflict levels over a subtractable good and the transaction costs of arriving at acceptable allocation formulae, group size may well exacerbate the problems of self-governing systems. Since there are tradeoffs among various impacts of size on other variables, a better working hypothesis is that medium-sized groups may succeed more often than very small or very large groups.

Heterogeneity

Many scholars conclude that only very small groups can organise themselves effectively because they presume that size is related to the homogeneity of a group and that homogeneity is needed to initiate and sustain self-governance. Heterogeneity is also a highly contested variable. Groups can vary along a diversity of dimensions including their cultural backgrounds, interests and endowments. Each may operate differently. Further, groups who are relatively homogeneous may also find themselves confronted with high levels of conflict when rules related to access to forest resources are not well defined. If groups from diverse cultural backgrounds share access to a forest, the key question affecting the likelihood of self-organised solutions is whether the views of the multiple groups concerning the structure of the forest, authority, interpretation of rules, trust and reciprocity differ or are similar. In other words, do they share a common understanding (A2) of their situation? New settlers to a region may simply learn and accept the rules of the established group, and their cultural differences on other fronts do not affect their participation in governing a forest. On the other hand, new settlers are frequently highly disruptive to the sustenance of a self-governing enterprise when they generate higher levels of conflict over the interpretation and application of rules and increase enforcement costs substantially.

When the interests of users differ, achieving a self-governing solution is particularly challenging. This problem characterises some fisheries where local subsistence fishermen have strong interests in the sustenance of an inshore fishery, while industrial fishing firms have many other options and may be more interested in the profitability of fishing in a particular location than its sustained yield. The conflict between absentee livestock owners and local pastoralists has also proved difficult to solve in many parts of the world. Differential endowments of users can be associated with both extreme levels of conflict as well as very smooth and low-cost transitions into a sustainable, self-governed system. Johnson and Libecap (1982) reason that the difference in the skills and knowledge of different kinds of users frequently prevents them from arriving at agreements about how to allocate harvesting quotas. Heterogeneity of wealth or power may or may not be associated with a difference in interests.

As discussed above, when those who have more assets share similar interests with those who have less assets (A4), groups may be privileged by having the more powerful take on the higher initial costs of organising, while crafting rules that benefit a large proportion of the users. Users may design institutions that cope effectively with heterogeneities. Thus, when they adopt rules that allocate benefits using the same formulae used to allocate duties and responsibilities (Design Principle 2A), users who differ significantly in terms of assets will tend to agree to and follow such rules.

Even in a group that differs on many variables, if at least a minimally winning subset of users from an endangered but valuable forest are dependent on it (A1), and they share a common understanding of their situations (A2), have a low discount rate (A3), include some with more assets among their members (A4), trust one another (A5), and have autonomy to make their own rules (A6), it is more likely that they will estimate the expected benefits of governing their forest to be greater than the expected costs.

Whether the rules agreed upon distribute benefits and costs fairly depends both on the collective-choice rule used and the type of heterogeneity existing in the community. Neither size nor heterogeneity is a variable with a uniform effect on the likelihood of organising and sustaining self-governing enterprises. The debate about their effect is focussing on the wrong variables. Instead of concentrating on size or the various kinds of heterogeneity independently, it is important to ask how these variables influence other variables as they affect the benefit-cost calculations of those involved in negotiating and sustaining agreements. Their impact on costs of producing and distributing information (Scott 1993) is particularly important.

Conclusion

The conventional theory of common-pool resources, which presumed that external authorities were needed to impose new rules on those users trapped into producing excessive externalities for themselves and others, has now been shown to be a special theory of a more general theoretical structure. For users to contemplate changing the institutions they face, they have to conclude that the expected benefits from an institutional change will exceed the immediate and long-term expected costs. When users cannot communicate and have no way of gaining trust through their own efforts or with the help of the macro institutional system within which they are embedded, the prediction of the earlier theory is likely to be empirically supported. Ocean fisheries, the stratosphere and other global commons come closest to the appropriate empirical referents.

If users can engage in face-to-face bargaining and have autonomy to change their rules, they may well attempt to organise themselves.

Whether they organise depends on attributes of the resource and the users themselves that affect the benefits to be achieved and the costs of achieving them. Whether their self-governed enterprise succeeds over the long term depends on whether the institutions they develop are consistent with design principles underlying robust, long-living, self-governed systems. The theory has progressed substantially during the past half century. There are, however, many challenging puzzles to be solved.

Further empirical research is needed to test the relevance and explanatory power for forests of the emerging consensus regarding the conditions conducive to effective self-governance of resources and for the design of more effective public policies. Given the number of variables that can independently and interactively affect the incentives and actions of local users especially when one focuses on forest resources systematic research conducted in a large number of locations obtaining data about the same set of variables is also extremely important. Hopefully, future policies will be constructed on the basis of an understanding of both the strengths and limitations of self-governance of forestry resources.

Bibliography

Allen, John C. and Dillman, Don : *Against All Odds: Rural Community in the Information Age*, Boulder: Westview Press, 1994.

Ashraf, A. : *Political Sociology : A New Grammar of Politics*, Universities Press, Delhi, 1983.

Basu, Prahlad K.: *Governance and Public Administration for Poverty Reduction*, Salvador, Brazil, 1997.

Batliwala, Srilatha: *Population Policies Reconsidered: Health, Empowerment and Rights*, Cambridge, Harvard University Press, 1994.

Carr, W. & Kemmis, S. : *Becoming Critical: Education, Knowledge and Action Research*, London, Falmer, 1986.

Chaklader, Snehamoy : *Sociolinguistics: A Guide to Language Problems in India*, New Delhi, Mittal, 1990.

Damon, William : *Social and Personality Development, Infancy through Adolescence,* New York: Norton, 1983.

Dennis Shirley: *Community Organizing for Urban School Reform,* Austin, University of Texas Press, 1997.

Elisabeth Relchert: *Social Work and Human Rights : A Foundation for Policy and Practice*, Rawat, Delhi, 2003.

Eysenck, Hans : *Psychoticism as a Dimension of Personality*, Pergamon, Elsevier Science Inc, Amsterdam, 1997.

Flavia Agnes: *Law and Gender Inequality : The Politics of Women's Rights in India,* Oxford University Press, 1999,

Fran Tonkiss: *Contemporary Economic Sociology: Globalization, Production, Inequality*, Manohar, Delhi, 2008.

Gagan Kumar Singh: *Administration for Rural Development Programmes in India*, Abhijeet, Delhi, 2003.

Gornick, V. : *Women and Science: Portraits from a World in Transition,* New York, Simon & Schuster, 1983.

Hajira Kumar : *Social Work, Social Development and Sustainable Development*, Regency, Delhi, 1997.

Howes, Elaine V. : *Connecting Girls and Science: Constructivism, Feminism, and Science Education Reform*, New York, Teachers College Press, 2002.

Iqbal, Shaikh Azhar : *Problems of Social Welfare and Social Work*, Sublime, Delhi, 2005.

John A, Marcell, *Handbook of Small Business Valuation Formulas and Rules of Thumb,* Valuation Press, 1993.

Kaur, Rajpal : *Developmental Psychology : New Trends and Innovations*, Deep and Deep, Delhi, 2006.

Kumar Sanal Velayudhan : *Rural Marketing : Targeting the Non-Urban Consumer*, Response, Delhi, 2002.

Lal, Shyam: *Caste and Political Mobilisation: The Bhangis*, Jaipur, Panchsheel Prakashan, 1981.

Lifton, R. : *The Nazi Doctors, Medical Killing and the Psychology of Genocide*, Basic Books, New York, 1986.

MacDonald, S.: *Evolutionary Perspectives on Human Development,* Thousand Oaks, CA: Sage Publications, 2004.

Mayoux, Linda: *Micro-finance and the Empowerment of Women,* Geneva, International Labor Organization, 2000.

Nussbaum, Martha: *Women and Human Development: The Capabilities Approach*, New York, Cambridge Press, 2000.

Omvedt, Gail : *Reinventing Revolution: New Social Movements and the Socialist Tradition in India*, New York, Sharpe, 1993.

Pamela Abbott, Claire Wallace and Melissa Tyler: *An Introduction to Sociology: Feminist Perspective*, Manohar, Delhi, 2008.

Pandey, R K : *Urban Sociology : Planning, Administration and Management*, Sarup and Sons, Delhi, 2006.

Rajesh S. Shinde : *Rural Marketing in India: Current Scenario*, ABD Publishers, Delhi, 2010.

Rao, M. S. A.: *Social Movement and Social Transformation: A Study of Backward Class Movement*, New Delhi, Macmillian Press, 1978.

Satyamurthy, T.V.: *Region, Religion, Caste, Gender and Culture in Contemporary India*, Delhi, OUP, 1996.

Shalinee Gusain: *Feminist Contributions to Indian Sociology: A Study of Select Texts*, Academic Excellence, Delhi, 2005.

Tzannatos, Z.: *Child Labor: Issues, and Directions for the World Bank,* Washington, World Bank, 1998.

Vaknin, Sam : *A Textbook of Organizational Psychology*, Dominant Pub, Delhi, 2010.

Walker, Kenneth R.: *Agricultural Development in China, 1949-1989,* Oxford University Press, New York, 1998.

Index

A

B

C

D

E

F

G

H

I

L

❑❑❑